AF893870

Nineteenth-Century Major Lives and Letters

Series Editor: Marilyn Gaull

The nineteenth century invented major figures: gifted, productive, and influential writers and artists in English, European, and American public life who captured and expressed what Hazlitt called "The Spirit of the Age." Their achievements summarize, reflect, and shape the cultural traditions they inherited and influence the quality of life that followed. Before radio, film, and journalism deflected the energies of authors and audiences alike, literary forms such as popular verse, song lyrics, biographies, memoirs, letters, novels, reviews, essays, children's books, and drama generated a golden age of letters incomparable in Western history. *Nineteenth-Century Major Lives and Letters* presents a series of original biographical, critical, and scholarly studies of major figures evoking their energies, achievements, and their impact on the character of this age. Projects to be included range from works on Blake to Hardy, Erasmus Darwin to Charles Darwin, Wordsworth to Yeats, Coleridge and J. S. Mill, Joanna Baillie, Jane Austen, Sir Walter Scott, Byron, Shelley, Keats to Dickens, Tennyson, George Eliot, Browning, Hopkins, Lewis Carroll, Rudyard Kipling, and their contemporaries. The series editor is Marilyn Gaull, PhD from Indiana University. She has served on the faculty at Temple University, New York University, and is now Research Professor at the Editorial Institute at Boston University. She brings to the series decades of experience as editor of books on nineteenth-century literature and culture. She is the founder and editor of *The Wordsworth Circle*, author of *English Romanticism: The Human Context*, publishes editions, essays, and reviews in numerous journals and lectures internationally on British Romanticism, folklore, and narrative theory.

PUBLISHED BY PALGRAVE:

Shelley's German Afterlives, by Susanne Schmid
Romantic Literature, Race, and Colonial Encounter, by Peter J. Kitson
Coleridge, the Bible, and Religion, by Jeffrey W. Barbeau
Byron: Heritage and Legacy, edited by Cheryl A. Wilson
Romantic Migrations: Local, National, and Transnational Dispositions, by Michael Wiley

FORTHCOMING TITLES:

The Long and Winding Road from Blake to the Beatles, by Matthew Schneider
Reading the Sphinx: Ancient Egypt in 19th Century Literary Culture, by Lynn Parramore

Also by the Author

Romantic Geography: Wordsworth and Anglo-European Spaces (Palgrave Macmillan, 1998)

The Last Striptease (fiction) (St. Martin's Press/Minotaur, 2007)

Romantic Migrations

Local, National, and Transnational Dispositions

Michael Wiley

palgrave
macmillan

ROMANTIC MIGRATIONS

Copyright © Michael Wiley, 2008.

The cover of this book includes an image of J. M. Probst's 1780 *Globus Terrestris*. The image is reproduced courtesy of the Lewis Ansbacher Map Collection, permanently housed in the Morris Ansbacher Map Room, Jacksonville (Florida) Public Library.

All rights reserved. No part of this book may be used or reproduced in any manner whatsoever without written permission except in the case of brief quotations embodied in critical articles or reviews.

First published in 2008 by
PALGRAVE MACMILLAN™
175 Fifth Avenue, New York, N.Y. 10010 and
Houndmills, Basingstoke, Hampshire, England RG21 6XS
Companies and representatives throughout the world.

PALGRAVE MACMILLAN is the global academic imprint of the Palgrave Macmillan division of St. Martin's Press, LLC and of Palgrave Macmillan Ltd. Macmillan® is a registered trademark in the United States, United Kingdom and other countries. Palgrave is a registered trademark in the European Union and other countries.

ISBN-13: 978–0–230–60468–1
ISBN-10: 0–230–60468–4

Library of Congress Cataloging-in-Publication Data

Wiley, Michael, 1961–
Romantic migrations : local, national, and transnational dispositions / Michael Wiley.
p. cm.—(Nineteenth-century major lives and letters)
Includes bibliographical references.
ISBN 0–230–60468–4
1. English literature—18th century—History and criticism. 2. Emigration and immigration in literature. 3. Self in literature. 4. National characteristics in literature. 5. Transnationalism in literature. 6. Romanticism—Great Britain. 7. Great Britain—Emigration and immigration—History—18th century. 8. France—Emigration and immigration—History—18th century. 9. North America—Emigration and immigration—History—18th century. 10. Africa—Emigration and immigration—History—18th century. I. Title.

PR448.E43W56 2008
820.9′3552—dc22 2007032128

A catalogue record for this book is available from the British Library.

Design by Newgen Imaging Systems (P) Ltd., Chennai, India.

First edition: April 2008

10 9 8 7 6 5 4 3 2 1

Printed in the United States of America.

For Julie, Isaac, Maya, and Elias

Contents

Preface

In 2008, the word "migration" describes the terror-driven diaspora from Darfur, the poverty-driven movement of fruit pickers, the post-Katrina departure from New Orleans, the transnational aesthetics of expatriate artists, even the seasonal patterns of Canadian geese and butterflies. It describes the prehistoric spread of hominids from Africa to Eurasia, the Hebrew exodus from Egypt, the Puritan crossing to the Massachusetts Bay Colony, and the flight of young Somalian women from compulsory genital mutilation. It describes emigrations and immigrations, the movements of the living.

But in 1754, as Nicholas Roe comments, "emigrant," in its modern sense, "was quite a new word."[1] Within only forty years, though, it was part of the public vocabulary. In 1793, Charlotte Smith used it to title her poem about French refugees. And in the mid-1790s, Thomas Poole speculated on the aesthetic and social gains that literary "emigrators" might achieve by leaving England.[2]

In a letter published in 1789, the naturalist Gilbert White argued to a skeptic, who, along with many contemporaries, believed exclusively in avian hibernation, that bird "migration certainly does subsist in some places."[3] In 1792, the British explorer Samuel Hearne described hunger-driven Indians wandering the Canadian wilderness as "migrants."[4] Also in 1792, the historian and travel writer Jeremy Belknap first used the word "immigrant" in print, though he acknowledged that "the strict letter of the English dictionaries" would not recognize it; and in 1809, Edward A. Kendall commented on the newness of the word to the English language.[5]

The new languages and meanings of migration arose as British emigration accelerated: from about 40,000 in the 1770s to about 80,000 in the first decade of the nineteenth century, to about 200,000 in the 1820s.[6] Immigration accelerated as well, coming from North America at the start of the Revolution in 1775, for example, from France in the decade following the French Revolution, and from Western Africa, often by way of the Americas or the British West

Indies, after 1772, when Lord Chief Justice Mansfield outlawed English slavery.

* * *

Romantic Migrations describes the literary origins of modern conceptions of British migration. At the end of the eighteenth century, when poets, novelists, and others affiliated with British literature crossed the British landscape, moved to or from Great Britain, or just imagined physical, spiritual, and aesthetic movement, the concept of migration acquired the complex semantic and ideological range familiar to the twenty-first century.

In the early 1790s Samuel Taylor Coleridge, Robert Southey, and Robert Lovell planned to emigrate to Pennsylvania to set up a Pantisocratic community. After travelling to Germany with William and Dorothy Wordsworth in 1798, and living in Malta from 1804 to 1806, Coleridge returned to England reluctantly. Wordsworth lived and started a family in France in the early 1790s and travelled to Germany with Dorothy and Coleridge, with no plans to return to England. Southey represented himself as a short-term resident of Spain and Portugal in *Letters Written during a Short Residence in Spain and Portugal* (1797) after accompanying his diplomat uncle to the Continent; and, fictionally, as a Spaniard in Britain in *Letters from England by Don Manual Alvarez Espriella* (1807).

Joseph Priestley emigrated to Pennsylvania after a mob burned his Bristol home and laboratory. Thomas Paine emigrated to North America in 1774 after losing his job as exciseman because of his political agitation, returned to Britain in 1787, fled to France under the threat of arrest in 1792, then returned to America in 1802, where he died in 1809. And William Cobbett moved to America and left three times, the last departure being in 1819 when he took Paine's bones back to Britain with him. John Keats's brother George and his wife emigrated to Kentucky; and Mary Shelley, widowed, considered emigrating to North America as well.

As a child William Hazlitt emigrated to America with his parents and lived in Pennsylvania and then Massachusetts for three years before returning to England. Leigh Hunt's father emigrated from the American colonies to England. Writers of African birth or heritage, including Ignatius Sancho, Ottabah Cugoano, and Olaudah Equiano, came to England by way of the Americas as well.

Frances Burney moved to France with her husband Alexandre d'Arblay and their young son in 1802 and returned to Britain only in 1812. Charlotte Smith, following her debt-driven husband, lived in France for only six months, though her daughter married a French émigré, and concerns with emigration color her poetry and novels. Helen Maria Williams lived in France following the French Revolution, establishing herself as an Englishwoman deeply knowledgeable about the new republic. Among the second-generation Romantic writers, Lord Byron, Percy Bysshe Shelley, and John Keats all migrated to Italy: Keats and Shelley to die there and Byron to die in Greece.

The West Indies attracted Robert Burns, who, troubled by debt, planned to emigrate to Jamaica in the mid-1780s, even booking passage on a ship. Matthew Lewis's father, born in Jamaica, owned a sugar plantation there, and Lewis himself died at sea while returning from the estates. William Beckford's father likewise was born in Jamaica, and Beckford owed his enormous wealth to the family's plantations. After the Pantisocrats failed to realize their plans in Pennsylvania, Coleridge also considered setting up a community in the West Indies.

With their diverse social, religious, economic, and political circumstances and their various geographical origins and destinations, these writers shared no single migrant disposition, but they and their texts exhibited interrelated patterns of migrant thought and behavior. For instance, many of the writers thought and wrote about selfhood, spatial position, and the power of the imagination and of empirical observation to help individuals and communities orient themselves within a world that, they understood, was disunited and still dividing. Nearly all the writers (or the characters within the writers' fictions) looked at the destinations of their actual or projected migrations as places of potential salvation, or political, economic, social, religious, and—often—millenarian regeneration. They thus contributed to a widely held belief that emigration would fundamentally transform individuals and societies. Hence, the decision by the British government to transport criminals and political discontents to Australia. And hence the social utopian planner Morris Birkbeck's need to warn Britons considering a move to his Illinois settlement in the 1810s that, against their expectations, "Emigration to the extreme limits of this western America will not repair a bad character."[7] When the destinations failed to fulfill the migrants' expectations, as they nearly always did, the writers grappled with a central Romantic concern: the relationship between ideality and material reality. Failed migrations are still attributable to this discrepancy between expectations and reality.

In addressing the migration literature of the late eighteenth century, *Romantic Migrations* builds upon a deep and rich critical tradition. Nigel Leask's *Curiosity and the Aesthetics of Travel Writing, 1770–1840*, Amanda Gilroy's edition of essays on *Romantic Geographies: Discourses of Travel, 1775–1844*, and Tim Fulford's eight-volume anthology of *Travels, Explorations, and Empires: Writings from the Era of Imperial Expansion, 1770–1835* have explained the philosophical, ideological, and aesthetic challenges faced (and often produced) by travellers into the same places where emigrants were moving. Leask's *British Romantic Writers and the East: Anxieties of Empire*, Saree Makdisi's *Romantic Imperialism: Universal Empire and the Culture of Modernity*, Fulford and Peter Kitson's *Romanticism and Colonialism: Writing and Empire, 1780–1830*, Rajani Sudan's *Fair Exotics: Xenophobic Subjects in English Literature, 1720–1850*, and Alan Richardson and Sonia Hofkosh's collection of essays *Romanticism, Race, and Imperial Culture*, along with work on Romantic literature and the slave trade, have studied imperialism and colonialism in these spaces.

Franco Moretti's *Atlas of the European Novel, 1800–1900 and* my *Romantic Geography* have provided a critical vocabulary with which to discuss literary spaces; and Celeste Langan's *Romantic Vagrancy*, Toby Benis's *Romanticism on the Road*, and Gary Harrison's *Wordsworth's Vagrant Muse* have added to that vocabulary.

Benis's essay "'A Likely Story': Charlotte Smith's Revolutionary Narratives," which deals with Smith's emigration novel *The Banished Man*, Tilar Mazzeo's "The Impossibility of Being Anglo-American: The Rhetoric of Emigration and Transatlanticism in British Romantic Culture, 1791–1833," and Katharina Rennhak's "Tropes of Exile in the 1790s: English Women Writers and French Emigrants" have further set the stage for *Romantic Migrations*. Their work, along with the work done on Romantic imperialism, Orientalism, and geography, has pointed to a conclusion that I pursue further: that "[w]hen all is said and done, [British] romanticism will turn out to be not only worldly, but also global, and to have been so all along."[8]

In reading British Romanticism as a global movement, Leask shifts the term "anxiety" away from Bloomian inter-authorial, intertextual, psychoanalytic meanings toward inter-cultural and linguistic ones. Lee writes of a "distanced imagination," which she defines as "a creative faculty at once expansive and self-sacrificing…[with] roots in the [British/global] change in moral consciousness that took place in the eighteenth century."[9] Sara Suleri writes of "a continually dislocated idiom of migrancy," and, intersecting with Lee and Leask, calls the Indian subcontinent "a tropological repository from which colonial and postcolonial imaginations have drawn—and continue to draw—their most basic figures for the anxiety of empire."[10] Building upon such ideas and continuing to develop a critical vocabulary that accounts for the global, *Romantic Migrations* situates literary Britain in the larger world and the larger world within literary Britain. As Richard Drayton comments, at this time the English metropolis "sat at the center of…[a] system of intellectual accumulation….But if one argues that everyone in the eighteenth-century empire lived in 'London's provinces,' one must equally concede that modern London was itself constructed within these new global arrangements."[11]

Seeing London and Britain this way unsettled contemporaries. If Britain was reassuringly at the center of British–World relations, the boundaries of Britain and British identity were in flux and uncertain. Even the boundaries of the British isles themselves showed instability. In the early eighteenth century, Jacobites rebelled repeatedly in the north; in 1797, the French attempted to invade England through Fishguard, Wales (and Britons feared further invasions throughout the French–British wars); and in 1707, an Act of Union united Scotland with England, with another Act of Union adding Ireland in 1800.

As nation-states and racial and ethnic taxonomies took their modern forms both inside and outside of Britain, complex questions arose about the unity, constancy, and solidity of identities and selfhoods. Writers about emigration faced these questions in their poetry and prose; and they redefined, renamed, and, often, aestheticized selfhood (individual, national, international, and transnational) in new ways. If writers such as Wordsworth and Coleridge often seem to have formulated selfhood as having a "consciousness" that "experienced a world that it ha[d] made somehow meaningful and coherent," as much Romantic criticism has suggested,[12] a counter-formulation opposed these ideas. This other selfhood had a nonintegrated consciousness, and, although this consciousness struggled to make the world "meaningful and coherent," it rarely succeeded in doing so. The identities and kinds of self-consciousness that *Romantic Migrations* discusses challenged beliefs in easily comprehensible meaning and coherence at the moment when the beliefs were taking definitive shape.[13]

To be—or to think like—a migrant in the late eighteenth century, then, was to move uncertainly through the world and to constitute the self through that movement; to be literally a work in progress; to have an inchoate identity, subject to the informing forces of other identities.[14] As the literature of Romantic migration shows, the minds and bodies forever turning inward—toward nation state, toward locality, and toward mental interiors—extended also outward into international and global spaces that shook and transformed the Romantic self. The shaking and transforming continue in 2008.

Acknowledgments

I owe thanks to many for helping me complete *Romantic Migrations*.

To Julia Burns for reading and critiquing early drafts of the manuscript. To Sarah Zimmerman for still earlier conversations about Charlotte Smith. To Regina Hewitt for reading portions of the manuscript and encouraging me to make them better. To readers at *Studies in Romanticism* and *European Romantic Review* who read and helped me improve article versions of my ideas about Olaudah Equiano and Charlotte Smith. To Andrea Richards for her thoughts on eighteenth-century sea bathing. To Dale Clifford and Shira Schwam-Baird for helping me find my way through historical France. To Sam Kimball for conversations that have kept me always aware of the dangers of critical complacency.

And many more thanks to Marilyn Gaull who has matched her committed good-spiritedness only with her consistently incisive editorial eye, as well as to Farideh Koohi-Kamali at Palgrave Macmillan for enthusiastically representing and tending to this book and Julia Cohen, also at Palgrave Macmillan, for clearing the way of various obstacles.

Also, thanks to the staffs at the British Library, the Newberry Library, the Lewis Ansbacher Map Room at the Jacksonville Public Library, and the Research Branch of the New York Public Library. To David Marchant of the East Riding of Yorkshire Council Museums. To Alisa Craddock at the University of North Florida Thomas Carpenter Library for helping me pursue rare books from distant locations. To David Wilson in the Center for Instruction and Research Technology for his invaluable help with illustrations. And to the University of North Florida for supporting the research and writing of this book with two summer research grants and a sabbatical.

In gratitude toward and memory of Paul Magnuson, whose conversations and writings continue to guide, though he is gone.

Introduction: Deposing, Disposing, Dispositioning

On the night of June 20–21, 1791, King Louis XVI and his family tried to emigrate from France, where the French Revolutionaries had held them as privileged captives in the Tuileries palace. Frustrated by his narrowing power and many perceived indignities, Louis set out for the northeast border of France, where he expected to cross from Montmédy into the arms of a gathering *émigré* army. But the Revolutionaries stopped him in Varennes and carried him and his family back.[1]

Although Louis wished to restore himself to power in France, the act of emigration would first have taken him both out of the nation and out of his identity as king of the nation. The disguises that he and his family wore that night show how radically they needed to remove themselves from their established identities to emigrate. The family traveled in the guise of Russians (they carried Russian passports), servants (the children's governess played a Russian baroness, the king her steward, the queen the governess to the two children), and crossdressers (the king and queen dressed their son as well as their daughter as a girl).

But the family also insisted on maintaining certain markers of their past identity, refusing, for instance, to travel in quick, light coaches that could have sped them to the border, choosing instead to go, attended by servants and bodyguards, in a six-horse carriage. That carriage, though, failed to carry them to the destinations (social and political as well as geographical) that they wished to reach. Partly because they chose the carriage, Louis and his family became disoriented in a France that no longer recognized their self-markings. Marie Antoinette became "lost in the dark alleys around the Tuileries" as she searched for the carriage.[2] Once underway, Louis "obsessive[ly]...plotted the journey on a specially prepared map," but "What evidently escaped Louis' attention as his carriage rumbled across northern France...was that the country he was travelling through was not the one he had inherited almost two decades earlier."[3] When they stopped to rest and refresh themselves, an officer needed to remind them that they would be "lost" if they lingered.[4]

But they already were lost (because they had remained too long in a place they thought, wrongly, that they knew well). The National Guard arrested them and returned them to Paris. In the meantime—literally overnight—Parisians dispossessed themselves of the king who, they had learned, had abandoned them in the emigration attempt. The Revolutionary leaders, who were completing a constitution that included a king, feared the national loss of Louis perhaps as much as Louis feared losing the nation, and so they promulgated a story that counter-revolutionary conspirators had kidnapped him; but Parisians, seeing through the falsehood, tore down and defaced official and commercial signs that included Louis's name or image.

* * *

In planning to emigrate, Louis sought to reorient both himself and France. Since France had started removing him from his position as head of state—that is, politically decapitating him—his single hope for regaining his position and reincorporating himself within (and as head of) the nation involved first taking his head from the French capital (de-capitalizing it) and then returning it later to the body of France on his own terms.

In other words, Louis had a *migratory disposition*, with all the contradictions and semantic play that inhere to the word "disposition." He dis-positioned himself by removing himself from his kingly position: by leaving Paris, by passing himself off as a Russian and a servant, by removing the head from the state. He effectively deposed himself ("depose" shares etymology with "disposition"). But he dispositioned himself also so as to engage with—and reposition himself within—the national body as the head of that body: that is, so as to demonstrate and reestablish his kingly disposition. He articulated the doubleness of his (dis)position upon his capture in Varennes. When Varennes authorities brought a country judge to identify the king and the judge dropped to one knee, thereby recognizing Louis in the position that Louis claimed for himself, Louis acknowledged, "I am indeed your King"; but when orders arrived from the Revolutionary government demanding that Louis return to Paris, thereby demonstrating that he no longer controlled either the state or even himself, Louis declared, "there is no longer a king in France."[5]

* * *

On the night of June 20–21, 1791, Louis and his family failed to emigrate from France in large part because they dispositioned themselves insufficiently. They moved too slowly, too hesitantly toward the border and toward a new identity. They held too tightly to the position they once had occupied. In the nineteen months that followed, the Revolutionaries, increasingly under the influence of Robespierre, learned the power of controlling the king's disposition. On the morning of January 21, 1793, they honored Louis's wish to leave, but left no opportunity for him to return. At the guillotine, they dis-positioned his head from his shoulders and from the body of the nation.

The death was bloody, and, according to many accounts, spectators came forth to take the blood for themselves, dipping pens, paper, handkerchiefs, pikes, and sabers into it.[6] According to some, spectators also tasted Louis's blood: one boy supposedly touched it to his tongue and said, "*Il est bougrement salé*": "It is damned salty."[7] At the end, the French, following the leveling tendencies of the time, effectively swallowed Louis's blood, repositioning his power and his identity into the republic itself.

* * *

Romantic Migrations studies the migrations and dispositions that preceded and followed these dramatic and traumatic events, focusing on accounts that appeared in British Romantic literature of the 1780s and 1790s.

The first chapter, "The French Immersion: Crosscurrents of Selfhood," addresses literature on the French migration to Britain especially in the early 1790s. This cross-Channel literature—written by Burney, Smith, Wordsworth, Mary Robinson, and Coleridge, among others—explores both the dangers and the radically beneficial potentials that migration posed to individual and national subjectivities in a condition of unsettled *betweenness.* In the accounts of these writers, France, submerged in Revolutionary and military violence, was socially, politically, and culturally displaced from its past, awash historically and geographically; and Britain, despite its appearance of relative peace, was no less so. The most promising solution tested by these writers involved committing to a deeper immersion in the *betweenness* that divided the nations. (Smith and Burney even considered the social and broadly ideological benefits of bathing in Channel waters.) The writers imagined that an immersion could result in a new world in which social, economic, and—most of all—linguistic differences no longer led to international misunderstanding and interpersonal violence.

The second chapter, "Imagining America," addresses the writing of British authors who generally sympathized with the early ideals of the French Revolution but who sought new spaces where they might realize these ideals after the September Massacres and the rise of Robespierre. This section focuses on Coleridge and Southey's Pantisocratic scheme for an emigrant community on the banks of the Susquehanna River in Northumberland, Pennsylvania. Also important are Priestley's actual settlement in Northumberland, Cobbett's various polemical positions concerning emigration to America, and later moves by Morris Birkbeck and George Keats to Illinois and Kentucky. Through the various North American emigration plans, Romantic writers tested the boundaries of idealism and empirical realism by imagining possible lives in a material space that even the most empirically minded observers agreed was still uncertain in its dimensions and thus still open to broad-ranging interpretation and speculation. Many of the writers extended social, political, physical, and spiritual self-representations and self-idealizations into North America. The failure of North America to sustain these representations and idealizations presented a crisis in selfhood (especially for Coleridge); and yet, the crisis was as productive as it was destructive, contributing to the Romantic analysis of the self and to dramatic tensions that helped to define Romantic aesthetics.

Chapter 3, "Consuming Africa," addresses a still deeper crisis in selfhood and identity for late-eighteenth-century Britain. This section deals with two sets of migrations, one by Britons to Africa, whether to set up residences or to engage in multi-year travels and explorations, and another by Africans to Britain. The British-born writers included the well-known James Bruce, Joseph Banks, and Mungo Park and the lesser-known Archibald Dalzel, John Matthews, and others. Writers of African birth or heritage included Ignatius Sancho, Ottabah Cugoano, and Olaudah Equiano, among others. As was also the case in the writings on the American and French emigrations, tensions between idealism and empirical realism shaped these writers' texts; and, as was the case with so much else in the writing on the African–British relationship, these tensions were often more extreme than elsewhere. So too were representations of what was at stake for British and African selfhood in the encounter. In the interpersonal violence to Africans that permeated the African slave trade and the lesser but still great devastation to the bodies and minds of British travelers who ventured into the African interior, these writers saw extreme challenges to ideas of an integrated self and of integrated political spaces (whether continents, nations, or smaller regions). The writers often figured the dangers to their selves—including the productive (albeit problematically productive) new selves that resulted from the violence and devastation—in terms of consumption: economic, but also corporeal and even (as also in the purported blood-tasting following the execution of Louis XVI) cannibalistic. As was the case in both the French and the American migrations, the selves that the (literary) African migration destroyed and created were, more than anything else, linguistic. Identity and selfhood in the literature of this migration are highly figurative, things of language as well as blood and bones.

As Romantic writers came to understand, physical, social, and imaginative displacement related in complex ways to emplacement. Running away (to Britain) from the guillotine or from the iron shackles of forced servitude represented a complicated form of engagement with the French Terror and colonial slavery. Imagining oneself in the Americas far away from British political, religious, economic, and social realities represented a complicated form of engagement with those realities.

The literature of Romantic migration was never simply escapist, no more so than a war refugee seeking a peaceful land or an ex-slave seeking a space of freedom would be simply escapist. Migration frequently is dangerous, and it always challenges the boundaries of individual and group subjectivities, as well as individual and group social, political, and linguistic processes. As this book will show, the literature of Romantic migration spoke—and continues to speak—at once forcefully and interrogatively about a world in conflict, a transforming and transformative world, a world with uncertain borders and an uncertain future.

Chapter 1

The French Immersion: Cross Currents of Selfhood

Great numbers of...Emigrants have got across to the English coast within the last fortnight; they have been seen on the roads from Dover, Hastings, Eastbourne, and Brighthelmstone, coming up to London in all the possible ways, on coaches, wagons, fish carts, &c. Some came walking....The streets of London now swarm with them.

—*European Magazine* (September 1792)

Inland, within a hollow Vale, I stood,
And saw, while sea was calm and air was clear,
The Coast of France, the Coast of France how near!
Drawn almost into frightful neighbourhood.
I shrunk, for verily the barrier flood
Was like a Lake, or River bright and fair,
A span of waters; yet what power is there!
What mightiness for evil and for good!

—William Wordsworth, "September, 1802,"
Poems in Two Volumes

Between France and England

Late-eighteenth-century British literature emerged from a geographical polarity. At a time when Britain was adopting its modern form as a nation-state and when British–French national animosities were cresting, the French Revolution, the most important event in the history of France as a modern nation, defined a movement of British national literature. The geographical categorization of literature according to nation, though making sense for linguistic, historical, economic, and cultural reasons, has obscured the spaces between France and England. The study of what one might term Channel literature—like the study of Romantic Transatlanticism and Romantic imperialism—reveals a more complex cultural and literary world than exclusively national studies. This chapter explores that literature, especially as it involves the French emigration to England that began with the Revolution and peaked in the early 1790s.

In the first days after the storming of the Bastille, a group of the French nobility, Louis XVI's brother, the Comte d'Artois, being the most notable among them, left France. Then, as the National Assembly stripped the aristocracy of long-held economic control over the middle and lower classes, more of the social elite emigrated to other nations on the European continent, to the Americas, and especially to England, as did other, middle- and lower-class people with a variety of political and sometimes legal motives.[1] In 1791 and, following the September Massacres, in 1792, an enormous flood of emigrants departed, and they now included the Catholic clergy as well as others seeking refuge from political dangers.[2] In all, well over 125,000 French emigrated. Although the most-recorded and best-known *émigrés* came from the nobility, more than three times as many members of the other social classes—including the upper middle class, the lower middle class, the working class, and peasants—emigrated.[3] The destabilizing effects of this emigration worked their way deep into the minds of the contemporary French and British populations alike and deep into contemporary imaginative literature.[4]

Wordsworth, concerned with many kinds of travels and migrations, addressed emigration directly in *The Prelude* (1805), "The Banished Negroes" (1802), "The Emigrant Mother" (1802), and "The Exiled French Clergy" (1827). Smith also addressed the emigration, especially in *The Emigrants* (1793) and *The Banished Man* (1794). Burney dealt with the issue in *Brief Reflections Relative to the Emigrant French Clergy* (1793) and her emigrant novel *The Wanderer* (1814). Coleridge—although famously thematizing exile in poems such as "Rime of the Ancyent Marinere" and "Christabel" and directly addressing Priestley's emigration "o'er the ocean" to Pennsylvania in his *Sonnets on Eminent Characters*—dealt directly with the French emigration mostly in political and religious prose, such as *The Watchman*, his *Lectures on Revealed Religion*, and essays published in the *Morning Post*.[5] Mary Robinson wrote about emigration in her novel *Hubert de Sevrac, a Romance of the Eighteenth Century* (1796) and in her related poem "The Alien Boy" (1800). Madame de Staël, Chateaubriand, and other non-British writers who emigrated to Britain also addressed emigration. Such writers—particularly Smith, Burney, and Wordsworth (writers who frequently focused on place and space)—explored how emigration displaces and reorients identity and subjectivity, both individual and national. In other words, such writers considered Romantic dispositionings. Smith, Burney, and the early Wordsworth critiqued nationalism and the nationalistic abuse of power; and they examined variations on a potential alternative to nationhood: an international, multilingual, meritocratic community. As will be clear in later chapters, such interests remained central in other emigration literature as well, particularly that of the African-British emigration.

Burney and, to a lesser extent, Smith connected personally to the French emigration. As Kristy Carpenter observes, "The Burney family were intimately involved with the French *émigrés*. Both Fanny's sisters knew and entertained *émigrés* and her father was closely involved with Relief effort[s]."[6] Dr. Burney encouraged Frances to write her *Brief Reflections Relative to the Emigrant French Clergy*; and Hannah More wrote another call for relief, *Considerations on Religion and Public Education* (1793). (Also, as part of this effort, Edmund Burke wrote "Case of the Suffering Clergy of France" [1792].) Burney married a French emigrant, Alexandre d'Arblay, and she spent time with him and Madame de Staël at Juniper Hall, where de Staël stayed while in England. Burney later emigrated to France with her husband and young son in 1802 before returning to England in 1812. In 1784, Smith likewise moved to France with her husband and their young children—in her case so that her husband could escape creditors—and returned half a year later, now with a newborn son. Her daughter Augusta married Alexandre de Foville, another French *émigré*, in 1793.

Wordsworth associated himself with the emigration just as extensively as Burney and Smith, but his interests have passed nearly unnoted.[7] In fall 1791, Wordsworth traveled to France intending to spend a few months improving his French so that he could work as a tutor to a wealthy young Englishman.[8] In *The Prelude*, he commented cavalierly on his motives for making the trip: after living "Free as a colt, at pasture on the hills," he "betook…[himself] to France, / Led thither by a personal wish / To speak the language more familiarly."[9] But once there he became deeply involved in national politics and in a romantic relationship with Annette Vallon, who had a daughter by him. Instead of making a relatively brief trip, he spent over a year in France—first in Paris, then in Orleans (a common destination of temporary British visitors), then in Blois (a less common destination for the British, but the home of Annette), and again in Orleans and Paris—before returning to England, apparently only because he needed to get money to support his life in France. All this is to say that Wordsworth, in his early twenties, showed a strong interest in expatriating from England. He describes his time in Orleans as his "more permanent residence," and he committed himself to this place, time, and people, though only for a short while, as intensely as he committed himself at other times to the English Lake District: "my heart was all / Given to the [French] People," he said, "and my love was theirs" (*Prelude* 9.81, 125–6).

When Wordsworth's Girondist political affiliations kept him from safely returning to France for a prolonged stay, Annette, who was a Royalist and belonged to a family much threatened by the new French government (her brother narrowly escaped the guillotine), might have been expected to emigrate to England to join her lover. She had a newborn daughter, making emigration difficult, but other women (Smith and Burney, for example) crossed the Channel with young children and newborns; and if major hazards stood in the way of emigrating in 1793, the political and personal incentives for doing so would have offset them. Biographers and critics of Wordsworth frequently have considered Wordsworth's blameworthiness for not returning to Annette and his daughter, in no small part because Wordsworth focuses so closely on abandoned mothers in his poetry; but, as these same readers of Wordsworth frequently point out, a timely return by Wordsworth to France likely would have meant his execution (resulting in another kind of abandonment much considered by Wordsworth: that which occurs through the death of a father).[10] Annette's emigration to England would have been comparatively risk-free.

Annette appears never to have attempted to emigrate, though, and while Wordsworth seems to have reestablished his love of England quickly, observers of him still emphasized his French connections. Annette began to call herself Madame Williams or Veuve Williams; and their daughter would take Wordsworth's name. In England, some who did not know Wordsworth perceived him as French. In the famous "Spy-Nozy" affair, for instance, when the Home Office agent James Walsh came to Alfoxden in August 1797 to spy on Wordsworth and Coleridge, he was following a lead indicating that Wordsworth and his companions were French emigrants in service to the French government.[11] Walsh wrote to the Home Office that his informant,

Charles Mogg, had related that

> some French people had got possession of the Mansion House.... Christopher Trickie and his Wife who live at the Dog pound at Alfoxton, told Mogg that the French people had taken the plan of their House, and that They had also taken the plan of all the places round that part of the Country.... Mogg spoke to several other persons inhabitants of that Neighbourhood, who all told him, They thought these French people very suspicious persons, and that They were doing no good there.[12]

Although the accusations are laughable, they also reveal much about the suspicious political and cultural atmosphere of this time and potentially still more about Wordsworth's self-representations. (Did he, Coleridge, and Dorothy Wordsworth communicate in French when in public, perhaps when speaking of matters they wished to keep private from nosy neighbors? Did Wordsworth wear French clothing or affect French habits?)

Notably, others also mistook Coleridge for a French emigrant in July 1794 when he took a walking tour through Wales.[13] He clearly was thinking about emigration at this time. During the tour, he wrote to Southey about their Pantisocratic emigration plans, including a joke about faux-French emigrants. At an inn where he stopped during the tour, he became

> sore afraid, that I had caught the Itch from a Welch Democrat, who was charmed with my [Pantisocratic] sentiments: he grasped my hand with flesh-bruising Ardour—and I trembled lest some discontented Citizens of the *animalcular* Republic should have emigrated.[14]

As such events show, the French emigration conditioned life in Britain during the 1790s, not only in London where the "streets... swarm[ed] with" emigrants, but in southern England's Somersetshire and in rural Wales where relatively few emigrants lived.[15]

The British responded variously to the emigration. In the early 1790s, Burney, More, and Burke represented the *émigrés* as victims of republican tyranny who deserved British support. Smith, writing with sympathy for republican ideals but disgust for republican excesses, also generally supported the *émigrés*. Coleridge, on the other hand, criticized writers like Burney, More, and Burke as he aligned himself with a "professing patriot" who commented that

> The Emigrants are forever held up as demanding Respect and impassioned Condolence and the French Legislators depictured as monsters for having expelled them from the bosom of the Republic and confiscated their property, and all this without one inquiry whether or no

> these emigrants from their private Depravity and political Intrigues were not such men, as no State in the act of settling itself could safely tolerate.[16]

Even as Coleridge swung away from his early, ardent support of the French Revolution, he remained suspicious of French emigrants, as when he suggested in a 17 February 1800 article in the *Morning Post* that either "a well-paid Anti-Jacobin" or an emigrant had been writing anti-French propaganda that had been passed off as coming from the pen of French soldiers.[17] Wordsworth, though, at first glance seems to have been ambivalent about the French emigrants. They generally were absent from his writing of the early 1790s, and when, in the first years of the 1800s, they did appear, they did so at least partially in the service of other interests that Wordsworth was exploring: for instance, the problem of Napoleonic tyranny ("The Banished Negroes"), the psychology of a mother separated from her child ("The Emigrant Mother"), or the virtues of an idealized England ("The Exiled French Clergy").

But the French emigration concerned Wordsworth—and Burney and Smith, too—both in and of itself and also as a metonymic figure for broader social issues. The emigration, for all three writers, revealed instabilities in the identities and subjectivities of the French emigrants, especially as those identities and subjectivities emerged from national spaces. And it also revealed instabilities in the identities and subjectivities of the British, including the authors themselves. The instability of the foreign others and of the authors themselves was dangerous: it might—and in the fictions usually did—tear people away from the places that had given root and meaning to their lives as they had known them. But it also frequently opened the possibility of a transformation of individuals and societies into something new and better. If a migration involved displacement, it also involved re-emplacement, albeit frequently a provisional and insecure re-emplacement.

The Geography of Displacement and Replacement in Charlotte Smith's *The Emigrants*

Near the end of *The Emigrants* (1793), Charlotte Smith draws a metaphorical map that offers an alternative to dominant geographical configurations of England and France in the early 1790s. From an eminence in the South Downs of Sussex, Smith looks at the land beneath her, "where boundless, yet [as] distinct, / Even as [on] a map, . . . are spread the fields/ [God's] . . . bounty clothes; divided here by woods/ And there by commons rude, or winding brooks."[18] On this map, naturalized lines formed by "woods," "winding brooks," and the "commons rude" circumscribe the space owned by humans: "the fields." In other words, this map replaces standard cartographic dividing lines, which demonstrate British institutional power over humans and over nature, with a naturalized alternative.

The lines are naturalized rather than natural since a commons, even a "rude" one, is not quite nature; since, as Arthur Young noted, the woods that mark the fields are likely "shaws" or coppices cultivated specifically for the purpose of showing property lines; and since a "map" itself implies human ordering.[19] The natural on this map, then, does not oppose the social; rather, the natural has a social purpose—in this case, a socially radical, reformist purpose.

Unlike this map, many other contemporary English maps overtly promoted the interests of the wealthy and socially powerful. These are county maps (or maps derived from them) that mapmakers sold by subscription to landowners who then appeared more prominently than their neighbors who neglected to subscribe.[20] In the cartouches, one finds coats of arms and pictures of buildings related to institutional power (major churches, for example). These other maps, then, promote an idea of a well-ordered physical and social nation, with institutional architecture or institutional topographic markings (which represent structures of power and ownership) providing orientation and direction.

On Smith's metaphorical map, the commons—the egalitarian space of the map—defines the owned property, rather than the other way around. The shaws, planted by property owners but then left to become "woods," define the cultivated, actively managed land around them. This kind of leveling nature promotes those lacking power over those who normally wield it: this nature contests the dominant British social order and asserts its own order based upon individual merit, regardless of socioeconomic or other institutional power. As Smith, quoting James Thomson, writes elsewhere in the poem, a peasant who "Displays distinguish'd merit . . . is a Noble / Of Nature's own creation" (1.240–4). The alternative offered by Smith's metaphorical map, then, re-codifies and re-institutionalizes the world according to Smith's principles of a politically reformist Nature.

Smith's alternative map also resists another kind of institutional mapping then in ascendancy. This other mapping would inscribe England with the lines of a militarized nation state. In 1792–93, the years in which *The Emigrants* is set, Captain William Mudge and Isaac

Dalby performed early, and conspicuous, work for the first national ordnance survey in Sussex. They "extended the primary triangulation of England and Wales westward along the crest of the South Downs, and fixed the position of key trigonometrical stations...within the area of the Brighton sheet."[21] The English map offered by Smith's poem stands against such militaristic configurations of Sussex and England.

In a discussion of Smith's emigrant novel *The Banished Man*, Benis observes that the political and ideological positions of Smith's characters are realized *spatially*.[22] Such is the case, too, in Smith's other writings of the 1790s and early 1800s. Geography—the writing of space—throughout *The Emigrants* provides directions toward a non-militaristic, reformist social order, an order possible only for people whose sense of national identity has been destabilized. Smith's representation of this potential order had evolved considerably from the French Revolutionary order that Smith supported in her novel *Desmond*, published a year earlier in 1792, the evolution perhaps reflecting less Smith's own ideological changes than changes in the socio-geographical delineations of nations during the French Terror and early weeks of French–English war. By the time that Smith published *The Banished Man* in 1794, Anglo-European circumstances—and Smith's geographical relationship to them—would shift again. Smith would reflect broadly on the specific geography of *The Emigrants* only in *Beachy Head* (1807), though, and here her social expectations would diminish.

Through its configuration of the Sussex coast, *The Emigrants* reveals the contradictions and shortcomings inherent in dominant late-eighteenth-century English and French geographical self-representations as well as in the material realities of England and France. In particular, the poem shows that the real uses of inhabited spaces, along with geographical self-representations—in maps and in newspaper and magazine accounts—alienated and displaced many of the people who constituted the two nations. And through both negative and positive example the poem offers a model of a preferable self-representation that might supplant the existing ones.[23] Smith's map in *The Emigrants* thus challenges the dominant organizations and significations of British and European spaces, offering instead a peaceful, egalitarian replacement, a replacement that, she suggests, is immanent in nature itself.

Smith's challenge is evident in her use of toponyms, like Sussex, Brighthelmstone (now Brighton), and the Downs south of the Weald of Sussex, through which she conducts a complex critique of the dominant geographies of nations and national identity. In naming and mapping the Sussex coast, Smith critiques the people represented in the poem (the French emigrants and the English, including, to a limited degree, Smith herself). These people, the poem indicates, need to move beyond their institutionally determined conceptions of their nations, which is to say beyond their current social and religious orientations, and reorient themselves according to the natural-political geography Smith proposes. While Smith herself sees the benefits of this natural geography, the emigrants who occupy her poem ground themselves in a class- and religion-based nationalistic geography that does not and cannot provide them adequate physical or social direction.[24] In *The Banished Man*, Smith's characters would achieve a transnational, transcultural state through international intermarriage and multilingualism, but that state remains largely unrealized in *The Emigrants*. Smith only hints at the future possibility of such a state in *The Emigrants* when she expresses hope, in her dedication to William Cowper, that the emigrants' "painful exile may finally lead to the extirpation of that reciprocal hatred so unworthy of great and enlightened nations; that it may tend to humanize both countries, by convincing each that good qualities exist in the other; and at length annihilate the prejudices that have so long existed to the injury of both" (p. 133). The poem exposes the emigrants' position as a current failure to move beyond prejudice: a failure deserving sympathy, but a failure nonetheless.

Smith's representation of the emigrants in Sussex highlights a specific nationalistic geographical configuration (with king at center of country and with lands divided according to aristocratic and Church interests) that may have provided the aristocratic and Catholic emigrants with a means of negotiating the world in pre-Revolutionary France but leaves them geographically disoriented, literally incapable of moving with purposeful direction, after the Revolution.[25] Though Smith suggests that these emigrants do move, describing them as wanderers "Thro' the wide World" (1.103), "Poor wand'ring wretches" (1.296), and "ill-starr'd wanderers" (2.436), they actually go virtually nowhere in this poem. They remain fixed on the configuration of France that they have lost, never proceeding beyond the coordinates of their lives under the reign of Louis XVI.[26] These ostensible wanderers "hang / Upon the barrier of the rock" (1.108–9). They "droop" on the cliffs, while only their "thoughts go back to France, / Dwelling on all . . . [they have] lost" (1.113, 127–8). They "recline" in a hollow of the cliff as "Fancy brings, / In waking dreams, that native land again" (1.200–2, 220–1). Their "aching eyes

[are]/ Fix'd on the horizon" toward France (1.216–17). They gaze across the Channel, and simply, without moving—or moving only to shift position a little on the cliffside—"wait / On this bleak morning" (1.159, 161–2). Although just fifty miles from London, the emigrants whom Smith sees on the cliffs to the east of Brighthelmstone appear literally on the edge of England and have in no way committed themselves geographically or ideologically to even a temporary life there (or any other place away from monarchist France). The emigrants, "waiting long / Some fortunate reverse that never comes," seem to sense—like the "little band" of Burkean politicians in Smith's *Desmond*—that if an "event . . . does not restore to the French their former government, there will be a blank in that portion of the map of Europe that *was* France."[27]

During the emigration years of 1792–93, though, in British newspapers, magazines, and other popular nonfictional representations with nationalist leanings, emigrants generally appear less disoriented; and (unlike the landscape of Smith's poem) the Sussex coast and downs generally appear as a threshold environment, a point of entry and transition to other places, rather than as a point of arrested movement. In contemporary periodicals, masses of French refugees move away from Brighthelmstone and other Sussex coastal towns, with "Emigrants . . . coming up to London in all possible ways, ... [t]he streets of London now swarm[ing] with them."[28] Although some emigrants did stay in Sussex, sometimes living in the houses of charitable residents (Smith among them), most found their way quickly to London, which Carpenter and others have described as the capital of emigration.[29] According to contemporary news accounts, rather than being fully debilitated by their spatial (dis)orientation as Smith's characters are, the majority of emigrants, while never giving up their idea of themselves as French or their idea of France as their own, in some sense moved on. In the early 1790s, instead of succumbing to arresting despair in the face of severe financial and social hardships, they had, Lord Auckland notes, a public reputation for "levity and gaity."[30] They were more likely to dance at the Vauxhall Pleasure Gardens than to prostrate themselves in a cliff-side hollow.[31] Records show that some set themselves up in business or in the arts; and another group of them likely moved undetected across England as spies for the Jacobins.[32]

The group of emigrants Smith describes, then, is not typical of the whole population of emigrants as her contemporaries would have understood it through newspapers and other popular accounts, but represents a specific way of understanding and engaging with—or failing to understand and engage with—the fast-changing late-eighteenth-century orientation of nations. Despairing—literally "Dwelling on all . . . they have lost" (in other words, dwelling on or inhabiting a place that is gone)—Smith's emigrants require, though they do not realize it, a newly configured set of geographical coordinates and a means to move between them. They require a new disposition.

The emigrants' geographical disorientation appears still greater because Smith locates them ironically "to the Eastward of the Town of Brighthelmstone" (p. 135), a place designation generally associated with luxury at the end of the eighteenth century and thus highlighting how far the emigrants (who no longer enjoy social privileges) have fallen since leaving France. Although "Brighthelmstone" may have compared poorly with the Versailles that appears in the "waking dream" of Smith's courtly woman lying in the cliff-side hollow, it did have its own "painted galleries, / And rooms of regal splendour" (1.221–2) and was fashionable enough among the English elite to indicate the irony of such a dream and of Smith's description of the woman's "drear reality" in this "cold rugged seat" (1.230, 232). Smith's representation of lingering malaise near the town challenges dominant nonfiction textual representations of the place in recent history. It highlights the failure of the English landscape to function in the ways—and for the people—that the English generally claimed it functioned.

Specifically, the English often claimed that in Brighton and its environs nature collaborated with society to benefit the social elite within existing social hierarchies, which is to say that nature maintained a class hierarchy there that inverted the one proposed by James Thompson and Smith. Through the last half of the eighteenth century, Brighton had become a famous spa town, a destination for members of the upper classes, including the Prince of Wales. Toward the end of the century, the wealthy came for the mild winters and the entertainments; since the 1750s they came mainly for a natural attraction: the ostensibly curative seawater. The Sussex physician Richard Russell promoted the medical benefits of bathing in and drinking Sussex ocean water in a 1750 dissertation, and he then set up a house in Brighthelmstone, where he treated patients. Eleven years later, Anthony Relhan published *A Short History of Brighthelmston, With Remarks on its Air, & an Analysis of its Waters*, detailing the high and purportedly curative salt and mineral content of the seawater at Brighton, calling it "as great, or perhaps greater, than is to be found in the sea water of any other port in England," thereby helping to set the town's reputation among the upper classes.[33] Many of Smith's contemporaries, such as William Lee in his 1795 *Ancient and Modern History of Lewes and Brighthelmston*, figure the region including and surrounding Brighton simply as "That healthful tract."[34]

Others, though, satirize the people who go to Brighton for the water cure, revealing that the healthfulness of the town is part of only one possible figuration and that it does not correspond with all of the various perceived (or advertised) realities of the place. These writers—usually writers of imaginative literature—satirize elite tourists who "with ails in heart or lungs, / In liver or in spine / Rush . . . coastward to be cur'd like tongues, / By dipping into brine."[35] William Cowper, to whom Smith dedicates *The Emigrants*, includes similar satire in "Retirement" (1782):

> Your prudent grand-mammas, ye modern belles,
> Content with Bristol, Bath, and Tunbridge-Wells,
> When health requir'd it, would consent to roam,
> Else more attach'd to pleasures found at home.
> But now alike, gay widow, virgin, wife,
> Ingenious to diversify dull life,
> In coaches, chaises, caravans, and hoys,
> Fly to the coast for daily, nightly joys,
> And all, impatient of dry land, agree
> With one consent to rush into the sea.[36]

Smith, without satire here, also plays against figurations of Brighton as a site of natural ease and curative waters for those born or raised into social privilege. For the formerly aristocratic and clerical emigrants who have become bewildered in post–Revolutionary France and England, the water offers no medicinal benefits, failing to revitalize them in either body or spirit. For the formerly courtly woman in the cliff-side hollow, the water is merely "dark'ning waves" (1.230). For all of them, it is "dim [and] cold," and "melancholy rolls its refluent tides" (1.158–9). Fixed within their no longer tenable social and national identities, they are beyond the benefits available in nature. According to Smith, even the English elite—who, still secure in their social positions, equate Brighton with curative waters—fail to connect to the genuine in nature and fail to sense the real benefits of natural waters. She writes, "one, who long / Has dwelt amid . . . artificial scenes / . . . [,] deems that splendid shows, / . . . and [the] pageant pomp of Courts, / Are only worth regard; forgets all taste / For Nature's genuine beauty; [and] in the lapse / Of rushing waters hears no soothing sound" (1.260–6).

Smith includes Britons like herself in the critique. The water off the Sussex coast has been "melancholy" for herself as well: she speaks of the "troubled waves," the "baffled wave" and the "restless Sea" (1.159, 2, 71, and 88). As readers have frequently noted, she describes the emigrants' condition and her own as nearly reflexive in the poem, going to great lengths to suggest a sympathetic connection between herself and them despite their ideological differences.[37] As Stuart Curran observes, Smith's "strategy" in the poem involves "connect[ing herself] . . . as center of perception" to the emigrants.[38]

One might expect, then, that she shares much of the emigrants' experience of space. But in nearly all senses, she configures for herself, at least prospectively, a different and preferable geographical space in Sussex. While the emigrants hang on rocks and huddle in cliff-side hollows, Smith in Book Two of the poem climbs to an eminence in the Sussex downs.[39] Like the emigrants, she may be "Lost in despondence" (2.6), but she gains a perspective that includes their own and also extends beyond it. (As she explains her "map" from that perspective, the ocean water even shows the potential of becoming beneficent to her as it alternates between the cold stormy waters she describes elsewhere and waters more ameliorative: the "waves . . . now / Swell with dark tempests, now are mild and blue" [2.402–3].) While Smith, as "a center of perception," clearly connects to the emigrants, the emigrants themselves occupy a less privileged position and have a more limited perspective. In other words, Smith's reformist map emerges from a position of ideological advantage.

Intriguingly, this reformist map differs from other reformist geographical configurations: for instance, those of radical and dissident writers such as John Thelwall and the early Coleridge, who configure an England centered around cottage life as a space that might transcend (or at least avoid) British and European difficulties. Smith finds the idea of a cottage-centered England attractive, but ultimately rejects it as a nonfunctional alternative geography. She "sigh[s] for some lone Cottage, deep embower'd/ In the green woods, that these steep chalky Hills/ Guard from the strong South West" (1.42–5). But she fails to find such a "guard[ed]" place: "Tranquil seclusion I have vainly sought," she says; "Peace, who delights in solitary shade, / No more will spread for me her downy wings" (1.65–7). She then reemphasizes the failure: "[T]he Cot sequester'd, where the briar/ And wood-bine wild, embrace the mossy thatch," cannot "shut out for an hour the spectre Care" (1.75 and 90).

While Smith indicates that personal circumstances have precluded "Peace," also important is the location of the cottage "[i]n the green woods, that these steep chalky Hills / Guard from the strong South West." The term "South West" in the eighteenth century could mean "south west wind," and that meaning fits here, but the term also could designate a local or regional place, especially when capitalized as in Smith's poem.[40] In what sense is the South West as a geographical region "strong"? Since the South West directly includes Normandy, its strength includes the strength of Robespierrist France.[41] Having shifted from her position in *Desmond*, in which the title character asserts happily that French "oppression is destroyed" with the fall of the monarchy and the Catholic Church, to an acknowledgment of the "horrors" and "infernal passions" of the September Massacres (and subsequent French events), Smith now also proposes that the hills might "guard" her from an increasingly bloody French leadership.[42] But from that strength there is no security since "Peace.../ No more will spread...her...wings." Smith's rejection of a secure English life centered on the rural cottage, then, follows from the fact that the integrity of English borders and English selfhood is uncertain in a time of military conflict. The war jeopardizes nationhood and the sense of secure identity within the nation.

Subsequent lines contradicting Smith's assertion of insecurity, though, complicate such a reading. In these lines, Smith associates herself with an equally common configuration of the Sussex Downs and England at large as a *peaceful* space safe from the dangers of France and Europe. "Peace is here," she writes, "And o'er our vallies, cloath'd with springing corn, / No hostile hoof shall trample," because "by the rude sea guarded, we are safe" (2.205–7, 210).

"Peace...no more will spread...her...wings," and "Peace is here." This is an odd contradiction, and the military history of Sussex highlights its oddness further. In 1793, other representations of the region indicate that there was much reason to doubt the claims for peace and security made by Smith on the South Downs.[43] While less frequently mentioned by newspapers or guidebooks than Brighton, the downs to the south of the Weald of Sussex appeared in contemporary print and were of popular interest and concern. When Smith made her contradictory claims about English peace and security early in 1793, peace and security were fragile in this part of Sussex. Foreign invaders had landed on the coast of Sussex in the past: the Norman invasion entered England through Pevensey Bay, and the Danes and Romans had been there as well.[44] If such incursions were distant history, they maintained analogical significance within the current British–French crisis, as Smith's poem *Beachy Head* would demonstrate.[45] Still more to the point, the government and the English populace increasingly recognized the Sussex coast as a likely landing place for invading French republicans in the current conflict, and they soon would militarize the South Downs in response.[46] As a correspondent to the London *Morning Herald* reported, by the middle of August 1793 (four months after the end of *The Emigrants*), the government had moved 7000 troops over the South Downs to "the hills over Brighton" and set up an encampment.[47]

In the face of much contradictory evidence (and in the face of her own contrary claims and tendencies), why should Smith configure a peaceful England? Perhaps because contemporary newspapers and other popular representations already configured an opposing representation of Sussex—a militarized one—as a space of English "delight." As the *Morning Herald* commented,

> The novelty of seeing near 7000 men, with their park of artillery, battalion guns, &c. in one line of march, drew out the whole town of Brighton. Innumerable carriages of every description, and crowds of people of the first fashion covered the hills, while the deep azure of the sea, on whose bosom rode a number of ships in full sail, the glittering of arms on the shore, and the beauty of the morning, added to the splendour of the scene, and filled the mind of every spectator with *delight* [My emphasis].[48]

A correspondent to the *Gentlemen's Magazine* for September, 1793, similarly called attention to militaristic "delight," which he connected to the waters of Brighton as well as to the aesthetic spectacle. During the troops' march toward Brighton,

> The irregularity of the Downs frequently gave an opportunity of seeing every regiment with a *coup-d'oiel.* Numbers of people came out to meet us. The town, with the sea, and the music, and the universal animation around, somewhat dissipated the fatigue of a long march.... We... wheeled round the town to our new ground, which appeared a little Paradise.... The water of our former stations has too much chalybeate in it to be pleasant.... [O]n our arrival here we had the luxury of finding it could not be better. This necessary part of the comforts of life... [complements] the *delightful* ground we are encamped upon [My emphasis].[49]

Smith, on the other hand, associates "delight" with peaceful nature. Not only does "Peace... delight... in solitary shade" (1.66), but solitary shade evidently delights in peace. She remembers the naturally "delightful landscapes" that she experienced when young;

and (unlike the newspaper correspondents) she indicates that natural delight is unattainable in a time of war: "What is the promise of the infant year, / The lively verdure, or the bursting blooms, / To those, who shrink from horrors such as War / Spreads o'er the affrighted world?" (2. 38, 43–6).

Smith's mapping, then, challenges the "delightful" militaristic configuration of Sussex and the nation, a configuration that contemporaries recognized as one that military leaders manipulated and achieved. As the *Morning Herald* writer noted, the military leaders attempted to inscribe the land with a specific ideological message, and they accordingly set up the Brighton Camp for the consumption of the spectator citizens, who saw the landscape the way that the military leaders wished them to see it. According to this writer, the "delightful ground" described in the *Gentlemen's Magazine* offered delights to the eye, but not to the rest of the body. The Brighton Camp

> has a fine appearance to the eye, and to preserve this effect the comfort of two regiments is destroyed, as . . . [these regiments] are encamped on a newly ploughed field, full of sharp flint stones. . . . [A]lmost immediately behind these two regiments they might have pitched their tents on the finest turf in England; but this would not please the eye so well.[50]

If Smith had acknowledged that this militaristic configuration of Sussex was coming to dominate—and delight—the popular imagination, her own natural, peacefully egalitarian configuration might have seemed beyond reach. Seven thousand troops and the whole appreciative town of Brighthelmstone would do much to trample nature, just as the militaries of Europe were trampling nature across the Channel. "*There*," in Europe, but not here, "the trumpet's voice / Drowns the soft warbling of the woodland choir; / And violets, lurking in their turfy beds / Beneath the flow'ring thorn, are stained with blood" (2.68–71). There, the Jacobins have broken "The laws of Nature and Humanity" (2.123).

In order to offer a model of reform—and a new, alternative subject position—even to France and Europe, Smith requires a figurative space, such as she offers in a demilitarized Sussex, in which her prospective natural ideal still *might* be realized currently. "Unhappy France!" she writes,

> If e'er thy lilies, trampled now in dust,
> And blood-bespotted, shall again revive
> In silver splendour, may the wreath be wov'n

By voluntary hands; and Freemen, such
As England's self *might* [my emphasis] boast, unite to place
The guarded diadem on *his* fair brow,
Where Loyalty may join with Liberty
To fix it firmly. (2.104–11)

The subjunctive is crucial. England *might* boast these Freemen, who *might* set an example that French citizens can follow to achieve a new kind of constitutional monarchy. As the rest of the poem makes clear, though, this possibility depends upon a reorganization of England itself. The freedom of the English "Freemen," after all, remains at present more of a vain boast—a "highly vaunted Freedom"—than an actuality (1.245). The English *might* set an example, but only if their own government learns to restrain its "power" (2. 424), only if their own rulers learn that "the poorest hind . . . / . . . / Is equal to the imperious Lord" (2.427–9), and only if their own land is occupied by "lovely Freedom," "equal Justice" (2.431–2), "public virtue" (2.439), and "Reason, Liberty, and Peace" (2.444). Smith wishes for England to "triumph," but away from the fields of conventional warfare: England's "laurels" should be "bloodless," she argues (1.365 and 369). In other words, before England will offer a viable substitute to France, the English must achieve values promoted (though not achieved) by the early French Revolutionaries themselves (egalitarianism, reason, liberty), along with a kind of peace asserted by Smith but little in evidence on the English land.[51] Only then *might* England's social and political system become an international one.

Smith's final assessment of England's progress toward such reform appears in her other long Sussex poem, *Beachy Head*, published fourteen years later, shortly after her death. Often viewed as a fragmentary revision or "reforging" of *The Emigrants*, *Beachy Head* likewise addresses the geography of England and Europe, and it also addresses, more than its precursor, the geography of the world and an extra-geographical, fanciful, and visionary space.[52] For the most part, though, it eliminates the prospective, reformist mapping evident in *The Emigrants.*

As it opens, the poem configures a coastal Sussex site in a way familiar from *The Emigrants.* The site is English, but Smith describes it in relation to France:

On thy stupendous summit, rock sublime!
That o'er the channel rear'd, half way at sea
The mariner at early morning hails,
I would recline.[53]

Smith comes to this spot overlooking the channel between France and England so as to "represent" the cause of England's particular geographical and geological situation, arising from the moment when

> the Omnipotent
> Stretch'd forth his arm, and rent the solid hills,
> Bidding the impetuous main flood rush between
> The rifted shores, and from the continent
> Eternally divided this green isle.[54]

As the poem quickly makes clear, though, Smith is interested in more than the geophysical (and divine) origins of England. She is interested in the social and military history that has intervened between the origins and the present time, effectively narrowing the physical divide at times and expanding it at others.

As Sarah Zimmerman notes, Smith here "commands a vast prospect literally and figuratively."[55] Along with England, the poem refers to Ireland, Normandy (historically called "Neustria, since called Normandy"), Brittany, France (historically "Gallia"), the Lake of Geneva, the Netherlands, Sicily ("anciently called Trinacria"), Norway, Sweden, Denmark, Lapland ("Scandinavia"), Naples, Salerno, Aversa, Spain (Iberia), Asia, Africa, Jerusalem, North America, and "some island of the southern sea," as well as Arcady and "visionary vales." And yet, the term "prospect," though also Smith's own ("The prospect widens"), misnames the general direction of the gaze, which is not forward, but—as the historical place names themselves indicate—backward.

Whereas *The Emigrants* mostly concerns present and future geographical circumstances, *Beachy Head* reads England and the world topologically: it reads the past in the present situation of the land and sea. The poem asks how England has arrived in its current circumstances more than how England might move beyond these circumstances into alternative, preferable ones. The poem nonetheless is as speculative as *The Emigrants*, the records of the past here often being as uncertain as expectations for the future. Like her "lone antiquary" contemplating "obliterated [burial] mounds," Smith only "perhaps may trace, / Or fancy [s]he can trace" the historical people and relations that have made England the place it is.[56]

Although the view that Smith obtains from her summit initially seems enormous—figuratively, global; literally, "So extensive . . . that only the want of power in the human eye to travel so far, prevents

London itself from being discerned"—it is nonetheless highly unstable and undependable.[57] As Anne Wallace has argued, *Beachy Head* "deliberately leaves us in the midst of... aesthetic uncertainty,"[58] and inasmuch as Smith's aesthetics integrally deals with history and geography, that uncertainty leaves the future relationship of nations (and particularly England and France) unclear. Smith's representation of that relationship—like the picture of the past and the present, and like the poem itself—is fragmentary. Smith best captures the contradictions and complications of the poem's extensive and uncertain perspective on England and the world through the figure of the poem's enigmatic second poet, the Sussex "stranger," thought by locals to have "injur'd senses, a singer of love songs and a writer of 'scatter'd rhymes, / Unfinish'd sentences,' or half erased."[59] He inhabits a space of actual physical "fragments" among the "ruins" of a "castellated mansion," and although he too conceives of an ideal hilly "prospect," the prospect is explicitly a false one, unachievable in his real world.[60]

Within *The Emigrants*, on the other hand, Smith's prospective view of both the present world and a future, reformed one still seems achievable for those who reorient themselves sufficiently. *The Emigrants* does more than "model... for readers the kind of sympathetic response toward the *émigrés* that [Smith] wants them to imitate";[61] it also maps a large-scale reformist critique that the British and the French must subscribe to. Within the poem's logic, only by accepting Smith's map might the French emigrants themselves—now internationals or transnationals instead of French nationals—"regain / Their native country" (2.437–8), albeit a country that looks little like the France that they have lost.[62] *The Emigrants* in this way is as much about the possibility of geographical re-placement as it is about displacement, though the re-placement requires still larger individual, social, and institutional displacements than any that the poem represents as having occurred.

A Banished Man Relocated

The Banished Man (1794) represents these further displacements and the ultimate re-placement in process, mostly through the French experience, as exemplified by the novel's hero D'Alonville, though also through the English, exemplified by Armand D'Alonville's friend Edward Ellesmere and D'Alonville's future wife Angelina Denzil; the Austro-Prussian, exemplified by the aristocratic Rosenheims family; and the Polish, exemplified by Carlowitz and his daughter Alexina.[63] These friends, as Benis observes, "have become estranged from their homelands, either by revolutionary instability or its mirror image, reactionary panic and intolerance."[64] As the group of international characters traverse much of the Continent and England, they must confront and then distance themselves from their nationalistic ideological positions before arriving at a resting place—albeit another unstable one—near Verona.[65] Still more than *The Emigrants*, *The Banished Man* represents a process of dispositioning: a displacement of identity, which is also a re-emplacement of it, though one that is provisional and unstable.

The novel opens a month after the September Massacres in a spot on a physical and political border zone: the Castle Rosenheim, seventeen miles from the French frontier, where the aristocrat D'Alonville arrives with his mortally wounded father in front of a pursuing French republican army.[66] The castle epitomizes many of the continuities and discontinuities of Europe at this time. The French army is "following the Austrian and Prussian troops in their retreat," and the castle is enemy territory: it not only is aristocratic but is the home of the Baron de Rosenheim, who is "a general in the Imperial Service . . . at Vienna," and of his daughter Madame D'Alberg, who is married to an Austrian Lieutenant Colonel (1.2 and 4). And yet the family extends hospitality to the Frenchman D'Alonville even before they know whether he is an enemy in disguise; and D'Alonville, "without a home, without even a country," takes full advantage of their hospitality: he buries his father in the castle garden and makes proprietary claims to the burial spot, saying, " 'I shall revisit this place again' " (1.15–17). Soon Madame D'Alberg encourages him to view her as his "elder sister" (1.17).[67] Despite political conflicts and despite national, cultural, and even social class differences, from the book's opening chapters it becomes clear "how nearly *the people* of all countries are alike" (2.43).

But before D'Alonville can act consistently and resolutely on this sentiment, he must examine more deeply an identity defined by now anachronistic nationalistic values (anachronistic since he no longer has "even a country," *his* country no longer existing in recognizable form) and now obsolete social class privileges.[68] D'Alonville's name signifies French emplacement (his family is of France, of the ville of Alon; they perhaps have come originally from the town of Allonville)[69] and yet also puns on a process of displacement (allons ville: allons à la ville?), and he must go out of himself and to his new self, but first he must stop within himself. Thus, his first stop after leaving the castle with the Rosenheim family and retainers is Koblenz, which contemporary readers would have recognized as a site circumscribed by the social and political power structures of monarchical France. In July 1791 the Comte d'Artois and the Comte de Provence, who later would become Louis XVIII, had set up an exiled government and court in this town; and so, when D'Alonville and the Rosenheim group arrive they unsurprisingly face "some difficulty in procuring lodgings in a town already crowded with persons who, driven from the frontiers, ha[ve]... taken shelter there" (1.108).[70]

In describing D'Alonville's experiences in Koblenz, Smith engages with a popular contemporary criticism of the profligacy of the exiled court. As quickly became apparent to the rest of the world, the French in Koblenz were living beyond their means. Expecting to return to France with an early victory over the republicans, many of the emigrants brought little money, but they nonetheless attempted to replicate their luxurious existence at Versailles.[71] D'Alonville benefits from the emigrants' willingness to spend and to give without expecting compensation as he seeks lodgings. He finds a "distant relation of his mothers, a Mareshal de Camp, who though by no means in high affluence himself, having saved very little, supplied him with money for his present support, and received him into a small apartment in the same house" (1.108).

While demonstrating the importance of generous social connections, D'Alonville's reliance on his "distant relation," like his reliance on the Rosenheim family, also shows that, once social and economic power becomes displaced from physical land and houses, it becomes tenuous. Characters may claim power in spoken or written language—they may call a stranger "sister" or offer shelter to a "distant relation"—but, without the solid land beneath them, the language of such claims becomes unstable, ungrounded. Families must refigure their relations; social communities must refigure theirs. When the Rosenheim family abandons their castle, for instance, their future social and economic power depends literally upon ungrounded language. Baron Rosenheim writes to his wife in Koblenz asking her if she has a set of papers that are " 'so material, that it would be a less loss to me to have [the Castle] Rosenheim destroyed, than to lose them' " inasmuch as his daughter's " 'and her children's succession to a great part depends upon these deeds' " (1.114). But the Baron's equation is faulty, backward: the loss of the castle also can lead to the loss of the deeds since the deeds are inside. Although the Baron's castle almoner, Heurothosen " 'ought to have... taken care' " to bring the deeds to Koblenz, he has not done so, and the French army subsequently has burned the castle (1.113, 145).

Except for the help of a poor, old man—once a domestic in the Baron's household and now, against the Revolutionary model, protecting his former master—the papers would be lost. D'Alonville, who comes back to the castle ruins in search of the deeds, finds the old domestic sitting on a pile of rubble. In this placeless place—in the wreckage of a castle surrounded by a wasted village—D'Alonville asks the man, "'Are you of this place, my friend[?]'...; 'Of what place?' replie[s]...the old man" (1.155). The (non)answer is apt since the domestic has lost "'all [his]...property...Everything [he]...had in the world'" (1.157). Nonetheless the old man helps D'Alonville find the papers in the ruins and agrees to accompany him back to Koblenz. The papers are of dubious value in this new nation, though, and before D'Alonville departs he reflects upon "the storms that [have] shake[n] to its centre the miserable kingdom of France" (1.169).[72]

In destabilized France, the previously dominant figurations of social space (with the castle at the physical, social, economic, and political center of the village and nation) that enabled both the upper class and the lower classes to orient themselves also have been shaken to their centers. One of the governing questions of the book is, Can the characters regain their now lost social orientation? That is, Can they return to the places from which they have been displaced? Although D'Alonville declares upon burying his father in the Rosenheim castle garden that he "'shall revisit this place again,'" his almost immediate return to the area while recovering the lost deeds requires reorientation in the already transformed topography:

> He found his way with some difficulty to the spot. The heat of the fire had withered the shrubs that grew around it; but from their remains, and his former observations, he found the very place where he so lately wept over the remains of his only parent. (1.168)

The poor man who guides D'Alonville through the castle ruins also concludes that "'the Baron will return no more'": that he and his family "'will never come back'" (1.158, 165). Fictional emigrant armies, following the example of the historically real ones, also try to reclaim the France that the emigrants have lost, but with no real hope of success (1.187, 3.174, and passim). And the Pole Carlowitz indicates the degree to which historical events can refigure nations, when he comments simply that his "country exists no longer" (2.51).

Although characters like D'Alonville and the servant wish to reestablish the places they have lost, they instead must find new places and reconfigure their understandings of particular national and regional spaces as well as the world at large. The novel's second, third, and fourth volumes track D'Alonville's progress as he reconceptualizes nation and world and as he re-identifies himself in relation to such spaces, a progress that results largely from his encounters with an international and transnational set of characters who also are transforming themselves as they cross through a range of European nations. He encounters Ellesmere—an Englishman (with a French name), who supports the principles but not the violence of the French Revolution—traveling "through Germany from Italy to England" (2.8, 9, 25, 34). D'Alonville and Ellesmere then meet the Pole Carlowitz, who has escaped to Germany from "the powers who had now the ascendancy" after "taking an active part in the late attempt of... [Poland] to regain its freedom" (2.39).[73]

In a sphere that is at once international and divorced from nationhood (occupied by men whose "country exists no longer"), national characteristics relate to each other in a kind of ideological play. Figurations of English "'half-savages'" (2.12) play off figurations of the English as "'enlightened,...respectable'" (2.13), "candid, generous, humane, and good-natured" (2.23), and "'hospitable'" (3.176). Figurations of French "'dissolute manners,'" lack of "'principle[s]'" (2.198), "'deceit'" (3.12), and treacherous politics play off D'Alonville's own impeccable manners, high principles, resistance to pretence (3.69, 154; 4.11), and bravery.[74] Like other Europeans, Germans may be either "inhuman" or humane (2.43). The institutional parameters of a nation similarly are up for grabs. For instance, when a Jacobin accuses D'Alonville of ignoring "'the laws of your country,'" D'Alonville responds, "'Not...the laws of my country,...but...the unjust and tyrannic ordinances of men who have usurped the government of that country'" (3.160–1). In this sphere, the characters who are progressing toward Verona reject "'prejudices, which affix to different nations different characters of vice,'" and believe, rather, that "'There is nothing so blind as national prejudice and national presumption'" (1.202; 2.199). If "the inferior class of the English [and other nations] have been taught to entertain [antipathy] toward every other nation" within formal or informal nationalistic ideological educational systems (3.85), the displacement from nation experienced by the characters in this novel teaches them otherwise.

Smith locates the best means for overcoming "national prejudice" in multilingualism.[75] In her linguistic solution, a basic attention to the other's language might obviate conflict. The Englishman Melton, who "could speak no language but English," is one of the novel's most bigoted characters, and Ellesmere asks him, "'might you not be better enabled to judge better of... [national] characters, if you could speak their languages?'" (2.14, 18–19). The French Marquis de Touranges simply does not "listen" to the English and thus views them as "a proud, ferocious, and hardly civilized people" (2.14).[76] As evidenced by the friendly conversations between D'Alonville, Ellesmere, and Carlowitz, speaking an other's language results in mutually beneficial peace and social support. Even more, as is clear from the relationships that develop between Ellesmere and Carlowitz's daughter Alexina and between D'Alonville and the English Angelina Denzil, multilingualism results in love. "'Alexina... is a very young scholar in your language,'" Carlowitz tells Ellesmere and D'Alonville, but even her "unsuccessful effort to express herself" leads Ellesmere to love her (2.49). Similarly, Angelina speaks "French imperfectly, and with extreme diffidence; but there was even in this defect a nameless enchantment; and her voice was so sweet, that whatever she said acquired a thousand charms only from the tone in which it was spoken"; and soon D'Alonville "fancied that the soft and expressive eyes of Angelina understood the language of his" (3.188, 204).

One must displace oneself—or be displaced—from one's home and search for a new place in order to progress ideologically in this novel, and one must displace oneself from one's own national language and seek to communicate in an other's language in order to sympathize with and love the other. One must live no place except with—and in—the loved other. Thus, when Angelina, in her unnaming French, asks D'Alonville where he lives, he at first tells her, "'I live no where'" (3.189). The answer accords with his earlier complaints about displacement: again, he says, "'I had once... a home and a country! but now I am... a wanderer upon the earth'" (3.189–90). Angelina, too, at first occupies a critical no place. Like D'Alonville, the banished man of the book's title, she and her family have been "banished" from their "place." (Her mother comments, "'the victims of injustice, oppression, and fraud, we are now banished from the rank of life where fortune originally placed us'" [2.205]). Although English themselves and residing in England, they, too, at times "live no where."

And so, D'Alonville determines to set up a household for Angelina in a place that is nearly off-the-map, in what Angelina describes as "a wild romantic country, far from any great town": in a cottage near the Welsh great house Rock-March, where D'Alonville serves as a tutor. This place—which looks at first like a no-place, or almost—fails to function as a critical alternative to the England that has victimized the Denzils, though. Rather, in Louis Marin's terms, this site is recognizable from "the philosophical discourse of [English and European] ideology, which is the totalizing expression of reality as it is given, and of its ideal justification," which is to say that at this site the victimization likely will continue.[77] Angelina imagines it as pastoral idyllic. In her view,

> the downy bloom of the sallows, the catkins of the hazel, spread slowly over the distant copses, while the sheltered hedges become partially green from the opening leaves of the elder and the hawthorn, and gradually the woods assume the verdant livery of spring. (4.212)

But in this place, a local man of wealth attempts to rape Angelina, using his social and economic power over her as a cover, and D'Alonville then faces the threat of the law after wounding Angelina's assailant in defense of her honor (4.286–305).

Angelina and D'Alonville must depart the place that Angelina has given the idealizing "romantic appellation" of "the Cottage of the Cliffs"; they must go over the cliffs (of Wales and of Dover) into a space that is alternative to either France or England. Angelina's mother speaks for them all when she says that she "'find[s] it impossible to stay in any part of England'" (4.305); and D'Alonville, in spite of his own romantic idealism, echoes Mrs. Denzil by declaring himself cut off from *all* national and institutional geographies. He will live instead in his love for Angelina and her family: "'Let us go, then.... Wherever Angelina is... is *now* my country'" (4.305). Thus, they "quit not only Wales, but Great Britain, for some part of the continent of Europe" (4.312–13).

Verona, their destination, is in many ways a peculiar choice. It is exactly the type of "'great town'" that Angelina wishes to avoid. The exiled French court, led by the Comte de Provence, left Koblenz shortly after the execution of Louis XVI and reestablished itself in Verona, where it remained until 1796.[78] Oddly, the D'Alonville-Denzils, seeking to avoid social and political conflict, head for the thick of it.[79]

French life in Verona, as English magazines and newspapers depicted it at this time, would be highly unattractive to a group such as the one led by D'Alonville. As Margery Weiner notes, when Lord Macartney, a British delegate, went to visit the French, he

> sent home a severe picture of Provence's court at Verona—the house barely furnished and with no comfort, the table served without elegance, the servants few and badly clothed, the barely disguised

> poverty—all that he recognized as the framework of exile and not without its own grandeur, but to him the real penury was the lack of intelligence in Provence's entourage, the sin against the spirit. In Macartney's view it was that which caused the monarchy to perish and it was that which condemned the emigration.[80]

Many others—including some emigrants—shared Macartney's perception of the Comte.[81] Sabatier de Cabre, a constitutionalist member of the citizen-nobility, commented at the end of November 1792 that

> It is infuriating to see such a man at the head of a cause that one would like to support. One wonders how he could have decided to escape [from France] and with what intention–to put himself at the head of a nobility flocking to him from all parts and whose efforts he negates by giving in to the intrigues of Mme de Balbi his mistress whom he has carted along with him.... This same man forgot the dossier which had all the negotiations of highest secrecy. He left it at Verdun and by this inconceivable stupidity he caused the loss of those who had shown him the most devoted loyalty. And it's this man who could be our King. When one thinks about it one is tempted to turn republican rather than be associated with people of this sort.[82]

What happens when the D'Alonville–Denzil group arrives in a place that is inconducive to their purposes of setting up a country of love separate from the other nations of the world? Finding the Rosenheim family and other emigrant friends (who seemingly have followed the Comte de Provence here), they set up what looks like an alternative court, a counter-court, whose interpersonal relations are based upon mutual affection rather than social class or economic power and in an environment that is natural rather than artificial.

The novel juxtaposes their model of a society with the actual society that existed currently in Verona and shows the advantages of their alternative. They take a house about thirty miles outside the city in "St. Isadore, near Roveredo [Rovereto]," though they know that "winter [will] oblige ... [them] to return to Verona" itself (4.328, 330). D'Alonville describes St. Isadore as a place that has a clear critical relationship to Verona (" 'we are too much delighted with the beauty and novelty of the objects around us, to think even of Verona with any wish to be there' "; 4.330), but Angelina's mother lets him know that his descriptive language still risks the kind of dangerous idealism that Angelina has exhibited in her representation of Wales. Saying that no Frenchman with the kind of education

D'Alonville has received "'has the least taste for the unadorned beauty of nature,'" Mrs. Denzil interrupts him and offers an alternative description. Her own description also figures the place—it highlights its own metaphorical adornments—but at the same time it calls attention to the failure of figurative description (and of language of any kind). She says,

> Figure to yourself these undescribeable mountains, so various in their forms, and so magnificent in their effect; *robed*, if I may use a woman's word, in many places with that assemblage of vegetable beauty, which in England is collected in the most ornamental gardens with difficulty. (4.332)

She then offers what appears to be her best effort at a non-figurative representation of her surroundings—a scientific inventory of the local flora: "'the citrus, the variety of antir[r]hinums, cedums, and faxapagar,'" and so on; flora seemingly "'calculated rather to attract the botanist, than the landscape painter'" (4.332–3).[83]

This ekphrasis is "unadorned" in the sense that it is "natural" or at least naturalized: the plants that would adorn an "'ornamental garden'" in England exist instead in nature in this space. In other words, England (and presumably much of the rest of Europe) strives toward such a space, but reaches it only in limited areas (gardens) and "with difficulty." It is a natural/naturalized alternative to the other spaces of the novel.[84]

Not only is the topography "'undescribable,'" but so is the house: Mrs. Denzil says, "'I cannot describe the house we inhabit'" (4.334). It is outside of the referential system of European places, even as it relates to those places as an alternative. It is a space emptied of institutional codings: it "'once contained a small religious society now dissolved'" (4.335). It is neither up nor down, "'not halfway up the stupendous mountain to which it clings'" (4.335). It opens toward utopian possibilities: it is an *ou topos*, which is also a *eu topos*, a critical alternative to the French court and also to the other European capitals of this time.[85]

As Benis observes, "D'Alonville's devotion to... [his] small circle of intimates dramatizes his newfound understanding that old French prescriptions about national duty require revision when the monarchy that underwrote those codes passes away."[86] This revision results in the reformist "'little society'" created by D'Alonville and his companions outside Verona (4.328).[87] This "'little society,'" promoted by the novel as an alternative to British and European societies, is not strictly egalitarian, but replaces social and economic hierarchies with natural and moral ones. To the end, D'Alonville remains

> proudly conscious . . . that, driven as he was from his home, his property and his rank, no local circumstances could level him, while he preserved his integrity and his honor, with . . . men . . . whose illiberal manners he saw and despised. (4.233)

Smith's " 'little society' " is a society of love, an alternative to the European societies of warfare, a space potentially habitable by people whose nations—and perhaps for whom ideas of nationhood and national identity—have become " 'insupportable' " (4.336).

FRANCES BURNEY AND THE "GIVEN WORD"

Published in 1814—well after Smith's utopian alternative of 1794 would have looked impractical to Europeans—and written by an author whose politics up to this time had been largely Tory as opposed to Smith's own Girondism, Frances Burney's emigration narrative, *The Wanderer*, challenges the idea that either internationalism or multilingualism can result in peace and contentment that transcend nationalist conflicts.[88] Equally, though, in a move that drew censure from English nationalist and Tory critics, the novel challenges nationalist self-representations of England as a preferred alternative to all other nations, especially France, even though in its final pages it shows a traditional English wedding in a happy English world.[89]

As Rose Marie Cutting notes, then, "It is wrong . . . simply to classify Fanny Burney with the conservative writers," and as Jacqueline Pearson says, "Burney is less confident of the evident superiority of Anglo-Saxon society" in *The Wanderer* than in her previous novels.[90] Margaret Doody adds that, in some senses, "*The Wanderer* is scarcely patriotic at all . . . ; it says England ought to change. It offers a somber view of deep-rooted wrongs in the structure of English social, economic, and sexual life."[91] And Deidre Lynch comments that Burney's novel "is preoccupied with *both* the enclosure and the crossing of geopolitical boundaries."[92] In other words, *The Wanderer* is deeply divided in its politics, and it thematizes its divisions both spatially and linguistically.[93]

Burney wrote the book over a period of fourteen years, mostly in France where she lived with her husband Alexandre d'Arblay. D'Arblay had served as an adjutant General to Lafayette in the Revolutionary government during the first days of the French Revolution, and he remained loyal to constitutionalist ideals shared by many moderates in the early revolution even after France and England descended into violence and warfare.[94] Nonetheless, he wished to fight for Napoleonic France, but Napoleon refused to commission him when he said he would not fight against England.[95] Trapped between divided loyalties, Burney and d'Arblay were compelled to remain in Paris until Napoleon's departure to begin the Russian campaign in 1812 enabled Burney to leave the country with her manuscript. Questioned about the contents of the manuscript at both the French and the English customhouses, she gave her word that it was politically neutral. In her dedication to the novel, she recalls that

> At the Custom-house on either—alas!—hostile shore, upon my given word that the papers contained neither letters, nor political writings; but simply a work of imagination and observation; the voluminous manuscript was suffered to pass, without demur, comment, or the smallest examination.[96]

Her "given word," her linguistic pledge, was enough. But it was also nothing, an empty signifier since the contents were in fact highly political and Burney really "was convinced that neither she nor her papers would have been given . . . permission to depart if Napoleon had been in Paris instead of advancing into Russia" (*Wanderer* 908n).[97]

The customhouse authorities would have had to read only the first sentences of the narrative to recognize the political character of the papers and to give the lie to Burney's words. Moreover, as this opening shows, language—spoken, written, unspoken, or unwritten; French or English—is uncertain and dangerous in this book. It leads to conflict and violence as easily as to peace of the kind discovered by the multilingual characters of *The Banished Man*. The novel opens,

> During the dire reign of the terrific Robespierre, and in the dead of night, braving the cold, the darkness and the damps of December, some English passengers, in a small vessel, were preparing to glide silently from the coast of France, when a voice of keen distress resounded from the shore, imploring, in the French language, pity and admission. (11)

One of the Englishmen warns the others to " 'Be lured by no tricks,' " and so, "no answer [is] . . . returned" (11). The long narrative that follows is all about the tricks of language, especially the language of national self-representation and self-identification.

The "voice of keen distress" comes from Juliet, the novel's protagonist. Although the narrative eventually identifies her name and blood as English, for most of the book she remains a nameless "Incognita." As she enters the boat, wearing blackface and speaking French to the English, she is literally a floating signifier of national identity (literally the feared "trick"). Doody asks the questions that the other passengers—and Burney's readers—must ask: "Is she French or English? . . . [I]s she West Indian? Is she African? The heroine . . . arrives [in England] as a nameless Everywoman; both black and white, both Eastern and Western, both high and low, both English and French."[98] And yet one must figure her equally as a No-woman, cut off from place and social connections and, therefore, cut off from whatever social identity she might otherwise have.

As the book's fourth volume eventually reveals, Juliet is at once a true French emigrant and an Englishwoman repatriating to Britain. She was born in England to English aristocratic parents, Lord Granville and his "concealed wife" (642–3). But her mother died while Juliet was still a baby, and her father, without ever publicly revealing his marriage and his legitimate child, took Juliet to France, where she grew up in a French convent, watched over by a Bishop friend of Granville's and as a companion of the Bishop's niece Gabriella (642–4). (Thus, she has "perfectly retained her native tongue, though she [has] . . . acquired something of a foreign accent," 643). Granville's intention to bring his adult daughter back to England with full legal claims to his name and social position has failed because of an accident (Granville's sudden death) and because of the outbreak of the French Revolution (which, in a moment reminiscent of *The Banished Man*, has led to a fire that has consumed all the papers showing Juliet's connection to Granville except one promissory note saved by the Bishop) (646). A Jacobin has subsequently compelled Juliet to marry him, threatening that, if she refuses him, he will have her protector, the Bishop, killed (740). The book begins with Juliet leaving France to join Gabriella, who already has emigrated to England (389), to establish her claim to inclusion in the Granville family, and to dissolve her marriage to the Jacobin once she has determined that the Bishop is safely out of his reach. Naming herself prematurely could jeopardize all of her goals (746–50).

Unable to publicly identify herself or her family connections, Juliet seeks an "inland letter" from Gabriella assuring her of the Bishop's safety (64). Juliet thus becomes associated with—though never fully placed in—the English post office, where she hopes to retrieve her letter and thereby to establish the letters of her name and identity. Landing in Dover and discovering that the post office there possesses no letter "left till called for" by her under the pseudonymous initials "L.S.," she seeks to travel to the Brighthelmstone post office (31).

The post office itself is a site of spatial and linguistic instability and displacement, a site of transition and uncertainty. In the earlier eighteenth century, it associated itself with high British authority, sending pro-government correspondence free of charge, for example; but, by the 1790s, it gave conflicting social and political messages, now "circulating, free of postage or restriction, opposition as well as government papers."[99] And yet it also operated as an organ of governmental intelligence gathering. The government "maintained a 'secret bureau' of [letter] openers and decipherers...in close contact with London," and "interceptions [of the mail] warned the government of the plans of disaffected subjects, such as...Horn Tooke, Tom Paine, Lord Edward Fitzgerald, &c."[100] Contemporaries associated the post office with men of economic and political power, and yet recurring scandals over financial corruption destabilized that power in the last decades of the eighteenth century.[101]

The post office connected other places but was itself without reliable grounding, then. In England, where unambiguous, well-rooted topographical (landed) and social place were keys to social power, Juliet's attachment to the post office thus is an embarrassment. When Juliet's sometime friend and sometime antagonist Elinor, offering to help her get to Brighthelmstone, says, "'I believe I know every soul in...[Brighthelmstone]. Whom do you want to see there?—Where are you to go?'"—Juliet looks "embarrassed, and with much hesitation, answer[s]..., 'To...the Post-office, Madam'" (31). Unable to imagine the post office as a destination in and of itself, Elinor asks, "'O! what, you are something to the post-master, are you?'" and Juliet must admit, "'No, Madam...I...I...go to the Post-office only for a letter!'" (32).

For a letter. One might think that the letter must not be an "I" since she has two of them already ("'. . . I...I . . .'"), though, in context, the double "I" suggests her uncertainty that she has any. What will this "inland letter" name the uncertain "I"? Will it call her by her pseudonym, "L.S."? Or will it call her "Mrs. Elless," the name into which another acquaintance mistakenly converts "L.S.," a name that, as Doody suggests, empties Juliet of agency, if not of identity, since it puns on "elle-less"? [102](81). Or will it call her "Ellis," the Anglo name that her other acquaintances—and the novel's narrator—then adopt for her? (82, 91).[103]

The Brighthelmstone post office does produce a letter for her, but it is a "foreign letter," rather than the domestic one she seeks, and this letter can neither name her nor place her properly. This failure amounts to having no letter at all, no place, and little sense of herself. She says, "'I have no letter, no direction from the person whom I had hoped to meet; and whose abode, whose address, I know not how to discover' "; and so she " 'dare[s] not say who, nor what I am,—hardly even know[s] it' " herself (63, 66; compare 673).[104]

As the "itinerant Incognita" bounces from household to household and receives illiberal treatment, which is at odds with contemporary British self-representations of English hospitality (208), Juliet's uncertain person continues to pose the question, What separates British identity from French?[105] Juliet thinks of England as her " 'loved, long lost, and fearfully recovered native land,' " but her belief, upon crossing the Channel, " 'that only to touch the British shore would be liberty and felicity' " bumps up against the reality that Britain offers no more "liberty and felicity" than France (751). The matriarch at one of the illiberal English households that mistreat Juliet comments that Juliet will " 'never know her place' " (550), an assertion that accords with Juliet's experience through most of the narrative. When the book finally names Juliet properly, it first reinforces, rather than alleviates, her placelessness by naming her in French, rather than English: her childhood friend Gabriella calls her "Julie" (the name by which she was known in France), rather than Juliet (her given name at birth in England) (387 and compare 933–4n).

How is a woman like Juliet to find her way in a world of politically and ideologically divided spaces? " '[A]ll we know of the world is only by bits and scraps; except, mayhap, what we can pick out of books,' " says an Admiral who is part of the crew crossing from France to England at the book's opening; and he adds that most books too are unreliable (832).[106] The worldview—the world knowledge—provided by most of Burney's own book makes clear the problems that arise when one subscribes to Anglo-centric or any other nationalist ideals. Such ideals lead to greater division and displace those (like Juliet) most worthy of confident emplacement.

And yet, *The Wanderer* finally does articulate a well-ordered and apparently stable world in which long-established, dominant English social hierarchies mesh fully with moral hierarchies. The good woman attains her proper place, a place prescribed for her not only by the reader's sympathies and by a transcendental moral system, but by English law and social custom. As the book nears its conclusion, Juliet regains a name, becoming "the Honorable Miss Granville," and then she marries an English aristocrat and solidifies her English identity by taking *his* "name, . . . mansion, . . . fortune, and . . . fate" (735, 870). She stops wandering and becomes "fixed" (870).

All of this happens in Brighthelmstone. Most of the book associates Brighthelmstone with the post office where Juliet has failed to find her letters and with property owners who fail to act generously toward her. As Smith does in *The Emigrants*, Burney criticizes the town. As Doody observes, "The world of Brighton . . . here is not, as the English think, a paradisal refuge from the disorders of France."[107] And yet, even early in the book, other characters note that Juliet seems "to be naturalized at Brighthelmstone" (241). And if Burney, like Smith, faults the people who come to the town for the ostensibly curative waters—one of the smallest minded and most ungenerous women goes there " 'to give her favourite lap-dog a six-weeks' bathing' " (a line that also recalls Cowper's "Retirement")—Burney at the same time has the sympathetic Gabriella make an "excursion for sea-bathing" there with her terminally ill child (400, 739; also see 410).

When Juliet's guardians contract to marry her to her aristocratic lover—to assure her a name and a mansion within the British social and legal system—they do so not in a utopian space on the margins of Verona, but in a place where, within dominant configurations of England, the English ostensibly can *fix* themselves in an English environment and with English water: in a bathing machine on the Brighthelmstone strand (864–5).[108] Bathing machines, a standard part of the English sea bathing culture until the late nineteenth century, were small wood houses on wheels. A bather entered, changed out of his or her clothes, and then was drawn, usually by horse, into the water, where an attendant—or "dipper"—assisted the bathing (figure 1.1).

Figure 1.1 'Sea Bathing, Bridlington Bay' (Reproduced by Permission of the East Riding of Yorkshire Council Museum Service).

As Burney notes in her *Diary and Letters*, contemporaries associated bathing machines with English nationalist and royalist principles. The machines at Weymouth, where George III was vacationing in July, 1789, for example, had the motto "God Save the King" inscribed on them. As Burney comments in a letter written on the day before the storming of the Bastille,

> The bathing-machines make it their motto over their windows; and those bathers that belong to the royal dippers wear it in bandeaus on their bonnets, to go into the sea; and have it again, in large letters, round their waists, to encounter the waves.... Nor is this all. Think but of the surprise of His Majesty when, the first time of his bathing, he had no sooner popped his royal head under water than a band of music, concealed in a neighbouring machine, struck up "God save great George our King."[109]

A bathing machine parked on the beach of Brighthelmstone is a committedly English site, even as it rests on the shifting sands of a border zone where emigrants arrive.[110] A marriage contracted within such a machine is a committedly English marriage.

And yet, as Burney's remarks on King George's experiences show, a bathing machine also is ridiculous; and Burney plays the wedding contract scene for comic as well as serious effect. One can look at the wedding party, as a nearby sailor does, "with a merry nod, and a significant leer" (864). The ridiculousness of a bathing machine as a location for making a marriage contract, then, at least partly undercuts the claim to Brighthelmstone and to England as a site of stable order. At least in relation to the bathing machine, the marriage between Juliet and her propertied aristocrat is laughable.

Not so laughable, though, is a prayer for "'UNIVERSAL PEACE'" that Juliet's guardian, the Bishop, having arrived safely in England, encourages upon the occasion of the happy reunion (857). If nationalism fails as a political philosophy and internationalism fares little better, Burney's novel nonetheless promotes the possibility of a peaceful social space that transcends contemporary worldly boundaries. The conclusion to Burney's novel, though, offers little direction toward this transcendental social space. Burney asserts that, after the marriage, Juliet's troubles ended:

> Here, and thus felicitously, ended, with the acknowledgement of her name, and her family, the DIFFICULTIES of the WANDERER;—a being who had been cast upon herself; a female Robinson Crusoe, as unaided and unprotected, though in the midst of the world, as that

> imaginary hero in his uninhabited island; and reduced either to sink, through inanition, to nonentity, or to be rescued from famine and death by such resources as she could find, independently, in herself. (873)

Despite these narrative claims, Juliet remains a divided figure. Though "name[d]" and reintegrated into her "family," her identity within the narrative remains subordinate to her uncertain role as "the WANDERER." Though Burney attributes to her a reality that contrasts with the artificial status of "that imaginary hero" Robinson Crusoe, she (a fictional character, too, after all) is no more real than he is. Though she survives through "such resources as she could find, independently, in herself," that self is an uncertain, hollow signifier until the end.[111]

Burney's Reflections on Alternative Englands

The England in which Juliet obtains her ideal marriage, her place, and her name is, after all, a divided and dividing space in *The Wanderers*, a space that offers little promise of integrated social or individual identity. As such, it looks much like one of the possible Englands that Burney imagines in *Brief Reflections Relative to the Emigrant French Clergy*, published in 1793, twenty-one years before *The Wanderer*. "Earnestly Submitted to the Humane Consideration of the Ladies of Great Britain," *Brief Reflections* asks the wealthy women of England to fund Catholic clergy who, Burney suggests, are on the brink of starvation; and, as part of her plea, Burney envisions future historical accounts of alternative Englands. In the first, England fails to support the clergy. In the second, England fulfills Burney's preferred idea of a nation. The second configuration accords with a dominant British self-representation—which is to say, with a nationalistic cliché: this is "Great Britain . . . in the fullness of its felicity, in the meridian of its glory, not more celebrated for arts and arms, than beloved for indulgent benevolence, and admired for munificence of liberality."[112] This version of Great Britain contrasts with the Britain through which Burney's later emigrant, Juliet, travels. The alternative is an uncivilized island, populated but otherwise much the same as the island inhabited by Robinson Crusoe:

> What was this land? some wild, uncultivated spot, where yet no . . . civilization [had] been spread, no benefits reciprocated? . . . Where novelty was the only passport, and where kindness was the short-lived offspring of curiosity? (*Brief Reflections* 15)

This island has " 'inhospitable shores,' " and its inhabitants are "a race so unapprized of all social, all relative ties, as to confer favours only where they may be expected in return, unconscious, or unreflecting that every unoffending man is a brother!" (15)[113] In other words, this island closely resembles the England Juliet discovers after washing up on the shores of Dover.

Although *Brief Reflections* promotes Tory, nationalistic political ideals considerably more than *The Wanderer* does—Burney in the earlier text seems optimistic that England, particularly the women of England, will prove benevolent and "munificen[t]... of liberality"—Burney already aims her nationalistic rhetoric toward goals that transcend nationalism. "O let us be brethren with the good, wheresoever they may arise!" she writes, "and let us resist the culpable, whether abroad or at home" (12–13). In 1793, she, like Smith, advocates a moral hierarchy rather than a political and social one, and she even seems to believe that multilingualism may help to bridge national divides, since she notes that "A translation of this Tract is preparing for the press" (27).

But *The Wanderer* indicates that the years following 1793 disappointed Burney in her hopes for England. Juliet, clearly a more sympathetic hero than an "old... infirm" French priest (*Reflections* 6), stands in for the clergy whom Burney sought to fund in *Brief Reflections*, but she still receives little social or financial support. Like Juliet, these clergy are "destitute wanderers" who have been "Driven from house and home, despoiled of dignities and honours, abandoned to the seas for mercy, to chance for support" (*Reflections* 3–4, 6). Their "mental strength alone"—like the "resources" that Juliet "find[s], independently, in herself"—has enabled them to deal with "an aggregate of evil" (*Reflections* 6–7). They too must depend on "FEMALE BENEFICENCE" (*Reflections* 4). And, as *The Wanderer* shows, they may not receive it.

In the 1793 tract, though, the female contributors to the emigrant fund, rather than the female wanderer, remain nameless. Here, instead of marking unstable selfhood, namelessness marks a transcendent identity: the contributors, after all, practice ideal British "indulgent benevolence" and thus have a greater claim to placedness and social identity than others, who misrepresent the nation. Thus, Burney praises the contributors for their social propriety in wishing to remain nameless, an apparent preemptive defense against those who might accuse them (as characters accuse Juliet) of suspicious evasion: "The Ladies who have instituted this [fundraising] scheme desire not to be named; and those who are the principal agents for putting it in execution, join in the same wish. Such delicacy is too respectable to be opposed" (5). Like Juliet, these women, when named, will turn out to be identical to ideal British self-valuations: their

> names...will ultimately be sought, for what is now benevolence will in future become honour; and female tradition will not fail to hand down to posterity the formers and protectresses of a plan which, if successful, will exalt for ever the female annals of Great Britain. (5–6)

Although shaken by an unstable identity in uncertain places, Juliet, although more French than English by education and social connection, at least approximates Burney's representative ideal British woman, whom these annals should exalt. She protects the French clergy (the Bishop who would go to the guillotine except for her) at great sacrifice to herself; she acts benevolently. Through her, Burney figures a Great Britain that stands as a preferred alternative to a Britain that fails to see beyond national borders.[114]

Wordsworthian Migrations

In *Brief Reflections*, as she argues for sympathetic understandings that cross English and French national boundaries, Burney comments that "We are too apt to consider ourselves rather as a distinct race of beings, than as merely the emulous inhabitants of rival states" (12).[115] This comment, which represents statehood as fluid but race as essential, links the French migration to African–British migration; and it helps to explain one of the most troubling features of *The Wanderer*: Juliet's decision to adopt blackface when crossing the Channel from Calais to Dover.[116] Within the context of the Napoleonic era in which Burney published *The Wanderer*, though not the Robespierrist era in which she set the action, Juliet's adoption of blackface highlights an international abuse of social power.

On board the boat crossing the Channel, Juliet removes her gloves, revealing "hands and arms of so dark a colour, that they might rather be styled black than brown" (19). Unsympathetic British characters mistreat her because of her apparent color. One calls her a "black insect" (27). Another, sensing sexual potential in her black body, comments, "She wants a little bleaching, to be sure; but she has not bad eyes; nor a bad nose, neither" (27). When she visits British houses, she finds that the aristocratic owners mistreat blacks there as well. A "young negro," for example, is a household "favorite, because the most submissive servant" (479). When he laughs at the woman of the house—failing to act submissively—she threatens to send him from servitude to slavery. She says,

> I will have you shipped back to the West Indies. And there, that your joy shall be complete, I shall issue orders that you may be striped till you jump, and that you may jump,—you little black imp!—between every stripe. (482)

While Doody and Mack rightly suggest that "*The Wanderer* exhibits . . . dissatisfaction with all forms of coercive power," Burney does treat skin color as a basic difference of another category than nationality.[117] She type-names the servant "poor Mungo" and caricatures him as a black showing "foolish mirth," even while criticizing the power relations that lead to his behavior (*The Wanderer* 482, 940n). And even as Burney faults the British for mistreating blacks, she, too, values skin color according to English conventions as she describes Juliet's skin once the blackening cosmetic has been removed as having "the brightest, whitest, and most dazzling fairness" (43). Skin color here is no more dependable as a signifier of goodness than language or nation, and yet is also a transcendental signifier of otherness, of essential difference.

The narrative never fully explains why Juliet adopts blackface for her journey. The blackface most obviously disguises her as she eludes capture by her Jacobin husband. And yet, in "the dire reign of the terrific Robespierre," when the narrative begins, her choice of disguise could hardly be worse. If she needs to avoid looking like the woman of aristocratic birth and education that she is, she might dress as a peasant or middle-class emigrant, since the vast majority of emigrants at the time were from these classes. But in the early 1790s, a black was unlikely to travel from France, where slavery was being debated (it would be abolished on 4 February 1794) and where some Revolutionaries, led by the Abbé Baptiste Henri Grégoire, were arguing for full legal, political, social, and economic rights for blacks.[118] Or if a French black were to travel from France, she most likely would avoid traveling to England, where a bigoted woman might threaten to " 'ship . . . [her] to the West Indies' " to be flogged, despite English laws ostensibly protecting blacks from such treatment.

But while Burney sets the novel in the period of Robespierrist rule, its publication in 1814 situates its narrative in relation to a later, Napoleonic context. If Juliet's adoption of blackface makes little sense in the early 1790s, it makes great sense in subsequent years. While Napoleon initially followed the general Revolutionary emancipationist program, by the first years of the nineteenth century he had begun to reduce black rights and to work toward the restoration of slavery in the Caribbean.[119] England, which outlawed the slave trade in 1807, became a clearly preferable alternative to France.

And yet, England's treatment of blacks—and its policies related to France's treatment of blacks—remained complicated and problematic. Unlike Napoleon's militaristic moves throughout Europe and other regions, to which Britain responded aggressively, his attempts to reassert imperial power over colonial blacks depended greatly upon British acquiescence.[120] Such acquiescence was consistent with long-standing policies that enabled the white British colonial plantation economy to prosper, even at the expense of British national security. As David Brion Davis has noted, "Even in 1795–1796, when the British colonies were most seriously threatened... by French armies that included large numbers of emancipated slaves, Parliament deferred to the West India planters and merchants."[121] Unsurprisingly, then, in 1802, even while contesting French occupation of other parts of the world, Britain willingly allowed the French to conquer Saint-Domingue.[122] The terms of the Peace of Amiens—a Peace that ostensibly could model future international peace (though all parties at the time generally recognized it as a lull in, rather than a permanent cessation of, British–French hostilities)—led to brutal fighting in the Caribbean. Only with this Peace did Napoleon have sufficient troops to crack down on the colonies. Because of these circumstances, "The attempt to reclaim Haiti emerged directly from the Peace of Amiens."[123] Even British and French peace, in other words, depended upon abuse of power, and vice versa.

By having Juliet adopt blackface and receive the treatment she receives from her fellow passengers from France, then, Burney highlights one of the central points of the novel: that the British as well as the French are guilty of abusing power, even in environments that appear peaceful and prosperous.[124]

Race in *The Wanderer* serves largely as a metonymic figure of the novel's larger concern with the abuse of social, political, and economic power. In many respects, such treatment of race recalls Wordsworth's. His writing, too, represents racial oppression as simply a single instance of widespread social, political, and economic oppression. Recalling the early 1790s, when the French Revolution still looked as if it might spark universal liberty (including Rights of Man for blacks), Wordsworth says that he became convinced that if the new France

> prosper'd good Men would not long
> Pay fruitless worship to humanity,

> And this most rotten branch of human shame [slavery],
> Object, as seem'd, of superfluous pains,
> Would fall together with its parent tree. (*Prelude* 10.222–6)

For Wordsworth, as for Burney, slavery—an extreme evil in itself, "the most rotten branch of human shame"—is nonetheless a figure (a "branch") of a larger evil.

As Wordsworth addresses racial difference, particularly in Africans, though also in American Indians, he generally continues to treat the abuse of people because of skin color as at once a subordinate and a paramount example of general oppression. Aside from the short *Prelude* discussion, in the early 1800s Wordsworth concentrates on racial politics most closely in a series of sonnets that he first published in the *Morning Post* in 1803, a series that draws upon the connection between the Peace of Amiens and Napoleon's attempt to reconquer the Caribbean.[125] These poems, too, deal with emigration and other forms of migration.

On 29 January 1803, the *Morning Post* commented under a title of "Poetry" that

> We have been favoured with a dozen Sonnets of a Political nature, which are not only written by one of the first Poets of the age, but are among his best productions. Each forms a little Political Essay, on some recent proceeding.[126]

The first two, "I grieved for Buonaparté" and "Is it a Reed," which had appeared already in earlier editions of the newspaper, were reprinted below the note. In subsequent months, five more poems appeared: "To Toussaint L'Ouverture," "The Banished Negroes" ("We had a fellow-Passenger"), "August 15, 1802" ("Festivals have I seen"), "It is not to be thought of that the Flood," and "When I have borne in memory."[127] The other five sonnets did not appear. Two of the sonnets, "To Toussaint" and "Banished Negroes," address race. One of these sonnets, "The Banished Negroes" (retitled "September 1st, 1802" in the 1807 *Poems, in Two Volumes*) is also an emigration poem. Three of the other sonnets in the sequence address migrations of different sorts. "Toussaint" is a transportation sonnet, questioning where Toussaint has gone when deported from Saint-Domingue. "Is it a Reed" questions the motives of Britons who have traveled to France during the Peace of Amiens. According to "It is not to be thought of that the Flood," Britain opens its shores to all who wish to "come and go."[128]

In particular, "The Banished Negroes," in its *Morning Post* version, speaks forcefully about the same trans-Channel—and, more broadly, global—abuses of power that concern Burney.[129] The "Negro Woman" whom the poem discusses appears less as an individual historical subject than as a figure for other, larger groups: French blacks generally (as in the plural "Negroes" of the poem's title); French emigrants, especially those, like Burney's Juliet, who are innocent of abusing power themselves but nonetheless have been forced into exile; and any others who have suffered under the "Dishonour'd Despots" of the world.

In this generalization from the particular woman, Wordsworth follows the lead of the Abbé Grégoire. Grégoire also sees black rights as an example—a central one—of a larger realm of human rights that the French Revolutionaries need to address.[130] In his 1789 *Memoir in Favor of the People of Color or Mixed-Race of Saint Domingue*, he argues,

> The people of color being equal in everything to the whites, one will surely not ask if they should be active in legislation and send deputies to the National Assembly. Subjected to the laws and to taxation, citizens must consent to the one and the other, without which they can refuse obedience and payment. If someone could claim to possess to a higher degree this right that is equal for everyone, it would be without doubt those who, having been more afflicted by long and multiple vexations, have more complaints to lodge.[131]

Grégoire, who was an "immediate catalyst of the French Republic" and also a key member of Les Amis des Noirs, lived in Blois at the same time that Wordsworth stayed there during his affair with Annette Vallon, and he participated in political meetings that Wordsworth likely attended.[132] Like Wordsworth, he was interested in poetry, already having established a regional reputation as a poet; and so the two of them would have found each other's conversation worth pursuing.[133] Further, two of Annette's cousins were *curés* in the diocese of Blois, and Grégoire made one of them a *vicaire épiscopal* in Loir-et-Cher.[134] Literary historians consequently have speculated about whether Wordsworth knew the Abbé personally.[135] As Roe has shown, "Grégoire appears to have had a striking influence on Wordsworth during 1792": Wordsworth seems to draw from Grégoire's speeches in his 1793 *Descriptive Sketches*, and he refers to him as "a man of philosophy and humanity" in his otherwise mostly anti-clerical 1793 *Letter to the Bishop of Llandaff*.[136] As the *Prelude* passage on slavery indicates by also referring to the "worship" of "humanity," Grégoire's influence on Wordsworth extends further, well into the 1800s.[137]

"The Banished Negroes" shows that influence as well. In this sonnet, commenting upon his return trip from France, where he had gone during the Peace of Amiens to visit Annette and his daughter Caroline, Wordsworth says,

> WE had a fellow-passenger who came
> From Calais with us, gaudy in array,
> A Negro Woman, like a lady gay
> Yet silent as a woman fearing blame;
> Dejected, downcast, meek, and more than tame:
> She sate, from notice turning not away,
> But on our proffer'd kindness still did lay
> A weight of languid speech, or at the same
> Was silent, motionless in eyes and face.
> She was a negro woman driv'n out of France
> Rejected, like all others of that race:
> Not one of whom may now find footing there.
> What is the meaning of this ordinance?
> Dishonour'd Despots, tell us if ye dare.[138]

In a headnote to the 1827 edition of the poem, Wordsworth explains that "the chasing of all Negroes from France by decree of the Government" exemplifies "the capricious acts of Tyranny that disgraced those times."

Despite this headnote—and despite the fact that critics of Wordsworth, of Romantic literature, and even of French–English history have assumed that Wordsworth refers to specific real events in 1802 (often treating the sonnet itself as definitive proof of such events)—Jared Curtis has shown that the poem has, at most, a tenuous historical basis.[139] No independent letters or journal entries by Wordsworth or his sister Dorothy support the sonnet account of meeting this woman; and French governmental records include no ordinances banishing "all" blacks during these years.[140] Rather, in summer 1802, Napoleon's government expelled a select group of blacks—those newly arriving on France's shores from the colonies or from foreign nations—and further denied colonial blacks of their rights.[141]

If Wordsworth's sonnet emerges, as it seems to, from a partial error in Wordsworth's awareness of political events, it also engages with a historical situation in which French, English, and African subjects were assuming new dispositions, a situation, in other words, in which subjectivities were migrating and national space was inherently unstable (no one—black or white—could "find footing there"). This is the situation explored by the emigration literature of this period, the literature (rather than abolitionist literature) that provides the sonnet's closest and most informative context. If the woman's "gaudy . . . array" implies a "recent West Indian connection,"[142] Wordsworth's description of this clothing as being "like [that of] a lady gay" indicates, rather, that the woman is dressing the part of a French aristocrat emigrant—one of those with a reputation for "levity and gaiety"—who dressed this way and crossed the Channel, according to the news accounts of the previous decade. But while such aristocrats may have shared some culpability for their banishment (because they occupied positions of social power in pre–Revolutionary France), this woman would seem to be guiltless.[143] Nonetheless, she is "silent as a woman fearing blame," a fear that may reveal her awareness that many gaily dressed emigrants are (as Coleridge points out) blameworthy, or that she is so fully displaced from home and self that she has internalized others' guilt for exiling her, blaming herself for her victimization.[144]

Like Juliet, she appears submissive, and her speech, too, seems uncertain, but in her un-selved state she may be impervious to further efforts to displace her, un-name her, and efface her. If she is "meek," she is also "more than tame," a characteristic with a key doubleness: in the racial typing of the time, which frequently represents blackness and Africanness as wild, tameness might occur to a black whose spirit has been broken, and a woman who is "more than tame" thus might be broken beyond recovery; but, on the other hand, a woman who is "more than tame" also might not be tame at all and, rather, have a quality that cannot be tamed. If the woman is "downcast" (an emotional metonym extending from her apparent facial direction) she nonetheless "turn[s] . . . not away." If France has ejected (and "Dejected" and "Rejected") her, moving her over the water from a place where she can find no "footing," she nonetheless is "motionless in eyes and face." If France has forced her to emigrate, and if she embodies the instabilities and contradictions inherent in the migratory subjectivity, she is also, in important respects, essentially unmovable in her current state. When Wordsworth makes his demands at the end of the sonnet—"What is the meaning of this ordinance? / Dishour'd Despots, tell us if ye dare"—the "Despots," like the "Negroes" at the poem's beginning, are plural and must include other European kings such as George III (not just Napoleon) and perhaps include all other abusers of social power. But, less obviously, the "us" to whom the "Despots" might speak (and give meaningful language) are also plural and must include the "Negro Woman" who is twice "silent" (4, 9) and otherwise is nearly wordless, as well as the poet who seemingly has power over language and yet also lacks "the meaning."[145] The "Negro Woman," depersonalized as she is by the oppression that leads to her flight from France, is a figure of all migratory subjectivities, including Wordsworth's own.

Curtis makes a related claim—that is, that Wordsworth's poem on the "Banished Negroes" is also about himself—when he says that "Wordsworth's keen sympathy for [the woman] . . . seems . . . to have at least as much to do with his feelings about 'banishing' Annette and Caroline from his family circle . . . as it has to do with his moral outrage at the . . . 'ordinance.' "[146] While the poem deals with Wordsworth's own circumstances, though, it turns the blame outward, not inward. A related poem, "The Emigrant Mother" ("Once in a lonely Hamlet I sojourn'd")—which Wordsworth wrote in March 1802, shortly before traveling to France and writing "The Banished Negroes"—confirms this pattern of outward blame and self-exculpation.[147] Here, Wordsworth similarly addresses circumstances related to his own and Annette's while deflecting blame from himself.[148] In this alternative scenario, a French woman, who (like the "Negro Woman") has been "driv'n from France," "dwell[s] . . . upon English ground."[149] This emigrant woman has left behind a baby son in France, and she now visits the baby daughter of one of her English neighbors and speaks longingly to the girl about her own child. The poem, too, assigns no guilt to Wordsworth for " 'banishing' Annette and Caroline from his family circle," but seemingly explores Annette's failure to emigrate a decade earlier to join him.[150]

Having seen the emigrant woman "clasp the [neighbor's] Child about / And take it to herself," Wordsworth's narrator seeks sufficient language to represent her. He wishes

> in my native tongue to fashion out
> Such things as she unto the Child might say:
> And thus, from what I knew, had heard, and guess'd,
> My song the workings of her heart express'd.[151]

By asserting that an Englishman might accurately "express" the feelings of the Frenchwoman, Wordsworth, like Smith, suggests that language in translation, or multilingualism, can bridge the divide between the populations of antagonistic nations.

But the rest of the poem indicates that the divide may be unbridgeable. Wordsworth's song of the emigrant's heart sounds much like that of his "Mad Mother" in the *Lyrical Ballads*. The poem shows that a family-dividing emigration may lead to the loss of one's mind as well as (or as part of) the loss of one's selfhood. While the emigrant wishes that her neighbor's daughter " 'would . . . be / One little hour a child to me!' " and while she asserts that (despite the conflict between France and England) " 'I'm no enemy,' " she fears that her own son will die without her in France, and these fears nearly lead her to act violently against the baby girl she holds. Wordsworth imagines her saying to the girl,

> Dear Baby! I must lay thee down;
> Thou troublest me with strange alarms;
> Smiles hast Thou, sweet ones of thy own;
> I cannot keep thee in my arms,
> For they confound me.[152]

When she feels compelled to add, " 'I cannot help it—ill intent / I've none, my pretty innocent,' " it becomes clear that the child is in danger.[153] An emigrant mother's displacement wrests a subjectivity fully away from its central characteristics, turning the loving mother into a potential abuser or murderer.

At the end of the poem, the woman, apparently seeking to neutralize her own alienation and potential for violence, performs an act of translation, much in the manner that Smith's characters do when facing national, cultural, and linguistic divides. She says to the girl, " 'I'll call thee by my Darling's name.' "[154] But such translation cannot succeed: the English girl cannot become the French boy. Translation at this moment is also an act of violence, committed by the woman against herself as much as against the child. She backs away from her choice to call the English girl by her French son's name, though, and concludes that her own child and the English child, rather than being identical, must have a family resemblance:

> Thou hast, I think, a look of ours,
> Thy features seem to me the same;
> His little Sister thou shalt be;
> And, when once more my home I see,
> I'll tell him many tales of Thee.[155]

If Wordsworth claims to be able to access the French woman's heart accurately from what he "knew, had heard, and guess'd," her own account of the English girl's heart clearly will be less accurate: it will transfigure the girl, translating her into " 'tales,' " perhaps making her into something unrecognizable as herself.

WORDSWORTH AT HOME

The degree to which the French emigration of the Revolutionary and post-Revolutionary years displaces and destabilizes human subjects, readying them for new emplacement as in Smith's writing in the 1790s and to a lesser extent Burney's novel and Wordsworth's poems of the early 1800s, becomes still more apparent when the texts of this period are viewed in contrast to Wordsworth's later handling of emigration in the 1822 poem "The Exiled French Clergy." This late poem appears in the *Ecclesiastical Sonnets*, and, in it, Wordsworth reasserts nationhood as an essential category that defines social and moral identity.

> EVEN while I speak, the sacred roofs of France
> Are shattered into dust; and self-exiled
> From altars threatened, leveled, or defiled,
> Wander the Ministers of God, as chance
> Opens a way for life, or consonance
> Of faith invites. More welcome to no land
> The fugitives than to the British strand,
> Where priest and layman with the vigilance
> Of true compassion greet them. Creed and test
> Vanish before the unreserved embrace
> Of catholic humanity:—distrest
> They came,—and, while the moral tempest roars
> Throughout the Country they have left, our shores
> Give to their Faith a dreadless resting-place.[156]

The poem does echo some of Wordsworth's earlier thinking. In asserting that the French clergy have been "More welcome to no land / . . . than to the British strand," Wordsworth recalls his comment in the 1803 *Morning Post* sonnets that Britain has been a place to which and from which "all might come and go that would." But the *Ecclesiastical Sonnets* poem counters Wordsworth's assertion in another of the *Morning Post* sonnets that "Happy is he, who caring not for Pope, / . . . can sound himself to know / The destiny of Man, and live in hope."[157] It also counters Wordsworth's description of the radical placelessness of the "Negro Woman" who (seemingly "fearing blame") appears unlikely to find a "dreadless resting place" in England. And it counters his generally anti-clerical arguments in his 1793 *Letter to the Bishop of Llandaff*, written during the main emigration.[158] The poem seems out of place and out of date in a collection written nearly twenty years after Wordsworth's *Morning Post* sonnets and a full thirty years after the beginning of the emigration that brought most of the French clergy to England. After all, in 1792, between 6,000 and 7,000 members of the French clergy fled to the British Isles, and from 1793 to 1800, "there was a mean figure of some 5,000 exiled clergy on the English mainland"; but by the 1810s the crisis was largely over, and in 1815, "as few as 350 remained."[159]

Wordsworth addresses the issue of belatedness directly in the first lines and indirectly throughout the rest of the poem. If the emigration has largely ceased and the clerical population has dwindled in 1822 ("while I speak"), the results of the revolutionary violence that precipitated the emigration remain apparent: "the sacred roofs of France" still "Are shattered into dust." In the lines that follow, the importance of the still-existing physical-geographical evidence of the clergy's displacement supercedes the importance of historical change. If one looks for the former place of the clergy—the churches and convents now reduced to dust—one sees evidence that contradicts the demographic figures on them. If the clergy cannot reclaim their former homes, then France's "Ministers of God" still "Wander." They seemingly must continue to wander unless they relocate themselves in Wordsworth's ideal England, the "dreadless resting-place."

To assert this stable nation-state, Wordsworth must neutralize English history more fully than he neutralizes the French Revolutionary destruction of Church buildings. He thus proleptically proclaims the end of England's Test and Corporation Acts, which would not be repealed until 1828;[160] and he neutralizes (or changes the case of) centuries of British religious sectarianism in favor of universal faith: as the British welcome the French clergy, he says, "Creed and test / Vanish before the unreserved embrace / Of catholic humanity." In other words, Wordsworth now suggests that England at large achieves the kind of "humanity" that he attributes to the Abbé Grégoire in his *Letter to the Bishop of Llandaff.*

Wordsworth's "Emigrant French Clergy" sonnet is a dream of British and French nationhood, a dream in which physical geography is constant, unchanging, stable. In such a geography, a displaced group can emplace itself and find a foundation for its identity simply by moving from a (constantly) bad site to a (constantly) good one. This geography, though, is inconsistent with the geography experienced by the characters described by Smith, Burney, and, in his earlier poetry, Wordsworth himself. It appears also to be inconsistent with the lived experience of the people who inhabited a fluid, unstable, increasingly international world.

Chapter 2

Imagining America

Seduced by these sublime enchanting scenes of primitive nature, and these visions of terrestrial happiness, I had roamed far.

—William Bartram *Travels*

In the vast & unexplored regions of fairyland, there is ground enough & uncultivated; search there, & realize your favorite Susquehan[n]a scheme.

—Charles Lamb *Letters*

[T]he humanity of the Unite[d] States can never reach the sublime.

—John Keats *Letters*

New Selves in New World Positions

While Romantic criticism long has regarded Britain's relation to France as crucial to the development of Romantic literature, it has paid less attention to the complex relation that the writers and the writing had to North America.[1] Those who have considered the relationship often have represented it as distant and tenuous. Paul Giles, for instance, suggests that

> the New World manifested itself within the consciousness of British writers at the turn of the nineteenth century more as an abstract conception than a material place.... British writers projected an image of

> America as an externalization of their own ideologies of emancipation, a utopian image of alterity and virtual fulfillment.[2]

While Giles names a large part of the British relationship with America accurately, he understates the degree to which British writers investigated the empirical details of America and to which their figurations of the place accorded with contemporary European conceptions of its material reality. The writers perceived in the physical, material reality of America a preferable alternative space to which one might emigrate, and this idea contributed importantly to their dispositions, whether in the Americas or still in Britain.

British Romantic writers engaged with the Americas extensively and deeply, at once personally and publicly. The most centrally canonical of them addressed America in their poetry and prose and also considered living there. Coleridge, Southey, Priestley, Wollstonecraft, Paine, Cobbett, Hazlitt, and Keats's brother George emigrated or made detailed plans to emigrate. Wordsworth, Charles Lamb, Charles Lloyd, and Mary Shelley speculated imaginatively upon emigration to America without making plans to move there personally. Unsurprisingly, the British writers most inclined to emigrate were political and religious radicals who (as Giles suggests) sought alternatives to the institutional life of Britain. French writers of mixed ideological orientations—including Chateaubriand, Brissot, and Volney—came, too, whether to live or to make extended visits.

Coleridge and Southey famously planned their Pantisocratic community on the banks of the Susquehanna River. Lamb, though suspicious of the emigration scheme, dreamed of joining the "heaven on earth along the shores of the Susquehanna," and he aligned himself philosophically with the Pantisocrats.[3] Lloyd, who became friends with Coleridge, Lamb, and others in their circle only after the passing of the Pantisocratic scheme, also wished that he "had liv'd in high-soul'd fellowship" with the group "of noble souls / Who deem'd it wise, e'en in the morn of youth, / To quit this world" and travel "beyond the Atlantic deep / To find those virtues" that were lacking in Britain.[4] The radical Unitarian scientist Priestley did emigrate and settle on the Susquehanna in 1794 after fleeing a mob who burned down his house and laboratory in Birmingham.[5] Wollstonecraft and Gilbert Imlay, shortly after starting their affair in 1793, planned to emigrate and set up a farm (Wollstonecraft's brother Charles already had moved to the United States).[6] Paine lived in North America intermittently from 1774 until his death there in 1809. Cobbett came to America and left three times. George Keats moved to Kentucky with his wife Georgiana. As a child Hazlitt emigrated to America with his parents and lived in Pennsylvania and then Massachusetts for three years before returning to England.

This disparate group had various, often divergent interests. But the emigration plans themselves drew them together. For example, Coleridge and Southey planned to establish their Pantisocratic community on the banks of the Susquehanna partly because Priestley was already there. On the other hand, Cobbett started his journalistic career in America by criticizing Priestley's emigration and politics in a pamphlet, *Observations on the Emigration of Dr. Joseph Priestley.*[7] Cobbett later published a pamphlet critical of Morris Birkbeck's Albion colony in Illinois, the colony where George Keats planned to settle with his wife until John Keats warned George to consider Cobbett's account.[8]

If a single common feature linked the emigration plans it was that the emigrants or would-be emigrants sought radically new material and spiritual conditions in the New World. In other words, North America became for many British radical writers a space to refocus their displaced political, social, and religious energy after France failed to fulfill its early revolutionary promise: a new space in which to establish new selves. In *The Prelude*, Wordsworth emphasized the importance of expending such energy in the real political and social world. After the French Revolution, he and others wished to work

> Not in Utopia, subterranean fields,
> Or some secreted Island Heaven knows where;
> But in the world which is the world
> Of all of us, the place on which in the end
> We find our happiness or not at all. (*Prelude* 10. 723–7)

Following France's failure, North America became for many (or in some cases became *again*)[9] the best prospect in the "world which is the world / Of all of us" for personal and world reform. More than France, with its long European institutional history, though, North America, with much of its geography still unsettled by and unknown to Europeans, was a space open to imaginative speculation.[10] Where a map was empty or where the geographical details were few, writers could project their own spatial schemes more easily than where a map already was inscribed with centuries of territorial markings, erasures, and re-markings.

In the most important and interesting cases, the Romantic writers founded their spatial schemes on close research into the available empirical evidence: in other words, the writers sought to avoid imagining "Utopia, subterranean fields, / Or some secreted Island" in North America. But literary history often has refigured these schemes nonetheless as the products of pure idealism and fantasy. The writers themselves frequently thematized the relationship between the real world ("which is the world / Of all of us") and ideal, purely fictional worlds. Even as some radical writers imagined North America as a preferable space to Europe, counter-voices (Cobbett's among them) argued that American reality was generally as harsh as or harsher than European. This tension between positive and negative representations was at the heart of the British Romantic literary understanding of America and often of the Romantic authors' direct experience of America as well. And since America, in its combined colonial past and present independence, was both other than Britain and a key to Britain's self-identification, this tension went also to the heart of British Romantic literature.[11]

An Ideal of Material America

In many respects the material circumstances of North America and particularly the United States and its territories allowed for—even supported—imaginative speculation in ways that those of Europe did not. The United States had divided itself from Britain and, with its geographically expansionist tendencies, appeared to many Europeans to be open to a wide range of possible inscriptions, especially socially and politically radical ones.

Major parts of the United States and its territories, as well as regions to the north, south, and west, remained unfamiliar to the British in the eighteenth century and thus remained open to imaginative interpretation. After the 1783 Treaty of Paris, U.S. territory consisted of everything east of the Mississippi River except Florida and the coastal areas of what now are Alabama and Mississippi; and throughout the Romantic period the territory continued to expand. The Louisiana Purchase in 1803 nearly doubled the size of the country; and the government then seized coastal Mississippi in 1810 and coastal Alabama in 1813. The Adams–Onís Treaty added Florida (and, legally, coastal Alabama and Mississippi) in 1819.[12] This acquisition of land far outpaced the British settlers' and would-be settlers' firsthand knowledge of it.[13]

Through the middle of the eighteenth century, maps show a North American landmass that becomes uncertain and often fragmented when one looks either much to the north or much to the west of the English colonies. R. Seale's 1748 *Map of North America with Hudson's Bay and Straights*, for an extreme example, represents these areas of North America as a set of disconnected or barely connected pieces of land. An apparently navigable waterway cuts through what now are the United States and Canada, connecting the Atlantic Ocean to the Pacific.[14] California is—as it is on many early-eighteenth-century maps—an island. Alexander Dalrymple's 1789 *Map of the Lands around the North Pole*, which includes the latest and best knowledge of North America (gleaned from recent explorations by James Cook and older ones by Vitus Bering), shows only a fragmentary Pacific coastline (even as it claims the area for the British by labeling it "New Albion"), very spotty representation of the northwest beyond what now is the Canadian border, and an expanse of white space west of the Mississippi.[15] As late as 1811, John Pinkerton would comment in *Modern Geography* that while "the geography of North America begins to open with more clearness,... some obscurity" remains.[16] Exemplifying its own claims, the 1811 text shows Greenland as attached to Canada by land, though an 1802 edition of the same work shows it as a separate landmass.

For many Britons in the eighteenth century, these uncertain regions of North America were spaces of imaginative play and desire. In these spaces, they speculated, they might discover material or spiritual riches. The waterway inscribed on Seale's 1748 map is just one of the ostensibly empirical manifestations of the imaginative space. The waterway, of course, is a Northwest Passage, and, if it really had existed where Seale represented it, it would have brought great wealth to the east–west traders who used it, saving them the dangerous and time-consuming voyage around Cape Horn. Although seventeenth-century explorers had concluded that the passage did not exist, eighteenth-century governments, explorers, and scientists—especially in Britain—took up the search with enthusiasm.[17] When mid-century explorations proved fruitless, the explorers—again, British explorers in particular—reoriented the search, moving it to the north.[18] Around 1770, the *London Chronicle* still could report that "'The practicability of the North-west passage is not to be disputed.'"[19] (Olaudah Equiano voyaged toward the North Pole in 1773 on what he termed an "expedition... to explore a north-east passage," clearly motivated by related thinking).[20] In 1775, the British government offered an award of £20,000 for the discovery of a northwest passage and another award of £5,000 to anyone who sailed within a latitudinal degree of the North Pole.[21] Hope for a navigable northwest passage through the far north remained strong into the 1790s.[22]

While the British clearly would have benefited commercially from such a passage, contemporary imaginative writers also considered moral, spiritual, and philosophical benefits. In *The Excursion*, Wordsworth's Solitary, having emigrated to North America to escape European corruption, looks for the extreme liberty that he believes men must enjoy as they walk "along the side / Of . . . that Northern Stream / Which spreads into successive seas."[23] In *Frankenstein*, Mary Shelley's Robert Walton searches for the passage even farther north (perhaps seeking another eastern route): he hopes to confer an "inestimable benefit . . . on all mankind to the last generation, by discovering a passage near the pole to those countries, to reach which at present so many months are requisite" and, along the way, to visit (against the logic of the earth's rotational wobble, but in keeping with his idealism) a "country of eternal light": a country that depends upon the imagination for its delineation inasmuch as "it ever presents itself to [Walton's] . . . imagination as the region of beauty and delight."[24] The discovery of a passage might even have saved the Ancient Mariner his spiritual trouble, since, in using it, he could have avoided the bad weather and albatrosses of the far southern Pacific.

Most Romantic writers concerned themselves, though, with the possibilities offered by American land, rather than water. They believed that American soil was uncommonly fertile, and that this fertility might support not only an easy agricultural livelihood, but a healthy life of the mind and spirit. The tract names on the "List of Land Purchases" in Priestley's Northumberland settlement, for instance, indicate how these writers often conceived of American space. The names include Fairfield, Fairview, Fertile Grove, Fertility, Pleasant Hill, Pleasant Valley, Richland, Rich Soil, Rich Treasure, Spring Grove, and Wheatland, and also Content, Equality, Fraternity, Friendship, Independence, Liberty, Partnership, and Respectability.[25] Other tract names, such as Eden and Edenburg, either assert a millenarian new paradise or borrow from a Rousseauvian concept of natural environs, or both. (Shelley's "Eternal Light" would fit on this list.) Still other names, such as Utopia, Elysian Field, and Happy Retreat, suggest that at least some Romantic-period emigrants and would-be emigrants were seeking, rather than avoiding, Wordsworth's "Utopia, subterranean fields" and "secreted Island[s] Heaven knows where," and yet that they also were attempting to realize such sites and situations *in* "the world which is the world / Of all of us."

At any rate, British emigrants at the end of the eighteenth century would have known that they were separating themselves dramatically from what was popularly conceived of as the reality of Britain. Even if America offered much that was familiar to the British—a common language, a population that at this time still was more than sixty percent English—the emigration would divide them from the lives they had known: it would destabilize national identity; it would constitute a trip outside of boundaries.[26]

American emigration was transgressive and it was potentially transcendental.[27] After the end of the American War of Independence in 1783, the British understood emigration to America as taking people away especially from British institutional life: they understood it to be anti-governmental and anti-Anglican if not altogether anti-British. Dominant political theory long had held that any loss of British population meant a loss of British strength (a position that Adam Smith's *The Wealth of Nations* [1776] and Thomas Malthus's *Essay on the Principle of Population* [1798] were just beginning to challenge), and the wars with France between 1793 and 1815 accentuated for many both inside the government and outside it the need to keep Britain's working and potentially fighting population at home.[28] The government actively promulgated an anti-emigration position, passing various disincentives to departure and incentives to return, the most important of these being the 1803 Passenger Act, which raised the price of transatlantic passage and thereby made emigration impossible for most of the working poor.[29] The naval activity of the French Revolutionary and Napoleonic wars also worked in the favor of the government's anti-emigration policy by stopping most British travel to America. As David Brownstone and Irene Franck observe, between 1793 and 1815, "the North Atlantic crossing was very unsafe..., and very few immigrant-carrying ships even tried to reach North America from Britain."[30] In late 1794, Mary Evans, whom Coleridge had courted unsuccessfully, tapped into the popular conception of American emigration when she wrote to him objecting to his Pantisocratic scheme and encouraging him to remain in England, saying, "'You have a Country. Does it demand nothing of You?'" and Coleridge himself considered the real possibility of emigration becoming "treasonable."[31] Cobbett likewise commented that "There is, in the transfer of our duty from our nation to a foreign land [through emigration], something violently hostile to all our notions of fidelity."[32]

Literary history largely has elided the real and perceived danger of American emigration, though, and schemes like Pantisocracy now may look merely like armchair fantasy. Admittedly, to many contemporaries the schemes looked this way as well, though even these contemporaries generally registered some of the real hazards. Cobbett warned in 1796, for example, that "beautiful descriptions so luxuriantly picturesque of American scenery warm the imagination: regardless of scrutinizing their veracity, the deluded adventurer hastily undertakes the project of realizing his sanguine expectations"; and when the adventurer arrives in America "the material object and pleasing fruition of his wishes 'vanishes into thin air,' and leaves him the desponding dupe of deception and credulity."[33]

But many others thought they saw empirical evidence that demonstrated the likelihood that they could realize high ideals after encountering real risk. Ultimately, though, America failed many of the British Romantics who sought a destination for a migration that would transcend British shortcomings. On the other hand, the textual tensions that arose—and still arise—from this failure, as positive representation of America played against negative, were—and are—productive ones. British Romantic poetry and important features of the British Romantic idea of the imagination drew from these tensions. In their engagement with the tensions, Romantic writers and their fictional characters resituated themselves aesthetically, morally, socially, ideologically, even if they remained physically in England.

Coleridge, Wordsworth, and the Poetry of American Migration

Most of the poems in the 1798 *Lyrical Ballads* are migration poetry, as are many other poems that Coleridge and Wordsworth wrote in the last five years of the eighteenth century. Although Wordsworth argues in "Expostulation and Reply" for the virtues of sitting motionless on a rock and although he takes a famous "stand" in "Tintern Abbey," the volume depicts great physical movement, and that movement frequently is to and from the Americas.[34] *Lyrical Ballads* opens with the Ancient Mariner traveling from and then returning to his "own Countrée" on a trip that passes around South America (603). In "The Foster-Mother's Tale," a man, who has suffered from European religious and political oppression, goes "on ship-board / With those bold voyagers, who made discovery / Of golden lands" in the "new world," then disappears up "a great river" into the American interior (71–3, 76, 79). "Lines Left Upon a Seat in a Yew-Tree" addresses a "Traveller" in England (1). In "The Female Vagrant," a family moves from the English Lake District across the Atlantic to "the western world," and then the mother returns alone to England (117). In "We Are Seven," two siblings "are gone to sea" (19). The narrator of "The Thorn" has only recently come to "this country" (and the 1800 "Note to 'The Thorn'" adds that he is—or is like—a retired

"Captain of a small trading vessel") (182). The narrator of "The Last of the Flock" has been in "distant countries" (1). The woman in "The Mad Mother" has come "far from over the main," presumably from North America since she speaks and sings "in the English tongue" and knows how to make "an Indian bower" (4, 10, 55). In "Old Man Travelling," a man journeys " 'many miles' " to see his mortally wounded " 'son, a mariner' " who has returned to England, perhaps from the French wars, perhaps, like the Female Vagrant, from the American (17–18). In "The Complaint of a Forsaken Indian Woman," a dying "Northern Indian" finds herself unable to continue on a journey in the Hudson Bay region. And "Tintern Abbey" describes a visit, followed by wandering, followed by a revisiting.

As suggested by the direct or indirect appearance of America in six of these poems, the imagination of the *Lyrical Ballads* is at least partly the imagination of American emigration.[35] Additionally, some of Coleridge's most famous lines on the process of writing the *Lyrical Ballads* echo in his discussions of American spaces. In *Biographia Literaria*, he explains "the two cardinal points of [the] poetry" in *Lyrical Ballads*, the first being "the power of exciting the sympathy of the reader by a faithful adherence to the truth of nature" and the second being "the power of giving the interest of novelty by the modifying colours of the imagination." [36] Coleridge returns to this language (which is figuratively geographical since the "cardinal points" are points on the compass rose) in an essay from *The Friend* as he recalls that his plans for an American Pantisocratic community led to his "clearest insight into the nature of individual man" and yet also involved the imagination's "shifting forms and glowing colours."[37] (Coleridge connects his American Pantisocratic scheme and the work of the poetic imagination further by then quoting Wordsworth's *Prelude* lines on "utopia, subterraneous fields, / Or some secreted island, heaven knows where!"[38])

The language and ideas of American emigration thus inflect Coleridge's and Wordsworth's poetry, especially during the late 1790s, and especially in the *Lyrical Ballads*. The *Lyrical Ballads*, I argue, is the product of displaced Pantisocracy: it is Pantisocracy at a distance.[39] The volume investigates both the promises and the failures of Pantisocratic spaces.

THE LOGIC OF PANTISOCRACY

Although Pantisocracy looks now like what Coleridge himself eventually would call the "building of air-castles," rather than a social plan developed according to the real-world principles that counterbalance the fantastic in *Lyrical Ballads*, Coleridge and the other Pantisocrats founded the scheme upon many of the perceived realities of the time.[40] Coleridge, convinced of the solidity of its empirical foundation, insisted upon the "practicability" of the Pantisocratic system (*Letters* 1.96). The practical logic of the emigrant community, to the degree that such logic existed, often seems ambiguous because Coleridge and the others failed to produce and publish a tract explaining Pantisocracy in detail (though they promised one repeatedly) and because the descriptions that do exist, mostly in personal letters, either are skewed by irony or enthusiasm, or—if the authors wrote them after the plan failed—are tempered by retrospective disavowals of earlier commitment (Coleridge, *Letters* 1.96, 115, 119). By 1847, Joseph Cottle—the sometime friend and publisher of Coleridge, Southey, and others involved in the Pantisocratic scheme—could dismiss Pantisocracy as "epidemic delusion."[41] But such a label obscures both the seriousness of purpose and the practical research that the planners put toward that purpose in the 1790s.[42] At that time, those who rejected the plan while also knowing a great deal about it and sharing the planners' sociopolitical perspectives were more measured in their opposition. If they viewed the scheme as unachievable they viewed it nonetheless as desirable, praiseworthy, and worthy of pursuit. Thomas Poole, whose correspondence provides one of the fullest contemporary accounts of Pantisocracy, commented, for instance, that "however perfectible human nature may be, I fear it is not yet perfect enough to exist long under the regulations of such a [Pantisocratic] system, particularly when the Executors of the plan are taken from a society in a high degree civilised and corrupted."[43] For Poole, Pantisocracy was not a "delusion" and was not "air-castles"; it was, he feared, simply a too ambitious scheme, though one that nonetheless showed great potential for the future and even possibilities for the present: "America is certainly a desirable country" to him, and he "should like well to accompany [the Pantisocrats]...to see what progress they make."[44] For others in the world as it was known—and as it was unknown—in the mid-1790s, the success of the scheme looked more plausible.

In composite, as Poole, Cottle, and the Pantisocrats themselves described the plan in their letters and retrospective published accounts, Pantisocracy would have looked like the following.

The Pantisocrats would have emigrated to America by ship, carrying tools to farm, including " 'ploughs, and other implements of husbandry.' "[45] In England, they would have raised money for the emigration voyage and for the settlement, Coleridge and Southey by publishing and giving lectures, others through other means. They would have shared their funds to enable those who earned less to join those who earned more (Coleridge, *Letters* 1.97).

Coleridge and Southey initially planned for "Twelve gentlemen of good education and liberal principles... to embark [for America] with twelve ladies," but the number of committed emigrants never appears to have matched their expectations.[46] In various groupings, at various times, and according to various lists, the Pantisocratic emigrants—Poole called them "the Emigrators"—included Coleridge; Southey; Southey's mother, brothers and their cousin Margaret (Peggy) Hill; Robert Lovell (a poet and Bristol friend); the four Fricker sisters (three of whom were married to Coleridge, Southey, and Lovell) and their mother; George Burnett (an Oxford friend who failed to convince the fourth Fricker sister to marry him); Robert Allen (a friend of Coleridge's from Christ's Hospital who introduced Coleridge to Southey); Heath (an apothecary) along with his unnamed serving man and that man's unnamed wife; and Shadrach (Shad) Weeks (in the role of Southey's servant, a role Coleridge strongly opposed).[47]

The group chose to settle on the banks of the Susquehanna, near Priestley's house, in Northumberland, Pennsylvania, after early plans to settle in Kentucky began to look impractical. Later plans to create a Pantisocratic community in a farmhouse in Wales were short lived.[48] In Pennsylvania, the group would have "purchase[d] a thousand acres, [and] hire[d] labourers to assist... in clearing it and building houses" (Southey, *Letters* 1.71).

They would have worked the farm just two hours a day, "the common ground [being]... cultivated by common toil" in an "equalization of labour" (Southey, *Letters* 1.70, 90).[49] They would have "criticise[d] poetry when hunting a buffalo"; they would have composed "sonnets while following the plough"; they would have "discuss[ed] metaphysics" while "sawing down a tree"; and they would have found "repose in an Indian wig-wam—or from an Indian tomahawk" (Southey, *Letters* 1.70, 72; compare Coleridge, *Letters* 1.99). After the two hours of necessary labor,

> The leisure still remaining, might be devoted, in convenient fractions, to the extension of their domain, by prostrating the sturdy trees of the forest, where "lop and top," without cost, would supply their cheerful winter fire; and the trunks when cut into planks, without any further expense than their own pleasant labour, would form the sties for their pigs, and the linnies for their cattle, and the barns for their produce; reserving their choicest timbers for their own comfortable log-dwellings. But after every claim that might be made on their manual labour had been discharged, a large portion of time, would still remain for their own individual pursuits, so that they might read, converse, and even write books.[50]

After the work, "The produce of their industry [would have been]...laid up for the use of all; and a good library of books [would have been]...collected, and their leisure hours...spent in study, liberal discussions, and the education of their children."[51]

Even if they expected to hunt buffalo and repose in wigwams, they would have avoided going very far back into nature; that is to say, they would have settled closer to town than to the frontier. They chose a site within reach of Philadelphia, which, as many writers at the time noted, maintained at least some of the social and commercial infrastructure familiar to Europeans. As Brissot commented in 1788, if an emigrant to America "clings to his European ways and wishes to satisfy his European tastes and needs society, his best choice will be Pennsylvania."[52] Poole said that the group were planning to move to "a delightful part of the new back settlements," but they selected a spot that was not especially far "back."[53]

Pantisocracy, as Southey defined it, would be "the equal government of all," and its famous guiding principle would be aspheterism, which Southey described as "the generalization of individual property" and Coleridge described as "an abolition of personal property" (Southey, *Letters* 1.75; Coleridge, *Letters* 1.96). The society would have eschewed money, which the Pantisocrats considered a "huge evil"; without money and under the system of common property, they expected that "none should be poor" (Southey, *Letters* 1.81, 70). This would have been a "Social Colony," a "liberalized" community, though it also would have entailed a hierarchical relationship to the rest of the world: the Pantisocratic community would have been one of natural nobility, a "society...of the most polishd order" (Coleridge, *Letters* 1.96; Southey, *Letters* 1.72).[54]

The group's planners were all male, but their community would have given females more authority than they often had in Britain at this time, including them centrally in the philosophical conversations and the cultural work of the group (Coleridge, *Letters* 1.115).[55] As Poole commented, "The employments of the women are to be the care of infant children, and other occupations suited to their strength; at the same time the greatest attention is to be paid to the cultivation of their minds."[56] Coleridge suggested that Southey's mother and the mother of the Fricker sisters could

> prepare the Food of Simplicity for us—Let the married Women do only what is absolutely convenient and customary for pregnant Women or nurses—Let the Husbands do *all* the Rest—and what will that all

> be—? Washing with a Machine and cleaning the House. One Hour's addition to our daily Labor. (*Letters* 1.114)

While Coleridge reported that returned emigrants were saying that "Women's *teeth* are bad" in America, Southey commented that the Pantisocratic women all would be "beautiful amiable and accomplished" (Coleridge, *Letters* 1.99; Southey, *Letters* 1.72).[57]

Although a key tenet of Pantisocracy would be the communal treatment of possessions and although Bristol gossip had the Pantisocrats practicing free love, aspheterism never did extend to marital relations. The community would practice monogamy. Each man who emigrated would be expected to bring a wife. Thomas Poole did note a possible basis for the Bristol gossip, though, since, he said, "The regulations relating to the females strike [the Pantisocrats]...as the most difficult; whether the marriage contract shall be dissolved if agreeable to one or both parties, and many other circumstances, are not yet determined."[58]

The community would have questioned, if not rejected, other British institutional conventions as well. Poole said that "Every one is to enjoy his own religious and political opinions, provided they do not encroach on the rules previously made, which rules, it is unnecessary to add, must in some measure be regulated by the laws of the state which includes the district in which they settle."[59] But religious toleration appears to have stopped short of Anglicanism, which perhaps the Pantisocrats "rule[d]" out: Coleridge indicated that the group would have actively opposed the "mongrel whelp" that passed for Christianity in England (Coleridge, *Letters* 1.123).[60]

Nonetheless, the goals and values of Pantisocracy were as explicitly and enthusiastically theological as they were political. In keeping with Blake, Paine and others who saw in America the possibilities of a new heaven on earth, the Pantisocrats saw millenarian potential in their movement.[61] According to Cottle, Lovell hoped Pantisocracy would "regenerate the whole complexion of society; and that, not by establishing formal laws, but by excluding all the little deteriorating passions; injustice, 'wrath, anger, clamour, and evil speaking,' and thereby setting an example of 'Human Perfectibility.' "[62] The work of Pantisocracy, Southey agreed, would involve "the toil and...the glory of regenerating mankind" (*Letters* 1.71). Coleridge anticipated that "the pure System of Pant[is]ocracy" must eventually "aspheterize...the Bounties of Nature" and poverty and hunger must end (Coleridge, *Letters* 1.84). Later, after the plans had lost momentum, Southey still hoped to see "'the establishment of a system which I still believe to be the panacea of all human calamities, & I expect a [future] promised millennium.'"[63] At this late point, Coleridge as well commented that "Pantisocracy is not the Question—it's [sic] realization is distant—perhaps a miraculous Millenium" (*Letters* 1.158).

Everything about the community's structure—from its principle of aspheterism to its location on the banks of the Susquehanna—would have tied directly to this wish to regenerate political and moral society. As a result of the commonality of property, Southey commented, "every motive for vice should be annihilated and every motive for virtue [should be] strengthened" (Southey, *Letters* 1.70). Coleridge likewise said, "The leading Idea of Pantisocracy is to make men *necessarily* virtuous by removing all Motives to Evil—all possible Temptations"—and added that the "similarity of Property . . . would amount to a *moral Sameness*" (Coleridge, *Letters* 1.114, 163).

Pantisocracy thus became a high "duty" for its participants (Southey, *Letters* 1.87). They were self-conscious enthusiasts, whose enthusiasm, they happily knew, might look to others like madness. Southey commented that "My mother says I am mad—if so, she is bit by me for she wishes as much to go [to America] as I" (*Letters* 1.75). Coleridge reported that a Cambridge acquaintance called him a "'madman of Genius!'" and noted that the Pantisocrats "are all highly charged with that enthusiasm which results from strong perceptions of moral rectitude, called into life and action by ardent feelings" (*Letters* 1.103, 97).[64]

Although the Pantisocrats considered setting up their community in Wales, Coleridge in particular argued that America offered an alternative to Britain and Europe, and so settling there was crucial to the scheme.[65] Coleridge shared his confidence in the exclusive promise of America with other radicals of the period. Thomas Paine, for instance, commented,

> The Revolution in America presented in politics what was only theory in mechanics. So deeply rooted were all the governments of the old world, and so effectually had the tyranny and antiquity of habit established itself over the mind, that no beginning could be made in Asia, Africa, or Europe, to reform the political condition of man. Freedom had been hunted round the globe; reason was considered as rebellion; and slavery of fear had made men afraid to think.[66]

Thus, Paine concluded, "America is the only spot in the political world, where the principles of universal reformation could begin."[67]

In Paine's and Coleridge's America, extraordinary things could happen. The extraordinariness of the Pantisocratic scheme ranged from its day-to-day activities—buffalo hunting in Pennsylvania, sleeping in wigwams, clearing and farming heavily forested land with just two hours' labor a day—to its overarching millenarian regenerative purpose. And yet this extraordinary America corresponded at least loosely with the America that appeared in many contemporary accounts and in some of the best radical political and economic theory of the time. Coleridge, Southey, and the other Pantisocrats tried to ascertain and prepare for the circumstances of settling in America, and as fanciful as their scheme may look now they based it upon the results of their research. When Coleridge, using bureaucratic language, asserted that Pantisocracy should have a fully developed "code of contracts [of the kind] necessary for the internal regulation of the society," he was dealing, if at a stretch, with institutional realities (Coleridge, *Letters* 1.96).

If the Pantisocrats expected buffalo near their settlement, they did so because they were reading the *Topographical Description of North America*, in which Imlay discussed the relation between "The bison of Scythia, and what is called the buffalo in America."[68] If they planned to work for just two hours a day, they planned to do so because their readings of Brissot's *Travels in the United States* told them that a two-hour workday was sufficient: Brissot said, " 'A man living in these areas still surrounded by wilderness works scarcely two hours a day to support himself and his family, and he passes almost all his time loafing, hunting, or drinking.' "[69] Their readings of Adam Smith's *Wealth of Nations* also encouraged them to think that such a workday was possible. Southey commented, "According to the computation of Adam Smith—one man in twenty is employed in providing the necessaries and comforts of life. He works ten hours a day and in consequence cannot enjoy his mental faculties, but divide that labour among the whole twenty and the sum of work is half an hour" (Southey, *Letters* 1.70).[70] If they expected to "write sonnets while following the plough" and to "discuss metaphysics" while "sawing down a tree," they at least intended to acquire knowledge about the physical part of the activity before setting out for America. Coleridge noted that they planned "to learn the theory and practice of agriculture and carpentry"; and George Burnett, who was a "temporary farmer," already had some experience (Coleridge, *Letters* 1.97).[71]

If Southey's comment about seeking "repose in an Indian wig-wam—or from an Indian tomahawk"—expressed real expectations of both Indian hospitality and Indian violence (i.e., if it resulted from more than an attempt at humor), it was consistent with the central concerns of Europeans looking to settle outside the main American cities at the time.[72] In a series of letters at the beginning of *Travels in the United States*, Clavière asked Brissot to

> Please try to let us have the most reliable information available on the Indians inhabiting all the areas of that vast continent, their numbers, customs, way of life, and the more or less inevitable causes which lead to a permanent state of war between them and the Americans. You know of course that the mere idea of Indians terrifies many good people.[73]

Brissot answered that Indians tended toward the good and quoted William Penn's description of them as " 'generous, brave, honorable, and hospitable' "—a description that he called "quite accurate"—though he also discussed the "tomahawk [which has]...killed so cruelly," albeit generally at the provocation of whites, and he described an unprovoked attack by Indian "savages," including an Indian with "a knife between his teeth."[74] Brissot's description of European settlers who were willing to face the potential dangers as well as the potential benefits of contact with the Indians could well have served as a template for Southey's casual comment on the alternatives of the hospitable wigwam and the murderous tomahawk: Brissot wrote that "The frontiersman is courageous, daring, unafraid of death, and contemptuous of the Indians. He can sleep as soundly in the middle of the forest as he would surrounded by neighbors."[75] In *Topographical Description*, Imlay also described hospitable "Indians, who...are friendly and appear very happy in meeting with the white people, and rendering them any service they possibly can," but likewise described a recent incident in which "barbarous savages" took whites captive and then "immediately after tomahawked one man and two women, and loaded all the others with heavy baggage, forcing them along toward their towns, able or unable to march. Such as were weak and faint by the way, they tomahawked."[76] In his *Travels*, William Bartram repeatedly took repose with Indians—who were "civil" and who "[a]s moral men...certainly...[stood] in no need of European civilization"—and yet he also observed that some of them "do indeed scalp their slain enemy."[77] The banks of the Susquehanna, then, attracted the Pantisocrats because of their reported "security from hostile Indians" (Coleridge, *Letters* 1.99).[78]

This area also drew them, though, because others with similar aims already were attempting to establish a regenerative society there: Joseph Priestley (who sailed for America in April 1794) was doing so, along with his sons (especially Joseph, Jr.), his friend and fellow scientist the "Manchester radical" Thomas Cooper, and their friends.[79] Even though this group's Northumberland settlement plans had fallen apart by September 1794, Priestley, his family, and (sometimes) Cooper remained there. They reported back to Britain on the virtues of American living, and they continued to encourage like-minded friends to join them. They embodied the promise that American emigration held for people like the Pantisocrats.

Priestley's group optioned the 700,000 acres north of Northumberland and hoped to use the land to establish a New World society. The full scope of the settlement scheme is uncertain, but Priestley's group seems also to have been following at least loosely the example of Brissot, who was a friend of Priestley's.[80] Theirs was to be a space of refuge for "friends of liberty in general."[81] The Pantisocrats would have liked to include themselves at the fringes of this group of friends, and Coleridge referred to their attempted settlement when he wrote that he, Southey, and the others planned to establish their community "at a distance, but at a convenient distance, from Cooper's Town on the banks of the Susquehanna" (*Letters* 1.97). (Even in 1800, long after the dissolution of the Pantisocratic scheme, Coleridge commented that if he had the money he "would go & settle near Priestley, in America"; *Letters* 2.710). If the millenarian hopes of the Pantisocrats were ultimately ill-founded, the emigrants at least would be in the good company of one of the foremost empirical scientists of the day.

Coleridge and Southey found Priestley's situation in Northumberland attractive, and Southey's commitment to the Pantisocratic community began to diminish at the same time that news of Priestley's abandonment of his settlement plans was spreading through England.[82] Before that time, the Pantisocrats would have confirmed for themselves that Priestley's settlement was about to realize Priestley's radical, dissenting principles spatially—on the land itself—by reading Cooper's *Some Information Respecting America* (1794). Coleridge read the book and then recommended that Southey "By all means read & ponder on" it (*Letters* 1.115). The book, at once a promotional tract and a how-to guide for potential emigrants, enumerated populations, distances, and the costs of living. Coleridge took particular interest in Cooper's discussion of land prices (*Letters* 1.115). Cooper's representations of life in America generally—and life on the banks of the Susquehanna especially—made this space appear conducive to the Pantisocrats' settlement plans. Americans, Cooper wrote, had cleared the ideological landscape of European corruption, opening it for the processes of regenerative religion and civil society:

> They have exploded those principles, by the operation of which religious oppressions and restrictions, of whatever description, have been afflicted upon mankind.... They have exploded, in like manner, those principles, by the operation of which, civil oppressions have been afflicted upon mankind.[83]

The area around Northumberland, in turn, appeared to be exactly the right kind of place, sufficiently distant from the exploded Old World institutions, to start a New World society. According to Cooper, it was "delightfully situated near the Susquehanna."[84] The houses were "comfortable and commodious": built of logs, and thus "uncouth" to the English, but nonetheless "as comfortable, and as clean, and as convenient, as any brick or stone house" in Britain, constructed and finished with wainscoting, paneled doors, and glazed windows at a cost of just 250 pounds.[85] And the area was a natural garden, the soil being "apparently excellent for almost any kind of vegetation."[86]

If the Pantisocrats had distrusted Cooper's representation of the place, they could have consulted Brissot, who commented likewise that "the lands watered by the Susquehanna are highly regarded"; and, while he acknowledged that various accounts of these lands (including Crèvecoeur's popular *Letters of an American Farmer* [1782]) exaggerated their virtues, treating them as "a sort of paradise," he suggested that, at least in the case of the area where the Pantisocrats were looking to settle, such "description is true." [87] For those who were interested in picturesque landscape aesthetics, the Susquehanna also offered "beautiful view[s]" and "magnificent spectacle[s]."[88]

Although Pantisocracy clearly would possess its own set of principles, these principles meshed well with Priestley's experiences, writings, and reputation, and consequently might find firm grounding in the same space where Priestley was living. Well before Priestley emigrated, British radicals associated him with the process of European and world displacement and re-emplacement (as well as regeneration) that they hoped would emerge from the French Revolution and that they so often associated with life in America.[89] In "To Dr. Priestley. Dec. 29, 1792," for instance, Anna Letitia Barbauld writes,

> Well can'st thou afford
> To give large *credit* for that debt of fame

> Thy country owes thee. Calm thou can'st consign it
> To the slow payment of that distant day,
> If distant, when thy name, to freedom's join'd,
> Shall meet the thanks of a regenerate land.[90]

Unsurprisingly, then, in Coleridge's sonnet "Priestley," which appeared in the *Morning Chronicle* for 11 December 1794 (eight months after Priestley left Britain and during the time when the Pantisocrats' own plans to emigrate were coming apart), the Northumberland settlers reject the institutions of Europe and tend toward a bright millenarian future. Referring first to the riot that burned Priestley's house and lab and to the underlying political cause of that riot, Coleridge says that "king-bred rage with lawless uproar rude / Hath driv'n our PRIESTLEY o'er the Ocean swell"; but now in his American millenarian "halls of brightness he shall dwell" as "Religion . . . / Disdainful rouses . . . / And flings to Earth" all that is "unholy," as "JUSTICE" vanquishes "th' Oppressor," and as "NATURE slowly lifts her matron veil / To smile with fondness."[91] And in *Religious Musings*—which a subtitle dates also during the height of the Pantisocratic discussions ("Christmas Eve of 1794"), though Coleridge really wrote most of it in 1796[92]—Coleridge represents Priestley as a martyr persecuted by Old World government and religion and turns him into a "saint" of a new religion in the New World:

> Lo! Priestley there, patriot, and saint, and sage,
> Him, full of years, from his loved native land
> Statesmen blood-stained and priests idolatrous
> By dark lies maddening the blind multitude
> Drove with blind hate. Calm, pitying he retired,
> And mused expectant on these promised years. (371–6)

The "promised years" are those of a millenarian "blest future" on a "renovated Earth" (357, 365).[93]

So, at the end of the eighteenth century, Northumberland looked like a highly practical place for an impractical community. Fittingly, Cooper planned to name the Priestley-Cooper settlement "Asylum."[94] An asylum is a site structurally differentiated from and yet still related to real-world institutional power structures, since a *syle* is a right or power of seizure and an *a-syle* is the neutralization of such a right or power: an asylum, then, is a space that institutional power cannot intrude into or violate. As Jedidiah Morse in *The American Gazetteer* commented in 1798, "a great many people ha[d] . . . emigrated to this part of the state," and although the motives for emigration were highly varied, many, like Priestley and Cooper and like the Pantisocrats, looked to the area as a space where they could escape the practical and ideological limits imposed upon their selves in their nations of birth.[95] (At the same time, along the Pennsylvania Susquehanna, another group of emigrants—consisting of Royalists fleeing from Robespierre—constructed more than fifty buildings, established a social colony in 1793, and also called it Azilum).

Such settlements and settlement plans were more solid than the airy schemes that Cottle described.[96] If the Pantisocrats' expectations diverged frequently and sometimes dramatically from the physical realities of what their situation would have been as settlers, they based them nonetheless upon some of the most recent (if not always the factually best) topographical description and social, economic, and political theory.[97] And they developed the expectations in critical relation to another reality, this one European: a reality in which, for example, the long workday experienced by the longest-working portion of the population nonetheless was leaving that portion poor, in which government policies and government-provoked violence dispossessed otherwise loyal Britons of their houses and their senses of place on British soil (the burning of Priestley's house being just one striking example), and in which government and religion disenfranchised those whose beliefs differed from those promoted by dominant institutional systems. In other words, the Pantisocrats developed their expectations of a new reality in a New World in relation to what they must have seen as a failed reality in the Old World.

If their expected new reality also failed, it still maintained its socially critical force, and, for that matter, its aesthetic force. For Coleridge, and then for Wordsworth, the social, political, religious, *and* aesthetic features of American Pantisocracy contributed centrally to the making of poetry through the end of the 1790s and into the first decades of the nineteenth century. As Leask points out, when the American emigration plans fell through, "Coleridge sought a substitute in the cottage community around Tom Poole at Nether Stowey"; and that community came to include Wordsworth and his sister Dorothy.[98] The community between the Wordsworths and Coleridge led, at the time of the publication of *Lyrical Ballads*, to further plans for German and other Continental travels that, at least in duration, at first resembled an emigration scheme. Although the traveling party eventually consisted only of the two Wordsworths and Coleridge, Dorothy reported that the group originally was to include Coleridge's wife and two children and that the group planned to remain on the Continent "for one year, at least; what we shall do afterwards it is impossible at present to say."[99] In the event, the group stayed in Germany—and never with much coherence—for less than a year, the Wordsworths from late September 1798 until late April 1799, Coleridge until early July 1799 (Coleridge, *Letters* 1.520n).[100]

Then, just a few months after returning to England, in December 1799, Coleridge told Southey that he saw "no impossibility of forming a pleasant little Colony for a few years in Italy or the South of France" (Coleridge, *Letters* 1.553). At the same time, Leask suggests, the Wordsworths were "discover[ing]...Pantisocratic values" in Grasmere; and Coleridge joined them there too.[101]

Then, in a March, 1801, letter to Poole, Coleridge reconstructed his plans for an American Pantisocracy:

> *O for a lodge* in a Land, where human Life was an end, to which Labor was only a Means, instead of being, as it [is] here, a mere means of carrying on Labor....It fills me with indignation to hear the *croaking* accounts, which the English Emigrants send home of America. The society is so bad—the manners so vulgar—the servants so insolent.—Why then do they not seek out one another, & make a society—? It is arrant ingratitude to talk so of a Land in which there is no Poverty but as a consequence of absolute Idleness—and to talk of it too with abuse comparatively with England, with a place where the laborious Poor are dying with Grass with[in] their Bellies. (*Letters* 2.709–10)

This new Pantisocracy seemingly would replicate the old one, though it would carry the Lake District community with it. Coleridge would like to

> go & settle near Priestley, in America....I say, I would go to America, if Wordsworth would go with me, & we could persuade two or three Farmers of the Country who are exceedingly attached to us, to accompany us—I would go, if the difficulty of procuring sustenance in this Country remain in the state & degree, in which it is at present. Not on any romantic Scheme, but merely because Society has become a matter of great Indifference to me—I grow daily more & more attached to Solitude—but it is a matter of the utmost Importance to be removed from seeing and suffering *Want*. (*Letters* 2.710)[102]

And, again, four months later, in July, 1801, Coleridge tried to interest Southey in yet another new emigration scheme, now including the wider group coming to be known in the critical press as the Lakers:

> Now mark my scheme!—St Nevis is the most lovely as well as the most healthy Island in the W. Indies—Pinny's Estate is there—and

> he has a country House situated in a most heavenly way, a very large mansion. Now between you & me I have reason to believe that not only this House is at my service, but many advantages in a family way that would go one half to lessen the expences of living there—& perhaps Pinny would appoint us sine-cure Negro drivers at a hundred a year each, or some other snug & reputable office—& perhaps, too we might get some office in which there is quite nothing to do, under the Governour. Now I & my family, & you & Edith, & Wordsworth & his Sister might all go there—& make the Island more illustrious than Cos or Lesbos. A heavenly climate—a heavenly country,—& a good House. The Sea shore so near us—dells & rocks, & streams—/ Do now think of this! But say nothing about it—on account of old Pinny.—Wordsworth would certainly go, if I went. By the living God, it is my opinion, that we should not leave three such men behind us. (*Letters* 2.747–8)

That Coleridge would wish to emigrate to the West Indies, a space associated by him and others with the slavery that he consistently abhorred, indicates perhaps less a change in his Pantisocratic values than a desperate attachment to those values.[103] Much later, in *The Friend*, he commented that "to the intense interest and impassioned zeal, which called forth and strained every faculty of my intellect for the organization and defence [sic] of this [Pantisocratic] scheme, I owe much of whatever I at present possess."[104] Through much of his life, then, Pantisocracy helped determine his thought and work.[105]

COLERIDGE'S POETRY OF PANTISOCRACY

In the September, 1794, sonnet titled "Pantisocracy," Coleridge showed that early "zeal" as he idealized the emigration scheme considerably more than he did in his letters (even as he included the poem first in a letter):

> No more my Visionary Soul shall dwell
> On Joys, that were! No more endure to weigh
> The Shame and Anguish of the evil Day,
> Wisely forgetful! O'er the Ocean swell
> Sublime of Hope I seek the cottag'd Dell,
> Where Virtue calm with careless step may stray,
> And dancing to the moonlight Roundelay
> The Wizard Passions weave an holy Spell.
> Eyes that have ach'd with Sorrow! ye shall weep
> Tears of doubt-mingled Joy, like their's who start
> From Precipices of distemper'd Sleep,

> On which the fierce-eyed Fiends their Revels k[eep],
> And see the rising Sun, & feel it dart
> New Rays of Pleasance trembling to the Heart. (Coleridge, *Letters* 1.104)[106]

Pantisocracy appears again in the version of "Monody on the Death of Chatterton" that Coleridge first published in 1796. The "Monody" includes the first eight lines of the sonnet "Pantisocracy" with few changes, and then Coleridge adds,

> O Chatterton! that thou wert yet alive!
> Sure would'st thou spread the canvass to the gale,
> And love with us the tinkling team to drive
> O'er peaceful Freedom's undivided dale;
> . . .
> Yet will I love to follow the sweet dream,
> Where Susquehana pours his untamed stream;
> And on some hill, whose forest-frowning side
> Waves o'er the murmurs of his calmer tide,
> Will raise a solemn Cenotaph to thee,
> Sweet Harper of time-shrouded Minstrelsy!
> And there, sooth'd sadly by the dirgeful wind,
> Muse on the sore ills I had left behind. (140–51, 158–65)

"To a Young Ass," which appeared in the *Morning Chronicle* in December, 1794, emphasizes the regenerative characteristics of Pantisocracy. Coleridge addresses a lethargic and oppressed young British ass, saying that he

> fain would take thee with me, in the Dell
> Of high-soul'd Pantisocracy to dwell,
> Where Toil shall call the charmer Health his bride,
> And Laughter tickle Plenty's ribless side!
> How thou wouldst toss thy heels in gamesome play,
> And frisk about, as lamb or kitten gay! (27–32)

A manuscript version of the poem emphasizes further the millenarian aspects of this place, where the lion shall lie down with the lamb or at least "Rats shall mess with Terriers hand-in-glove / And Mice with Pussy's Whiskers sport in Love" (33–4).

"Pantisocracy" and "To a Young Ass" are minor poems and the portion of the "Monody" that deals with Pantisocracy distracts, at least in part, from the poem's main themes, but in these texts as well as in his other Pantisocratic writings Coleridges set forth the landscape and the aesthetic principles to which he returns in some of his most famous poems. Pointing to the Pantisocratic orientation of this later poetry, Leask comments that "the principles of Pantisocracy had an enduring significance in the later thought of Coleridge."[107] Eugenia, too, suggests that "to the [Pantisocratic] scheme...may be due much of the beautiful and fantastic imagery of [Coleridge's]...richest literary work."[108]

The most obvious place to look for Pantisocracy may be "Kubla Khan: Or, A Vision in a Dream," a poem in which Coleridge explores the possibilities of an imagined space and community that is other than Britain or Europe. As Tilar Mazzeo recently has proposed, this poem demonstrates "Romanticism's engagement with American emigration,"[109] and the poem's intertextual relationships indicate that the text engages specifically with Pantisocratic emigration. For instance, Mazzeo suggests persuasively that—along with Imlay's *Topographical Description*, which influenced Coleridge in his detailing of the Pantisocratic plan—Coleridge likely knew Imlay's 1793 novel *The Emigrants* and that this novel's representation of an American site called *Bellefont* (named for a fountain whose water "gushes from a rock," pours down in "pliant rills," "float[s] over a bed of crystals," and in a "meandering course moistens the flowery banks") "shaped the language of Coleridge's own utopian fountain community" in "Kubla Khan."[110] The river Alph, both in its turbulence and its placidity, may draw too from the circumstances of the Susquehanna near Northumberland. Cooper comments that "the Susquehanna sometimes roll[s]...through rich valleys, and sometimes wash[es]...the base of stupendous rocks."[111] Although the Susquehanna at Northumberland is calm, the water upriver is notorious for its waterfalls and difficult passage.[112]

More important than such loose connections, though, is the linguistic character of both Xanadu and the planned Pantisocratic settlement. The "Kubla Khan" dream vision is a speech-act since "In Xanadu...Kubla Khan / A stately pleasure-dome decree[d]" (1–2); and, as Victoria Meyers argues, in the Pantisocratic scheme, too, "Coleridge's and Southey's words [were to]...become speech-acts with power to bring a real world into being; their arguments [were to]...become performatives and the invention of a term like 'aspheterism' or 'pantisocracy' [was to be]...tantamount to 'Let there be light.'"[113] Likewise, Fulford comments, "Coleridge's power of speech was the basis of the [Pantisocratic] scheme"; and, James McKusick observes, in Pantisocracy "Language [would]...provide an invincible means of mastery over the colonial Other."[114] In "Kubla Khan,"

Coleridge states once more that he wishes to migrate away from the limits of a British national subjectivity and inhabit a better space and identity, which is to say, that he wishes to be a Pantisocrat.

Other Coleridge poems from the late 1790s also deal with Pantisocracy. As Roe notes, for instance, the Pantisocratic "idea of 'dwelling in the dell' persisted, relocating millenarian idealism in the personal, the private, the homely—in poems such as Coleridge's 'Frost at Midnight.' "[115] One might object only that with all the emphasis on the private pleasures of domestic life—with the construction of "comfortable log-dwellings," the warmth of "cheerful winter fires," and Coleridge looking forward to "cleaning the House"—Pantisocracy within its communitarian context already valued "the personal, the private, the homely." But certainly the life of "wander[ing] like a breeze" that Coleridge anticipates for his son in the poem, the rejection of the institutional education that he himself received (or at least the preference for the "lore" that one might learn in "far other scenes"), and the general removal—the migration—of the central religious and philosophical meditation from the British landscape and society that surround him (when "Sea, hill, and wood, [and] / This populous village" become as "Inaudible as dreams") are consistent with Pantisocratic principles (54, 50–1, 10–11, 13).[116]

Of Coleridge's poetry from this period, "Reflections on Having Left a Place of Retirement," written in 1795 and published in the October 1796 *Monthly Magazine*, most fully relocates Pantisocratic ideals to an English cottage. "Low was our pretty Cot," the poem opens, recalling the roughness and the allure of the anticipated American houses: "We could hear / At silent noon, and eve, and early morn, / The Sea's faint murmur" (1–4). In many ways this cottage and its surroundings look like the Susquehanna landscape in miniature:

> the little landscape round
> Was green and woody, and refresh'd the eye.
> It was a spot which you might aptly call
> The Valley of Seclusion! (6–9)

The cottage even shows some of the socially regenerative potential of the Pantisocratic settlement. From the cottage, Coleridge once saw

> A wealthy son of Commerce saunter by,
> Bristowa's citizen—he paus'd, and look'd
> With a pleased sadness and gaz'd all around,
> Then eye'd our cottage and gaz'd round again,
> And said, it was a *blessed little place.* (11–15)

In the 1797 version of the poem, Coleridge added that the sight of the cottage grounds seemed to "calm" the man's "thirst of idle gold, / And made him muse / With wiser feelings" (13–14).

But when Coleridge climbed out of the "low Dell" away from the "Low...Cot," up to a "stony Mount," he saw a "goodly scene" that included the topography both of nature (the mountain, a river, a woods) and of British social, political, and religious life (an abbey, a "faint city spire," the Channel between England and France) (27–36). From the removed perspective of the mountaintop—a Mountain of Seclusion that corresponds with the "Valley of Seclusion"—Coleridge saw what looked "like" a beautiful world, a world that "seem'd" like a new, regenerate one: "It seem'd like Omnipresence! God, methought; / Had built him there a Temple: the whole World/ Was *imag'd* in its vast circumference" (38–40). The world Coleridge saw was more than a microcosmic reflection; it was an imaginary space (the primary meaning of the verb *to image* still at this time being *to imagine*) and perhaps, like the Pantisocratic New World itself, a planned space (a secondary but still current meaning being *to devise, plan*).

Despite the similarities to the planned emigrant settlement in America, though, the "quiet Dell! dear Cot, and Mount sublime!"—a "Valley[, a cottage, and a mountain] of Seclusion"—were unlike that settlement and thus ultimately were not Pantisocratic. While the Susquehanna valley initially would have secluded the Pantisocrats from European—and even most American—social and political conflicts and while the Pantisocrats would have concerned themselves with the personal and the private, they planned to aim their work directly at engaging with and regenerating Europe. Migration differs greatly from seclusion. Migration entails spatial relationality: migrants move from point X to point Y, and their differential relation to point X conditions their habitation of point Y. (Once that differential relation ceases to matter, they no longer can be thought of as migrants). On the other hand, people who seclude themselves break their relation from point X. To seclude—to se-clude—is to take oneself apart from, to isolate oneself from: it is to become autonomous, shut off from the surrounding world. Coleridge finds that he must leave the cottage, and, in explaining his motives for leaving, he returns to the language of labor that he, Southey, and the other Pantisocrats used so often when describing the work of Pantisocracy. Southey celebrated "the toil and...the glory of regenerating mankind," apparently a more rewarding toil than the physical work that the Pantisocrats would limit to two hours a day (*Letters* 1.71). Coleridge celebrated even the limited "Toil of the Field" in the Pantisocratic settlement (*Letters* 1.122). And now in "Reflections" Coleridge asks, "Was it right, / While my unnumber'd brethren toil'd and bled, / That I should dream away the trusted hours / On rose-leaf beds . . . ?" (44–7) Instead, he concludes, he must "go, and join, head, heart, and hand, / Active and firm, to fight the bloodless fight / Of Science, Freedom, and the Truth in Christ" while praying a millenarian prayer that all might live in a world that resembles the one he has inhabited in the little cottage: "It might be so—but the time is not yet. / Speed it, O Father! Let thy Kingdom come!" (69–70). His plans and hopes for Pantisocracy too were these.

Coleridge's four contributions to the 1798 *Lyrical Ballads*, especially "The Foster-Mother's Tale" and "The Dungeon," both excerpted from his 1797 play *Osorio*, also explore the possibilities that Pantisocracy offered. "The Rime of the Ancyent Marinere," while addressing the spiritual and political psychology of migration in as fine of detail as any other Romantic text, speaks only indirectly about Coleridge's Pantisocratic concerns.[117] As the poem opens, the Mariner's ship leaves behind the institutional/regulatory guideposts of his home country, rounding the earth and dropping "Below the Kirk, below the Hill, / Below the Light-house top" (23–4). After his passage takes him around the Americas and into the south Pacific, the mariner eventually returns to his home country, though now his orientation is uncertain, the government-constructed guidepost, the religious marker, and even nationality itself having become unstable: he asks,

> is this indeed
> The light-house top I see?
> Is this the Hill? Is this the Kirk?
> Is this mine own countrée? (464–7)

Since "contree" and "cuntree" have roots in English but "contrée" and "cuntrée" have French roots, the geographical disorientation remains even as the Mariner steps onto (presumably) English soil: "now all in mine own Countrée / I stood on the firm land!" (570–1). A Hermit (in the role of English religious guide) and a harbor Pilot with his boy assistant (physical guides to a landing on English soil) offer little assistance. Upon encountering the Mariner, the Hermit, who seemingly should know exactly where he is on Britain's religious and institutional ground, "scarcely could . . . stand"; the Pilot, likewise disoriented, "fell down in a fit"; and the Pilot's boy went "crazy," his eyes rolling "to and fro" (573, 561, 565, 567). The apparent confidence the Mariner experiences in his position standing on "the firm land" fails quickly: he now must "pass, like night, from land to land" (586).

The "Ancient Mariner," in other words, is a poem of acute displacement. Although the Mariner comes to some wisdom and even to a provisional reorientation—a theological reorientation summed up tidily in the moral: "He prayeth best who loveth best, / All things both great and small: / For the dear God, who loveth us, / He made and loveth all" (614–17)—the moral and therefore the reorientation insufficiently answer to all that has occurred elsewhere in the poem. His return to Britain has been also uncertain. In some senses, he never has quite reached the Britain that he left at the poem's beginning. Rather, he occupies a state of in betweenness. He says in the present perfect that "this soul hath been / Alone on a wide wide sea" (597–8). He has not completed the action: he remains effectively "on a wide wide sea," not in Britain, not in the Americas, but displaced from both.

If the Mariner's situation speaks indirectly about Coleridge's own as his emigration voyage to America failed and as he continued to project schemes that would have taken him away from Britain's shores in the late 1790s, "The Foster-Mother's Tale" and "The Dungeon" emerge directly from and address the values of Pantisocracy. "The Foster-Mother's Tale," set in Spain but with themes and imagery that resonate with those of the English landscapes of poems like "Frost at Midnight" and Wordsworth's "We Are Seven," describes a child who grows up in nature and with nature as his best teacher, though he eventually suffers from religious and governmental oppression. When planning the Pantisocratic emigration scheme in 1794, Coleridge had worried that the children who accompanied the group would be "already *deeply* tinged with the prejudices and errors of Society" and that, even upon emigrating, the children would learn a prejudiced form of Christianity from the mothers of the Fricker sisters and Southey (*Letters* 1.119, 123). But the child in this poem is, from birth, a natural child (probably in both senses of the term), discovered "wrapped in mosses, lined / With thistle-beards" (24–5). With an apparently innate predisposition that overpowers European social and religious imperatives, he is

> most unteachable—
> And never learnt a prayer, nor told a bead,
> But knew the names of birds, and mocked their notes,
> And whistled, as he were a bird himself. (29–32)

When a friar eventually does succeed in taking the child out of himself by teaching him, the boy's "brain turn[s]" and he has "unlawful thoughts of many things" (43–4).

While Coleridge never specifies in writing the form of education the Pantisocrats would use to teach children to reject "the prejudices and errors of Society" and of religion, it seems safe to conclude that, set in an environment where discussions of metaphysics would coincide with "sawing down ... tree[s]" and the criticism of poetry would coincide with "hunting a buffalo," the education would integrate nature, and that religious understanding, by European standards, would be heterodox, "unlawful." It seems likely that the Pantisocratic children, like Hartley in "Frost at Midnight," would learn by "wander[ing] like a breeze / By lakes and sandy shores, beneath the crags / Of ancient mountain, and beneath the clouds" and would

> See and hear
> The lovely shapes and sounds intelligible
> Of that eternal language, which ... God
> Utters, who from eternity doth teach
> Himself in all, and all things in himself. (54–6, 58–62)

At any rate, the child in "The Foster-Mother's Tale" receives such an education. When institutional authorities hear about the young man's "heretical and lawless talk" and they throw him into a dungeon "hole," he thus turns back to nature, and specifically American nature (as Europeans configured it), rather than consoling himself with any religious lessons that the friar may have imparted (55, 57). He sings

> a doleful song about green fields,
> How sweet it were on lake or wild savannah,
> To hunt for food, and be a naked man,
> And wander up and down at liberty. (61–4)

And when he escapes from prison, he unsurprisingly heads for America, a place for which nature has prepared him and where he will escape from European oppression. Having sailed to the "new world," he

> seized a boat,
> And all alone, set sail by silent moonlight
> Up a great river, great as any sea,
> And ne'er was heard of more: but 'tis supposed,
> He lived and died among the savage men. (71–3, 76–81)

The young man's landfall is almost certainly in Spanish America. But the mention of the "wild savannah," likely gleaned (by Coleridge in his reading, if not the child in his) from Bartram's description of Georgia, tends toward the north. And if the "great river" is not the Susquehanna, it resonates with it nonetheless as a place where one might—as in Southey's speculations about life in Pennsylvania—"find repose in an Indian wig-wam–or from an Indian tomahawk."

When Coleridge describes the young man as a "poor mad youth" whose mind has "turned" in the poem, he avoids suggesting that the man's concept of an ideal America—or even his general thought process—is faulty (75). After all, Coleridge had cheerfully reported that some of his acquaintances during the months when he was promoting Pantisocracy the most strongly considered him, too, a "madman." Rather, the fault lies in the European institutions and teaching that either destroy the mind of such a man or alternatively represent him as mad. And if Maria, who hears the tale in the poem, considers much of the account of the foster-child merely "a sweet tale: / Such as would lull a listening child to sleep, / His rosy face besoiled with unwiped tears" (68–70), one must recall the importance of children's education in the poem. Rather than dismissing the tale as trivial, Maria's description calls attention to its educative potential: to its ability to train children in a counter-ideology to the prejudiced one promoted by European religion and schooling.

The key representation of the space of institutional Europe in this poem appears in one word: the "hole" into which the authorities throw the young man for speaking heretically and lawlessly. As "The Dungeon" likewise shows, this space is antithetical to that of Pantisocracy as Coleridge projected it in the mid-1790s. The poem draws much from contemporary debates over prisons, debates in which Coleridge participated as early as 1789 in "Destruction of the Bastille" and in which others involved in exploring the possibilities of experimental American communities also played a part. Brissot, for instance, includes a brief but important discussion of "The Philadelphia Prison" in his *New Travels*, which helped define the parameters of Pantisocracy. For Brissot, the presence of a prison in Pennsylvania initially appeared to be uncomfortable evidence that America might not be a site of moral regeneration. But the prison here, he concluded, amounted to little more than an ideological colony of institutional Europe. Noting that the British had used transportation laws "to rid themselves of all the bandits infesting their island by setting them loose in the United States" and that the "number of foreign adventurers" had increased in recent years, Brissot calculated that "less than a tenth of the prisoners in Philadelphia" were born in America and decided that "if there were no foreigners there would be no need of a jail."[118]

For Brissot, as for Coleridge, prisons were "tombs in which men are buried alive," and they were specifically European tombs from which America could redeem the living: "If there is any country where one could and where one ought to change this system, it is indeed the United States."[119] The Pantisocrats conceived of the United States similarly and sought to obviate the need for any penal policy. If aspheterism eliminated "every motive for vice" and strengthened "every motive for virtue" as anticipated, there would be no crime to punish.[120] A paragraph from Brissot's account, juxtaposed with Coleridge's representation of a dungeon, indicates both Brissot's influence on Coleridge and the degree to which Coleridge's dungeon critiqued an institutional Europe that was opposed by American—Pantisocratic—possibility (figure 2.1).

Figure 2.1 Brissot's account juxtaposed with Coleridge's representation of a dungeon.

Brissot's *New Travels*	Coleridge's "The Dungeon"
"Prisons are destructive to the health, liberty, and goodness of man. To be healthy, a man needs fresh air, frequent exercise, and good food.	In a prison, "Each pore and natural outlet [of the prisoner is] shrivell'd up / By ignorance and parching poverty, / [And his]...energies roll back upon his heart, / And stagnate and corrupt" (6–9).
In prisons the air is foul, there is no room for exercise, and the food is often detestable.	A prisoner lives in "the steams and vapour of his dungeon" (15).
A man is healthy only when he is with those who love him and whom he loves; in prison he is with strangers and evil men. There can be no social relationship between prisoners; and if there is, one of two things must happen:	Prisoners live in "uncomforted / And friendless solitude" among "groaning and tears / And savage faces" (12–14).
either he must ceaselessly struggle against the fearful influence of these evil men and thus engage in constant and agonizing battle; or else he becomes like them, which subjects them to equal torments. A man who lives with madmen becomes mad. Everything in life is contagious and interrelated."[121]	The prisoner "lies / Circled with evil, till his very soul / Unmoulds its essence, hopelessly deformed / By sights of ever more deformity" (16–19).

For Brissot, Europe could solve the problem of crime by following the example of the Indians. Indians have no prisons, he wrote, "and do not suffer from the lack"; rather, they "let each man's house be his prison," if necessary posting "a sentinel at his door" for security.[122] For Coleridge, Europe could solve the problem of crime by conceiving of the criminal as a child and re-educating him in the ways of nature, rather than in the rules of society and religion. It was best, it seems, to give the criminal the kind of education that Coleridge would have wished to give children in a Pantisocratic settlement (or to give Hartley in the England of "Frost at Midnight"). Or, at a greater extreme, it may have been best to give the criminal the kind of natural education that prepares the child in "The Foster-Mother's Tale" to live with the Indians. In "The Dungeon," Coleridge argues, nature's "soft influences, / . . . sunny hues, fair forms, and breathing sweets, / . . . melodies of woods, and winds, and waters" will "Heal" the "wandering and distempered child" far better than prison (21–4).

While the fourth of Coleridge's *Lyrical Ballads* poems, "The Nightingale," offers little direct or indirect comment on Pantisocracy, its message resonates with the messages of "The Dungeon" and the "Ancyent Marinere." Nothing in nature is melancholy, the poem argues, except from the perspective of a man like the disoriented Ancient Mariner—who seemingly has "done an hellish thing" in killing a bird and now must "pass, like night, from land to land" (91, 586)—or like the "distempered" criminal of "The Dungeon." Thus, the poem says, poets often represent the nightingale's song as melancholy only because

> some night-wandering Man, whose heart was pierc'd
> With the remembrance of a grievous wrong,
> Or slow distemper . . .
> . . .
> First nam'd these notes a melancholy strain. (16–22)

Others who live unreflectively within the social and cultural structures of Britain (spending their evenings in "ball-rooms and hot theatres")—that is, those who, within the context of Coleridge's *Lyrical Ballads* poems and of the Pantisocratic scheme, are socially and spiritually disoriented—share in this melancholic conception of the nightingale's song (37). Only a select society, consisting of Coleridge, William, and Dorothy Wordsworth ("My Friend, and my Friend's sister"), and Coleridge's yet-to-be-educated son ("My dear Babe"), have learned or will learn the "different lore" that, once again, nature teaches (40–1, 91). If this select group is not necessarily a Pantisocratic society, it nonetheless removes itself from Britain's dominant cultural and ideological logic.[123]

Wordsworth's Counter-Argument

Wordsworth rejected Coleridge's scheme, or at least major parts of it. Like Coleridge's poems, Wordsworth's *Lyrical Ballads* poems promote alternatives to the social and political values that dominated in Britain at the end of the eighteenth century, and they promote a natural basis for those alternatives; and, it is true, both of these features are recognizably Pantisocratic. But his poems also show great skepticism about America as an alternative to Britain and about all idealizations of spaces, whether Anglo-European or not. If "We find our happiness or not at all" in "the world which is the world / Of all of us," that world, in Wordsworth's poems, includes Britain and the Continent, if a transformed Britain and transformed Continent. Any scheme that requires people to neglect of these spaces is suspect. Wordsworth's poems instead promote spaces that are alternative to those defined by dominant British and other European institutional powers while nonetheless remaining on British or European land. If Coleridge's Pantisocratic community critiques—and is structured so as to regenerate—Britain from the outside, Wordsworth's textual spaces critique and work to transform Britain from the inside.[124]

Some of his *Lyrical Ballads* poems do pick up on and extend the Pantisocratic arguments of Coleridge, though. For instance, while many readers have observed that "The Convict," which Wordsworth probably wrote in mid-1796 and first published in the *Morning Post* in December 1797, articulates a Godwinian position concerning punishment of criminals, the poem also is consistent with the Brissotist tendencies of Pantisocracy.[125] When Godwin argues that legal punishment largely perpetuates rather than eliminates evil—that such punishment is "the voluntary infliction of evil upon a vicious being," or "pain inflicted on a person convicted of past injurious action"—he formulates a position also familiar in other radical writing of the time.[126] Wordsworth's poem rehearses many of the same arguments about prisons familiar from Coleridge's "The Dungeon" and Brissot's discussion of the Philadelphia Prison. It describes a dungeon as a living tomb (the convict wears "fetters that link him to death") and comments on its unhealthy atmosphere (the convict's "bones are consumed, and his life-blood is dried") (16, 21). And even if it blames crime upon corrupt British or Continental society less quickly than Coleridge's and Brissot's texts—Wordsworth represents the convict as *both* a social "victim" *and* a man (rather than a "distempered child") guilty of a "crime [that]... / Still blackens and grows on his view"—Wordsworth's poem, too, represents a life in nature as a better remedy to crime than prison (45, 23–4). If Wordsworth were called upon to exercise his skill as a government leader, he, like Coleridge and Brissot, would reform the penal system and thereby rehabilitate the convict: " 'if the arm of the mighty were mine,' " he tells the prisoner, he " 'Would plant thee where yet thou might'st blossom again' " (51–2). The geography of the poem as well as its time scheme even gestures toward Coleridge's and Brissot's preferred American site for millenarian regeneration since Wordsworth sets the action late in the day when "The glory of evening... [is] spread through the *west* [my emphasis]" (1).

"Last of the Flock," too, like Coleridge's letters on Pantisocracy, indicates that other nations may provide preferable alternatives to Britain. These other nations, Wordsworth suggests, avoid Britain's mistake of creating circumstances that lead to the poverty and distress of citizens who otherwise would be among the most productive. At least they do not do so openly, publicly, on the main thoroughfares of economic and social life, with the tacit approval of the government. Wordsworth writes,

> In distant countries I have been,
> And yet I have not often seen
> A healthy man, a man full grown,
> Weep in the public roads alone.
> But such a one on English ground,
> And in the broad highway, I met. (1–6)

This man—carrying a dead sheep, the last of what once was a flock of fifty, and thus suffering under English poor laws that dictate that he receive no public relief as long as he owns any real property–suffers within a specifically English legal system and social ethos. If he were to emigrate to another nation, the poem suggests, he might escape such suffering.

And yet, even as the poem strongly criticizes England and English law, it hesitates to specify an alternative nation where the situation is already better. Wordsworth has been in "distant countries," but he does not name them. The distance from England—which is also to say the relational *difference* from England—seemingly is the key.[127]

England has a problem that requires movement ("distant" movement) toward an alternative socioeconomic system. But the poem refuses to offer either of the obvious alternatives, that of Revolutionary France or that of America. France, after all, was no longer the France of the promising first days of the Revolution. And America—despite the Pantisocrats' expectation that a man like the one in "Last of the Flock" could thrive on just two hours of manual labor a day and despite the ways that a socio-economic system such as aspheterism would eliminate the man's troubles—had its own problems for Wordsworth.

"The Female Vagrant" details those problems as well as problems with other principles in the Pantisocratic scheme more clearly than any other poem in the 1798 *Lyrical Ballads*. Although Wordsworth drafted most of this poem as part of his 1793 version of *Salisbury Plain*, the new portions that he wrote for the 1798 *Lyrical Ballads*, along with his decision to publish the poem in the volume, show a deep engagement with and critique of Coleridge's emigration scheme.[128]

Like "Last of the Flock," this poem deals with government-sanctioned legal processes that lead to the loss of individual property. The Female Vagrant first becomes a vagrant when a wealthy owner of a Lake District mansion seeks to purchase her father's "old hereditary nook" and, upon failing to persuade the father to sell, subjects him to "cruel injuries" until

> all his substance fell into decay.
> His little range of water was denied;
> All but the bed where his old body lay,
> All, all was seized. (44, 47, 50–3)

In the context of the poem, the solution to this problem clearly is not the Pantisocratic-aspheterist one of making all property common. Rather, this poem—and, for all its criticism of the poor laws, "Last of the Flock," too—champions individual ownership of property. "The Female Vagrant," following capitalist rather than communitarian logic, argues that individual property is not necessarily, as Coleridge considered it, a "Motive . . . to Evil" but that it promotes social stability and good. Here the loss of the "dear-loved home, alas! no longer ours" destroys the daughter's religious faith: after the loss, she "could not pray" (62–3).

The poem indicates, instead, that a new home, possessed and occupied, can best resolve physical, social, cultural, and spiritual disorientation; and the Female Vagrant and her father obtain such a home when she marries a childhood friend. Her religion returns (the family engages in "constant prayer"); and, with labor that much exceeds the Pantisocratic minimum (they have "constant toil"), the household remains content and productive for "Four years" (82–3). A "sad distress" brings this second household to ruin, and this "distress," as opposed to the earlier economic injustice, is unnamed (87). Wordsworth does name the underlying problem, though, and again it is economic: like the man in "Last of the Flock," when faced with poverty, they "no relief could gain" (92).

Again, in this poem, the best solution is not the Pantisocratic one. When faced with socioeconomic and political injustice in Britain, the Pantisocrats turned toward America for new life. The Female Vagrant's family turns there, too, as her husband joins a British regiment headed there to fight the rebelling colonists. The Female Vagrant's ship follows—and compresses—the first part of the path taken by the Ancient Mariner.[129] If the "Ancyent Marinere" describes "How a Ship having passed the Line was driven by Storms to the cold Country toward the South Pole," the Female Vagrant's ship "drove" onward as "the equinoctial deep / Ran mountains-high before the howling blast" ("Argument," "Female Vagrant" 110–11).[130] But, unlike the "Ancyent Marinere," "The Female Vagrant" shows what happens if one lands on the American shores instead of continuing onward around Cape Horn. Set during the war for independence, this poem represents an America that looks nothing like the place envisioned by Coleridge and the other prospective emigrants. Instead of new life, the Female Vagrant and her family discover death: they "reach. . . the western world, a poor, devoted crew" and shortly thereafter her husband and children succumb to "sword / And ravenous plague" (117, 132–3). Every part of America denies refuge, even natural areas removed from cities: the family suffers whether "In wood or wilderness, in camp or town" (129). If Pantisocratic America looks sometimes like a happy dream-vision, this America looks like a nightmare; and when the Female Vagrant departs, now without her family, she "wake[s]" on "A British ship…, as from a trance restored" (135).

On board this ship, she is caught between continents, between nations. And she takes a certain comfort in the betweenness of a space that seems to be neither here nor there. But it is a false comfort. Although the ship appears to be separate from the British and American power structures that have destroyed her family, those power structures include it too. She may think that the Britain-bound ship can "restore" her. She may perceive from the perspective of the ship that the ocean is as "Peaceful as some immeasurable plain" (136).

She may feel "transported to another world" (164).[131] In other words, she may sense that through a process of dispositioning she has become first displaced and then re-emplaced, returned to firm grounding. But the ship is a site of violence, and it is fully part of this world—which, this poem suggests, is composed of an Old-World/New-World amalgam—and it offers no enduring relief from the life she has lived on either Atlantic shore. If she thinks that, on board, she has found "at last . . . a resting place" where she can "Roam. . . the illimitable waters round" far from Britain or America, she thinks so only because the ship has failed to "restore" her to herself: rather, she remains "robb'd of my perfect mind" (172–3, 175).

The poem shows that the ocean does have limits, and while the American limit seems worse than the British one when the Female Vagrant first arrives, the British is as bad as the American upon her return. She is "homeless near a thousand homes," she is famished "near a thousand tables," she is "Helpless as a sailor cast on desart rock," and, once again, she lacks relief from either governmental or religious institutions (179–80, 181).

At this point, though, the best solution at last does appear to be Pantisocratic, but with irony. In lines that Wordsworth added to the Female Vagrant's account for the 1798 publication, she receives her "first relief" from a group of British Aspheterists living in nature among "the trees," rather than from the government or church (214, 218). This group holds property in common ("all belonged to all") and they practice a perfect democracy ("each was chief") (221). Labor, for them, is minimal. If the Pantisocrats would write sonnets "while following the plough" and would reap the fruits of agriculture and nature in the Susquehanna valley by working only two hours a day, the working life of this group is still more leisurely:

> No plough their sinews strained; on grating road
> No wain they drove, and yet, the yellow sheaf
> In every vale for their delight was stowed:
> For them, in nature's meads, the milky udder flowed. (222–5)

Casting aside the institutional limits and prejudices that have afflicted people like the Female Vagrant in both Britain and America, this group offers "food, and rest," and even "joy" (216, 229).

The only problem with this Pantisocratic group is that they are thieving gypsies. The fields provide them abundant labor-free food because they get it through "midnight theft" (236). Aspheterism here fails to create the condition in which "every motive for vice should be eliminated"; rather, vice is the condition that makes aspheterism possible. Staying outside the laws of British society enables the "wild brood" to rise above the limits and corruptions of that society, but it also makes them outlaws (215). Of course, when Coleridge worried that an upbringing within Britain's social system would "*deeply* tinge... [children] with the prejudices and errors of Society," he was not advocating an alternative system that would encourage children to treat property as the group in "The Female Vagrant" does. But Wordsworth's poem highlights the complexity—even the contrariness—of social ideologies, suggesting that some of the same lessons that lead to "prejudice and error" (e.g., to dispossessing the poor of their limited property) also might lead to moral codes that prohibit wrongdoing. Such is the way that the Female Vagrant's upbringing works for (and against) her, the poem indicates. "[B]rought up in nothing ill"—taught by her father to "kneel beside [her]...bed" and pray as soon as she started to speak, taught by him to read, and raised within sight and sound of a church—she determines that the life of the vagrant group, for all its benefits, "ill...suit[s]" her (242, 13, 235, passim). She consequently returns to a life as a solitary vagrant.

Her vagrancy represents, among other things, the failure of transatlanticism: it has an origin, but no destination, least of all America. If Wordsworth nods toward the hopeful geography of Pantisocracy when, in "The Convict," he describes "The glory of evening...spread through the west," here he disputes that geography. As the poem ends, the Female Vagrant watches, "In tears, the sun towards that country tend / Where my poor heart lost all its fortitude" (263–4). Pantisocratic America or any other idealized America, the poem says, is as unstable and unreliable as the "other world" of the woman's shipboard dream. The principles of the Pantisocratic emigration scheme might offer much good that is absent within Britain's institutional structures (food, rest, and joy for the poor), but those same principles also might lead to moral failure. For Wordsworth by the late 1790s, movement from Britain's shores is part of the problem: America as settled by Europeans—and as contested in war by Europeans—promises nothing better than Britain or Europe, just more suffering. Two years later, in "Home at Grasmere" and the *Poems on the Naming of Places*, Wordsworth would offer spaces that at once are on British land and yet function according to alternative rules and offer a potentially positive alternative to the currently dominant British institutional rules.[132] But in 1798, working provisionally toward such spaces in "Tintern Abbey" (in Wales, where the Pantisocrats considered setting up their community when their plans to travel to America fell apart),

Wordsworth explored and, for the most part, rejected the possibility that America could serve as an alternative to Britain.

Among the other *Lyrical Ballads* poems, "The Mad Mother" and "The Complaint of a Forsaken Indian Woman" most directly address North America, and, in both, the New World offers little that might benefit the British. In "The Mad Mother," the references to America are brief, but important. Each of the first two sentences of the poem concludes with information that situates all that follows in the poem in relation to America. The mad mother looks like a typical late-eighteenth-century British portrait of an American Indian, but in England:[133]

> Her eyes are wild, her head is bare,
> The sun has burnt her coal-back hair,
> Her eye-brows have a rusty stain,
> And she came far from over the main. (1–4)

She looks like a stock American Indian, and she lives in the environments where the Indians live; and yet she is in England, she speaks English, and she seems to be English herself:

> on the green-wood stone,
> She talked and sung the woods among;
> And it was in the English tongue. (8–10)

Since the poem repeats the connection later, when the Mad Mother promises to build her child "an Indian bower" (55), this Englishwoman seemingly acclimated herself fully to Indian life while she lived in America.

The Mad Mother's madness appears to have originated in her geographical situation as it relates to her sexual and marital circumstances. Unlike Coleridge (the mad genius) or the ecstatically mad Pilot's Boy in the "Ancyent Marinere," the woman suffers from mental and physical sickness, making her dangerous to herself and to her child; and the sickness apparently results both from the failure of institutional Britain to be sufficiently expansive in its thinking (as Coleridge's ostensible madness does) and from a disjunction between a husband's errant behavior and British institutional rules regarding marriage.[134] The mother suffers deeply because she expects her husband's presence, but he is "gone and far away," perhaps still in America (80). The mother, meanwhile, is divided between geographical cultural codes. She lives in and English version of American nature and would have her child be a child of American nature, but she worries about British moral strictures against those who do not abide by British social and religious laws. Telling her child to ignore those who might call him a bastard, a natural child, she says, "Dread not their taunts, my little life! / I am thy father's wedded wife" (71–2).[135] She is torn between that which is English in her and that which is American and of the American wilderness. The poem indicates a danger in displacing the Englishwoman into an environment where British ideological codes do not apply. In this case, doing so corresponds with taking her out of herself, out of her mind.

"Complaint of a Forsaken Indian Woman" addresses the same geographical divide between Britain and America, at once insisting that certain principles are transatlantic (foremost among them, a mother's love for her child) and proposing that American life and experience are radically other than British. In many senses, this poem is a companion piece to "The Mad Mother," and the women in these poems speak to each other and sometimes against each other across the Atlantic divide.[136] The Indian Woman and the Mad Mother both live in nature, cut off from social and sexual support, and in danger of imminent death (the Indian Woman from whatever ailment afflicts her, the Mad Mother from suicide). The Indian Woman's tribe has "forsaken" her, and she says that she has "forsaken" her "poor . . . child" (65). The Mad Mother's husband likewise has "forsake[n]" both her and her "sweet boy" (75). Both women speak to their boys, each of them an infant, treating them as comprehending auditors, even though the Indian Woman's child is absent. The women use similar epithets for their children, the Indian Woman calling her boy "My little joy! my little pride!" (41), the Mad Mother calling her boy "my little life," "my little lamb" (71, 91). Both women fantasize about their boys fulfilling the roles of adult male sexual partners: as the tribe removes the boy from the Indian Woman, she sees "A most strange something . . . ; / —As if he strove to be a man, / That he might pull the sledge for me" (36–8); and the Mad Mother asks her son to "still be true" to her, replacing her (false) husband, and she offers the child the place at her breast that her husband once occupied (58, 61). Both women see their infant boys potentially saving them from death.

But despite the Indian Woman's desperation (and she, finally, faces more desperate circumstances than the Mad Mother), she remains sane. She, too, apparently lacks a husband, but she, unlike the Mad Mother, does not hold her child's father accountable for her situation; in fact, she does not even mention him. He is absent, but, within the world she occupies, he has not "forsaken" her or her child: within the social world of Wordsworth's two poems, that apparently is what the husbands of English women do, not necessarily those of Indian women.[137]

For all the sadness that the Indian Woman feels and for all her desire to reunite with her child and her social community, she exhibits little of the (geographical) alienation from self exhibited by the Mad Mother. Although she is a recognizably and sympathetically human character, the Indian Woman lives and thinks in ways that differ from English conventions of reality as Wordsworth's poetry represents them: in Fulford's words, despite her familiar maternal behavior, she is "admirably alien," a "sublime other."[138] After all, as Alan Bewell notes, according to this poem she "inhabits a nature that has not yet been shaped into an adequate human environment," which is to say a British or European environment.[139] Much as Wordsworth adds a subtitle to "Goody Blake and Harry Gill" declaring that events and behaviors that seem out of the realm of possibility in England nonetheless are from a "True Story" ("founded," he adds in the Advertisement to the *Lyrical Ballads*, "on a well-authenticated fact which happened in Warwickshire"), he here adds an authenticating forenote explaining that the story of the Indian Woman comes from Samuel Hearne's account of America, *A Journey from Prince of Wales's Fort in Hudson's Bay to the Northern Ocean*.[140] While Wordsworth's English wilds include danger—the Mad Mother is working to calm herself as well as her child when she tells him not to "fear," since she will be "Bold as a lion . . . ; / And . . . always be thy guide, / Through hollow snows and rivers wide" (51–4)—Wordsworth's Indian Woman, though she is sad at the loss of her child and though she clearly desires to live, fears neither "hollow snows" nor more predatory nature:

> My fire is dead, and snowy white
> The water which beside it stood;
> The wolf has come again to-night,
> And he has stolen away my food.
> For ever left alone am I,
> Then wherefore should I fear to die? (55–60)

If she speaks to her son using endearments familiar to English mothers, she speaks of death by nature in a truncated, stilted parataxis that was already becoming established as a language of otherness, of the English-speaking American Indian, an English language inherently different and distant from the language of England: "My journey will be shortly run, / I shall not see another sun" (61–2).[141] The maternal character is transatlantic, the poem says, and the Indian mother is as sympathetic as the British; but the life of the Indian mother (or, by extension, Indian life generally, perhaps even American life generally) fails to offer an alternative that the British can adopt to lessen their own hardships. Life in the American wilderness is different from and distant from British life, and yet it entails its own equally great suffering.

"Ruth," which Wordsworth wrote in Germany shortly after the publication of the 1798 *Lyrical Ballads* and then published in the 1800 *Lyrical Ballads*, brings together much of his 1798 critique of the American alternative proposed by Coleridge and the Pantisocrats. Ruth is English by birth and plans to go to America, but fails to go there, the promise of America being an empty dream. Having suffered because of British social conventions—as a child she was "slighted" when her mother died and her father remarried—she, like the Pantisocrats, becomes attracted to an image of an ideal America presented to her as an alternative to the British "world of woe."[142] The attraction, importantly, is not false or "feign'd": the man who attracts her to America—"a Youth from Georgia's shore"—is equally convinced of the authenticity of his representation of the New World (151, 13).

His America is a space away from the corruptions of European law. In no small part, it emerges directly from the most Rousseauvian passages written by another youth who spent time on Georgia's shores, William Bartram. In *Travels*, Bartram comes upon "swelling, green, turfy knolls, embellished with parterres of flowers and fruitful strawberry beds" where

> companies of young, innocent Cherokee virgins . . . lay reclined under the shade of floriferous and fragrant native bowers of Magnolia, Azalea, Philadelphus, perfumed Calycanthus, sweet Yellow Jessamine and cerulian Glycine frutescens, disclosing their beauties to the fluttering breeze, and bathing their limbs in the cool fleeting streams; whilst other parties, more gay and libertine, were yet Collecting strawberries or wantonly chasing their companions, tantalising them, staining their lips and cheeks with the rich fruit.[143]

Ruth's lover, too, describes Indian

> Girls, a happy rout,
> Who quit their fold with dance and shout
> Their pleasant Indian Town
> To gather strawberries all day long,
> Returning with a choral song
> When daylight is gone down. (43–8)

As poems ranging from "Last of the Flock" in 1798 through "Michael" and "The Brothers" in 1800 demonstrate, Wordsworth resisted such idyllic ideas of agrarian life in England. As Ruth's failure to achieve the idyll demonstrates, he resisted them in America too.

After all, Ruth's American dreams (like the Pantisocrats, she apparently never makes the voyage) result in madness, rather than the "quiet bliss" that her lover promises her (75). Perhaps still worse in the scheme of the *Lyrical Ballads*, the dreams result in imprisonment. Even if Ruth has been, by British standards, a child of nature, having wandered "over dale and hill / In thoughtless freedom bold" after losing the attention of her father and stepmother, and even if (or because) she herself has had a childhood in an environment that in some respects has resembled one of unreconstructed British pastoral idyll—playing "a pipe of [oaten] straw," building "a bower upon the green"—she finds herself ill-prepared for the life of nature outside of British law that she anticipates because of her love for an American man (5–7, 10). For all her "freedom bold," she agrees to go to America only after following British social codes and marrying her lover in the English Church, telling him, in the only lines that she speaks in the poem, " 'And now, as fitting is and right, / We in the Church our faith will plight, / A Husband and a Wife' " (98–100). Having lost her connection to British society through a marriage (her father's remarriage), she reestablishes that connection through her own British marriage—which she expects to give her "lawful joy" (107)—just as she prepares to leave Britain behind.

As is the case for the Mad Mother, this marriage marks a geographical and psychological divide in Ruth. Her lover, having lived among men in America who know "no better law" than that of wild nature, is himself "lawless," and so, when they go to the shore to make their voyage to America, he "Desert[s]... his poor Bride" (140, 162, 167). The desertion, in turn, takes her out of herself, out of her mind, and "she in half a year was mad/ And in a prison hous'd" (170–1). Even when she escapes from prison, the "other ministrations" that Coleridge promises from nature in "The Dungeon" and the new "blossom" that Wordsworth himself promises in "The Convict" fail to materialize ("Dungeon" 20; "Convict" 52). Interrupted by the promise of a better place—a better nature—in America, her life in Britain cannot improve from or even return to what it once was. Now, "That oaten pipe of hers is mute / Or thrown away," replaced by a "flute made of a hemlock stalk" (211–12, 214). The promise of American emigration here at best distracts from the real work to be done in Ruth's Britain: the work of redressing social structures of the kind that "slight" her in the first lines of the poem and, equally, the work of incorporating the nature that supports her after the "slight" into new social structures. One must become dispositioned within Britain, the poem argues, instead of by departing from the country; and the collective nation must disposition itself from its current social and institutional state. The poem seems to anticipate the progress if not the completion of this work as, in the final lines, it foresees a day—albeit the day of Ruth's death—when institutional Britain (including British institutional soil) will incorporate rather than exclude Ruth:

> in hallow'd mold
> Thy corpse shall buried be,
> For thee a funeral bell shall ring.
> And all the congregation sing
> A Christian psalm for thee.— (224–8)

The solution to Ruth's troubles, for Wordsworth, must appear in Ruth's old world, rather than the New World: it must appear in Wordsworth's "world which is the world / Of all of us." Instead of finding alternatives in other real nations, other spaces, Wordsworth works toward transforming British institutional spaces, as well as the perception, understanding, and use of them.

In later years, as Wordsworth's poetry increasingly champions an *untransformed* Britain, his critique of America as an alternative to Britain becomes stronger and more explicit. *The Excursion* (1814), for instance, argues at length against representations of America as a land where people can emancipate themselves from European corruption. In Books 2–4, the Wanderer and the Poet encounter the Solitary, who has spent most of his adult life in a constant (and failed) search for new or alternative worlds.[144] In the early days after the French Revolution, the Solitary looks to France as a " 'new world of hope' " only to see the nation descend into the Old-World ways of the Terror. [145] Next he sails for " 'a City / Fresh, youthful, and aspiring' " in the " 'Western World' " where he hopes to " 'roam at large' " and avoid " 'servitude,' " only to find that the city " 'on nearer view' " shares many of the faults of the old world (134–6). So he looks toward the American frontiers in the mid-continent, in Canada up toward an elusive Northwest Passage, and in Bartram's Georgia—" 'along the side / Of Mississippi,' " along " 'that Northern Stream / Which spreads into successive seas,' " and across the " 'wide Savannah, vast / Expanse of unappropriated earth' "—where he expects to find and live with an Indian "'pure Archetype of human greatness'", but discovers,

> in his stead, . . .
> A Creature, squalid, vengeful, and impure;
> Remorseless, and submissive to no law
> But superstitious fear, and abject sloth. (137–8)

The Solitary's solution is to return to Britain and to take a house in the Lake District, where, however, he remains discontent with the "'visible fabric of the World'" (138). Although *The Excursion* clearly criticizes the Solitary's character and opinions, the nationalistic quality of the poem as a whole authorizes his comments on America. *The Excursion*—with a title and a content that mark the importance of migration in the development of poet and non-poet alike—also contains perhaps Wordsworth's most committed argument against emigration.[146]

THE PERSISTENCE OF AMERICA

In the meantime, the Napoleonic Wars were nearing an end, and, with the end, emigration to America increased greatly, and Britons established new social communities there. Among the communities were the "British Settlement," established in the late 1810s in Susquehanna County, Pennsylvania (to the north of Northumberland); Birkbeck's "Albion" settlement, established also at that time in Illinois; and the "New Harmony" settlement, established by Wordsworth's friend Robert Owen in the mid-1820s in Indiana. Although the political, social, and religious beliefs of the founders of these and other communities varied greatly, the goals—and the still-strong tensions between the ideal and the real—often accorded with those of the Pantisocrats from the 1790s.[147]

In the 1819 *Letters from the British Settlement in Pennsylvania*, for instance, Charles Britten Johnson advertised the kind of agricultural bounty anticipated by Coleridge and Southey: in "Susquehanna county," he wrote, "the first crop usually pays more than all the expenses of clearing and fencing the land, and of sowing, harvesting, and threshing the grain."[148] At the same time, though, perhaps tempered by anti-emigration arguments such as Cobbett's, he warned British readers not to come "with the absurd hope of finding a place where idleness may repose itself, while the earth shall produce its fruit spontaneously."[149] The Settlement would be open to emigrants of all social classes, and here, as in the Pantisocratic community, there would be "unexampled prosperity" and therefore "no poor."[150] The Settlement's founders also emphasized aesthetic as well as practical and philosophical matters and thus hoped to "unite utility and beauty" in the community design.[151]

Likewise, Birkbeck, a British farmer before emigrating to America to found Albion in 1817, sounded much like radical Coleridge and Southey, minus their impulses toward world reform, as he explained his reasons for leaving Britain. "[W]ith half its population supported by alms, or poor-rates, and one fourth of its income derived from taxes, many of which are dried up in their sources, or speedily becoming so," he wrote in *Notes on a Journey in America*, Britain "must teem with emigrants from one end to the other: and, for such as myself, who have had 'nothing to do with the laws but to obey them,' it is quite reasonable and just to secure a timely retreat from the approaching crisis–either of anarchy or despotism."[152] On the other hand, those who joined him in Illinois, he promised in *Letters from Illinois*, would find a pleasant and prosperous life: "The comforts and luxuries of life we shall obtain with ease and in abundance."[153] If the Illinois prairies would be rougher than pastoral idyllic fields, they nonetheless would offer their own delights: "Such is the field of delightful action lying before me, that I am ready to regret the years wasted in the support of taxes and pauperism.... I am happier, much happier in my prospects, I feel that I am doing well for my family: and the privations I anticipated seem to vanish before us."[154] Still, though, like the Pantisocrats, Birkbeck emphasized that his community was only for those with good moral character; after all, "Emigration to the extreme limits of this western America will not repair a bad character."[155]

Mary Shelley's 1835 *Lodore* appears to draw directly from Birkbeck's account. When Mr. Fitzhenry arrives at the Illinois settlement,

> Like magic, a commodious house was raised on a small height that embanked the swift river–every vestige of forest disappeared from the immediate vicinity, replaced by agricultural cultivation, and a garden bloomed in the wilderness. His labourers were many and golden harvests shone in his fields.[156]

A similar place attracted George and Georgiana Keats, but upon arriving in America they discovered that Birkbeck already had sold the choicest plots in his settlement (plots with access to the "swift river") and that the settlement offered less than they anticipated. They settled in Louisville instead.

In establishing the New Harmony social colony, Robert Owen—although paternalistic and morally more rigid than the Pantisocrats—was motivated by many similar social, political, and philosophical principles, including millenarian ones. Addressing the inhabitants of New Lenark in Britain, about a decade before establishing New Harmony, he commented,

> What ideas individuals may attach to the term "Millennium" I know not; but I know that society may be formed so as to exist without crime, without poverty, with health greatly improved, with little, if any, misery, and with intelligence and happiness increased a hundred-fold; and no obstacle whatsoever intervenes at this moment, except ignorance, to prevent such a state of society from becoming universal.[157]

The Millenarian impulse (albeit in his case a secular one) and the impulse to spread the principles of a limited social community throughout a new world would have attracted the Pantisocrats.

WRITING NORTH AMERICA

Because of its material circumstances, North America long remained a space into which British writers projected alternatives to their own national realities. The institutional alignments of North America, especially outside the main metropolitan areas, were uncertain for Europeans at the turn to the nineteenth century, and imaginative writers evidently expected that they themselves could inscribe the new markings of a New World. When Wordsworth wrote that we must "find our happiness" "[n]ot in Utopia, subterranean fields, / Or some secreted Island Heaven knows where; / But in the world which is the world / Of all of us," he was discussing a situation at the beginning of the French Revolution when, for him apparently, the real world and worlds of the imagination seemed uncommonly proximate. In this account, as the French Revolutionaries dismantled many familiar institutional structures, imaginative writers and thinkers were "call'd upon to exercise their skill" in developing the new French government and running it (10.722, 695). When France, descending into the Terror, stopped calling, many Romantic writers heard the call from North America instead.

The North America of their imaginations offered as much possibility for revolutionary change as 1789 France. According to their writing, the space would shift the social, spiritual, and moral centers of the emigrants. In British Romantic North America, the material often met the ideal, or else (as in Wordsworth's and Cobbett's writing) it tended toward it but failed to meet it: the tension between these two possibilities was more typically Romantic than either simple idealism or the denial of it. In British Romantic North America, human subjects transcended the physical and cultural limitations that Britain imposed upon them, or else (again, as in much of the work of Wordsworth and Cobbett) they failed to do so.

And, again, the tension between the two possibilities typified what was—and still is—most interesting and complex in Romantic representations of selfhood. The British Romantic literature of North American emigration, like the literature of the French emigration, spoke—and speaks—of movement and the failure of movement: of the ability and inability of the human to go beyond national, regional, local, and individual situation.

Chapter 3

Consuming Africa: Embodying Antithesis

> This is Africa! That is Europe—There is *division*, sharp boundary, abrupt Change!—and what are they in Nature—two Mountain Banks, that make a noble River of the influent Sea,... existing & acting with distinctness and manifoldness indeed, but at once & as one—no division, no Change, no Antithesis!
>
> —S.T. Coleridge, *Notebooks*

> [Africa is]
> A world of wonders,—where creation seems
> No more the works of Nature, but her dreams;
> Great, wild and beautiful, beyond control,
> She reigns in all the freedom of her soul.
>
> —James Montgomery, *The West Indies*

Observing and Imagining Africa

If many British Romantic writers imagined that the Americas promised a natural space of savagery and danger or else political, spiritual, and material wealth, Africa generally seemed to them a space still more natural than—or even beyond the nature of—either Europe or America in its potential for both barbarity and riches. The British represented the Americas as displaced Europe, Europe with a (natural) difference. They represented Africa not quite as pure otherness—in many firsthand accounts of Africa, African societies have recognizable social hierarchies (ranging from kings down to slaves); the emotional life of black Africans (though not of "tawny" Arabs) often appears much the same as European emotional life[1]; etcetera—but so far removed from European norms as to require the aid of the imagination or, for those who rejected the authority of the imagination, adventurous, life-endangering empirical exploration. The explorer William George Browne, in his *Travels in Africa, Egypt, and Syria, from the year 1792 to 1798* (1799), commented, for instance, that one needed either a "creative imagination" to "draw . . . animated pictures" of Africa or "a mind . . . disposed to observation" to "collect . . . facts and incidents."[2]

Insofar as Europeans like Coleridge could conceive of the nature and especially the human nature of Africa as at once sharply separated from and continuous with the nature of Europe—having both "*division*" and "no division"—Africa called European identity into question and demonstrated to Europeans the instability of their own self-representations. If, as Marianna Torgovnick suggests, "to study the primitive brings us always back to ourselves, which we reveal in defining the Other," the uncertainties that Europeans saw when they looked at Africa (which many contemporary accounts represented as "primitive") brought them back to uncertain European selves, albeit ones that often made overdetermined assertions of confident selfhood.[3] Or, as Fulford, Debbie Lee, and Peter Kitson observe in relation to Wordsworth's representation of African exploration, "Africa . . . is the place where a[n] . . . Englishman has . . . stepped beyond the social networks in which . . . [his] personality is normally constructed, to find, *in extremis*, his deeper selfhood."[4]

Late-eighteenth- and early-nineteenth-century writers likewise understood that when they explored Africa and Africans they also explored themselves. Archibald Dalzel—who emigrated to Guinea in 1763, working as a surgeon for the Company of Merchants Trading to Africa and as a slave trader, and (after some time back in England) becoming governor at Cape Coast Castle in 1792—commented in his *History of Dahomy* (1793), for example, that "The contemplation of man, in the various situations and under the different circumstances in which he from time to time presents himself . . . immediately leads to that self-knowledge which deservedly holds the pre-eminence over all others, and which cannot be obtained without it."[5] "Primitive" men—for Dalzel, specifically the West African men of Dahomy—were among those from whom one most could benefit:

> To arrive at a just knowledge of human nature, a progress through the history of the ruder nations is essentially necessary. It is from the

> actions of mankind, when seen under little other controul than that of their own will, that the tendency and effects of the passions appear more truly, than when under the influence and restraint of laws of refinement.[6]

Browne wrote additionally that "The character of every nation merits the attention of the philosopher; and the less the nation resembles ourselves, the more its distinguishing features require our investigation."[7]

The British (as well as the African) self that emerged from such contemplations was, for the writers, complex, heterogeneous, sometimes contradictory, despite writers' frequent claims to self-confidence and assurance in their power over Africa. Lee rightly argues that "to say that the literature of the period portrays confident, expanding British selves at the expense of [African] . . . selves who submissively disappear is not entirely correct. For there also exists, among some writers, an unstoppable desire to see this expansive British self become *not-self* in the face of the other."[8] For British writers who either emigrated to or sojourned in Africa, these two impulses—toward expansion of the self and toward self-destabilization or even self-abnegation—depended on each other and some of the writers who "portray[ed] . . . confident, expanding British selves" also revealed a desire for or a tendency toward the "*not-self*."

In turn, Anglophone writers from Africa or of African heritage who migrated to Britain (usually as freed or soon-to-be freed slaves and by way of the British colonies) often represented their own identities at once as highly unstable "*not-sel[ves]*" and as confident political, intellectual, cultural selves. Speaking with voices that had been conditioned by British ideas of Africa and Afro-Britishness, these writers nonetheless embodied powerful textual identities.[9] Britons and in particular Afro-Britons understood this process of simultaneous unselving and selving—a dispositioning into a self through difference from and absence of selfhood (especially native selfhood)—through a model of *consumption*. In this model, Britain consumed Africans materially (socially, economically, *and* corporeally). And, having been consumed into Britain, Africans—now Afro-Britons—consumed Britain as well.

As Colin Cambell and others have shown, European nations at the end of the eighteenth century experienced a "radical transformation" in modes of consumption: a consumer revolution.[10] Late-eighteenth-century literature often addresses this transformation and its implications, revealing what Timothy Morton has called "the birth of self-reflective consumer subjectivity."[11] Writers about Africa frequently demonstrated that their own "self-reflective consumer subjectivit[ies]" resulted from cultural cannibalism, from a radical process of dislocation and relocation. By exposing how the *incorporated nation* had a corpus composed of the consumed bodies and subjectivities of its population, these writers participated in the consumer revolution and in the struggle to understand geographical identity.[12]

As this section of *Romantic Migrations* shows, British emigrants, explorers, and imaginative writers consumed and produced Africa through figurations of its land and people and thereby constituted their own uncertain selves; and Afro-Britons in turn consumed the British figurations of them and thereby constituted themselves as well.

AFRICAN POTENTIALITIES

Because British religious and governmental officials, geographical explorers, and merchants perceived stark differences and yet also strong continuities between Africa and Europe, they declared a need to know Africa at the end of the eighteenth century (which is to also say, to know themselves), to inscribe the African continent and control it on European maps and in European narrative and descriptive accounts. At the beginning of the Romantic period, the best knowledge that most Europeans had of much of the African interior was, after all, nearly 300 years old, coming from the *Description of Africa* (1526) by Leo Africanus, a Spanish-born African scholar captured by Italians and put into the service of Pope Leo X. No other extended firsthand account of the interior had appeared in Europe since then.

Nearly every contemporary European description thus figures the geography of the African interior as a blank, as unknown or unwritten. While a small population of Britons did move to Africa—generally in religious or governmental service, as transported convicts, as traders, or as proponents of African repatriation schemes—to the general mindset of Romantic Britain, migration to Africa was inconceivable, or no more conceivable than a migration to an imaginary "world of wonders" or of dreams. At most, Britons might travel temporarily to Africa. They might chart out what they perceived as valuable to them in this space before returning to Britain (if they were among the few travelers who survived explorations). Despite long-standing trade and other cultural contact with Africa, Europeans rarely ventured inland. Typical of European practices at this time were those on the Gold Coast. As Robin Hallet notes, "over thirty European forts and factories" dotted the coast, many of them involved in expropriating gold; but even though "gold mines lay less than a hundred miles inland . . . by the end of the eighteenth century no European had ever been known to have set eyes upon them."[13]

When accounts of Africa represent the interior as a large bare space, the bareness nearly always signifies as much a European as an African lack. For instance, in the inaugural records of the African Association—which formed in 1788 with plans to explore and exploit the markets of the African interior—Association Secretary Henry Beaufoy wrote,

> [M]uch of Asia, a still larger proportion of America, and almost the whole of Africa, are unvisited and unknown. . . . [N]otwithstanding the progress of discovery on the coasts and borders of that vast continent, the map of its interior is still but a wide extended blank, on which the geographer . . . has traced, with a hesitating hand, a few names of unexplored rivers and of uncertain nations.[14]

Mungo Park, whose two expeditions into the interior the African Association sponsored, commented similarly in his *Travels in the Interior Districts of Africa* (1799) upon his "passionate desire to examine into the productions of a country [the African continent] so little known; and to become experimentally acquainted with the modes of life, and character of the natives."[15] In a 1796 letter, Frederick Hornemann, also sponsored by the Association, thanked Joseph Banks, who led the Association, for "enabling me to satisfy my desire to travel in unknown parts of the world. I entertained . . . from childhood a great desire to travel in unknown regions of the globe, which ever increased with growing age."[16] Banks himself commented on European "ignorance" of the African interior.[17]

Along with other contemporary imaginative writers, Wordsworth worked within this figuration of an "unknown" Africa in the Prologue to *Peter Bell* (1798).[18] In early manuscript versions of the poem (MSS. 2 and 3), "a little boat" that is capable of transporting him to " 'the world of fairy' " and other spaces of the pure imagination offers also to take him to places in the real world, like the "land of snow" near the North Pole and the African interior, spaces that Europeans had yet to visit and thus that they had figured mostly in their imaginations.[19] The boat speaks to Wordsworth:

> I know a deep romantic land,
> A land that's deep and far away,

> And fair it is as evening skies,
> And in the farthest heart it lies
> Of deepest Africa. (91–5)

The first published edition of the poem stresses more fully the qualities of Africa that were unknown to Europeans. The boat declares,

> I know the secrets of a land
> Where human foot did never stray;
> Fair is the land as evening skies,
> And cool,—though in the depth it lies
> Of burning Africa. (101–5)

The boat's ability to "know" and to give the poet knowledge of this "'deep...deep...deepest,'" "'far...farthest'" land is almost as extraordinary as its access to "'the world of fairy'" in the context of the poem. The interior of Africa is, for the narrator, nearly otherworldly, and he tells the boat that it "quite forget[s] / What in the world is doing" (MSS. 2 and 3; 109–10).

Park's *Travels* appeared the following year, bringing a portion of the African interior into view for European readers (including Wordsworth, who read Park by 1804),[20] but even then most Europeans only could speculate about and imagine Africa. In 1820, James Grey Jackson, who had emigrated to Africa and had lived there for about sixteen years, wrote in *An Account of Timbuctoo and Housa Territories in the Interior of Africa* that "The continent of Africa, the discovery of which has baffled the enterprise of Europe, (unlike every other part of the habitable world), still remains, as it were, a sealed book, at least, if the book has been opened, we have scarcely got beyond the title-page."[21] As his account makes clear, Jackson—like Park and others interested in African exploration—wished to do more than read the "sealed book" of Africa: he wished to write it.

Doing so could bring explorers and investors many benefits. The African Association had at least two motives for going to Africa: Association members believed that they could advance geographical and general scientific knowledge, and that they could earn great wealth from that knowledge by gaining access to gold, ivory, slaves, and commercial markets for British goods. These interests were closely connected: the Association viewed geographical and scientific knowledge itself as a trade secret that they must guard carefully, and so, the governing committee resolved not to "disclose, except to the members of the Association at large, such intelligence as they shall, from time to time, receive from the persons who shall be sent out on the business of discovery."[22] Park, for one, expected to share in the riches that resulted from his discoveries (68). Likewise, in 1791, Major Daniel Houghton, another explorer supported by the Association, wrote expectantly to his wife from the head of the Gambia River that "gold, ivory, wax, and slaves, may at all times be had here for the most trifling articles; and a trade, the profit of which would be upwards of eight hundred per cent can be carried on . . . without the least trouble."[23] (Houghton's explicit enthusiasm for the slave trade is an exception among those actively involved in the African Association: most Association-related texts refrain from either supporting or opposing slavery, or else hint at opposition).[24] Usually the explorers imagined that they would become rich on African gold; and they usually expected to find it deep in the African interior, often in the city of Timbuktu. Beaufoy described the place as a "luxurious city."[25] As Kate Ferguson Marsters notes, many other Britons at this time also thought that Timbuktu was "full of gold," and they considered Africa more broadly as a "land of gold."[26]

While gold might provide Europeans with quick wealth and while some European dreamers of a wondrous African interior actively pursued it, many other British writers represented the market and trade potential of Africa as ultimately the more sustainable and realistic source of both European and African prosperity.[27] Britons who invested in African exploration clearly would benefit most from commerce with Africa, though British speculators often represented Africans as gaining more. Jackson, whose *Account of Timbuctoo and Housa* argued for abolition of slavery, nonetheless maintained that the British must establish trade before ending slavery. He argued, "The abolition of the slave-trade cannot be effected until we shall have substituted some commerce with the Negro countries, equivalent at least, or that shall be more than equivalent to it, otherwise the negro sovereigns of Sudan will never be induced to relinquish so great a source of profit."[28] Eventually, he said, commerce must negate the power of these sovereigns, and black Africans must achieve full independence: "commerce . . . will *enrich the negroes, enable them, by a supply of arms, to contend with and gain ascendancy over their Muhamedan oppressors.*"[29] Likewise, the poet James Montgomery wrote in his epic *The West Indies* (1809) that "Commerce abroad [would] espouse [Africans] . . . with mankind" (331).

If Montgomery saw a lack of commerce as keeping Africans out of contact with "mankind"—by which he seems to have meant out of contact with Europeans—others projected into the "unknown" spaces of Africa the social and cultural as well as economic riches of civilizations as advanced as or more advanced than those of Europe. An Arab informant reported to Banks, for instance, that Housa was "'one of the first cities of the world'" and said that "'It is evident there is a very considerable Empire in the internal part of Africa and judging by the manufacture and size of [Housa's]...walled capital, arrived at a high degree of civilization.'"[30] Park said that the African interior had governmental and cultural institutions as complex and well-ordered as those of Europe.[31] Contemporary Swedenborgians took ideals of civilization in the African interior to the greatest extreme: for them, the interior was "the promised land, peopled by survivors of the most ancient and celestial Adamic church."[32] Non-Swedenborgians occasionally approached such idealism too, though, as when Park described a valley of happiness and innocence that he visited in his travels:

> I descended into a delightful valley, and soon afterwards arrived at a romantic village called Kooma. This village is...the sole property of a Mandingo merchant.... The adjacent fields yield him plenty of corn, his cattle roam at large in the valley, and the rocky hills secure him from the depredations of war. In this obscure retreat he is seldom visited by strangers, but whenever this happens he makes the weary traveller welcome. I soon found myself surrounded by a circle of the harmless villagers. They...brought corn and milk for myself, and grass for my horse; kindled a fire in the hut where I was to sleep, and appeared very anxious to serve me. (224–5)

Other representations of Africa offset such idealism, however, and showed the continent as an uncultivated space that could be exploited through unequal relations (albeit ostensibly for mutual good).

In the positive representations, though, Africa—like Coleridge's Pantisocratic America—was a place of plenty, where there were resources enough for everyone, African and European alike, and obtainable at very little effort or cost. As Major Houghton wrote to his wife,

> You may live here almost for nothing: ten pounds a year would support a whole family with plenty of fowls, sheep, milk, eggs, butter, honey, bullocks, fish, and all sorts of game; I am tired of killing them. I want for none of these things, and I wish I could send you only what I have to spare, which would more than supply your family at home.[33]

In *Lecture on the Slave-Trade*, delivered while the Pantisocrats were planning their American community, Coleridge described African life as explicitly Pantisocratic, complete with an aspheterist treatment of property and labor practices that benefitted the intellect:

> The Africans, who are situated beyond the contagion of European vice—are innocent and happy—the peaceful inhabitants of a fertile soil, they cultivate their fields in common and reap the crop as common property of all. Each family like the peasants in some parts of Europe, spins weaves, sews, hunts, fishes and makes basket fishing tackle & the implements of agriculture, and this variety of employment gives an acuteness of intellect to the negro which the mechanic whom the division of Labour condemns to one simple operation is precluded from attaining.[34]

Here Pantisocracy met Rousseau and emerged as a fantasy of prelapsarian social intercourse. Less grounded than American Pantisocracy in the material politics and reports (often false) of empirical observations of the late eighteenth century, Coleridge's Africa still did relate to the material realities of Britain and Europe. Despite his later assertion in his *Notebooks* that between Africa and Europe there was "no Antithesis!" he did look to Africa to represent the self antithetically: Africa was beyond "the contagion of European vice," but Britain was not; and so on.

In "Sonnet IV" of *Poems Concerning the Slave Trade* (1794), Southey also represented Africans as innocent and happy when surrounded—and identified—by African nature, though their innocence and happiness apparently looked to him more primitive than Pantisocratic. "[H]appy Negroes join the midnight song / And merriment resounds on Niger's shore," he wrote, adding that Africans in Africa were a "cheerful throng."[35] The antithesis in this sonnet turns upon the alternative life of Africans in the British slave colonies, rather than directly upon England. Then, fifteen years later, in Montgomery's *The West Indies*, Africa revealed something about both Britain and the West Indies. Africa once again contained natural bounty and a happy life within it:

> —Is not the Negro blest? His generous soil
> With harvest-plenty crowns his toil;
> More than his wants his flocks and fields afford:
> He loves to greet the stranger at his board. (308)

The image of this Negro contrasts with that of oppressed and unblessed Britons who must work hard for their harvests; and the passage promotes the advantages of cultivating African land (in a world that includes European–African commerce, rather than slavery) over agriculture in the West Indies.

More African Potentialities

If, in some representations, Africa was fertile, in others it was overly so, overly sexualized, overly fecund. In these representations, African nature was too extreme, too natural. The sun did more than warm the earth; it burned. The rains did more than quench thirst and make life possible; they drowned both human and land. The cool night air failed to refresh; it brought fever and disease. Here, qualities that elsewhere might contribute to beauty and health became beastly or, when present in great magnitudes, contributed to what Felicity Nussbaum has described as "the monstrous racial fictions that erroneously and egregiously mapped . . . domestic and imperial regions" at this time.[36]

In representations of African men and women, beastliness and monstrosity often took the form of either exaggerated anatomy or animal-like behaviors and physical features (especially sexual ones).[37] Thus, in *Travels to Discover the Source of the Nile* (1790), Bruce repeatedly represented the sexuality of African women—and Africans in general—in extreme terms. At a dinner in Gondar, he wrote,

> anarchy prevailed. . . . All the married women ate, drank, and smoked, like the men; and it is impossible to convey to the reader any idea of this bacchanalian scene in terms of common decency. I found it necessary to quit this riot for a short time, and get leave to breathe the fresh air of the country, at such distance as that, once a day, or once in two days, I might be at the palace, and avoid the constant succession of these violent scenes of debauchery, of which no European can form any idea.[38]

After dinner, he added, "those within are very much elevated; love lights all its fires, and every thing is permitted with absolute freedom. There is no coyness, no delays, no need of appointments or retirement to gratify their wishes; there are no rooms but one, in which they sacrifice both to Bacchus and to Venus" (81). These behaviors, along with the specific dishes consumed, Bruce indicated, made the Africans monstrous, like Homer's Cyclops: the banquet was "Polyphemous" (79). No less than with the purportedly positive representations of Africa, Bruce's was a geography of antithesis, one that inscribed Britain and Britain's ostensibly superior morality on a map more clearly than it inscribed Africa.

On the other hand, in a famous scene from *Travels*, Park also used African female sexuality to establish a comparative geography, though his scene avoided the beastliness and monstrosity of Bruce's. In Benowm, he wrote,

> a party of [Moorish women]...came into my hut, and gave me plainly to understand that the object of their visit was to ascertain, by actual inspection, whether the rite of circumcision extended to the Nazarenes, (Christians,) as well as to the followers of Mahomet....I observed to them, that it was not customary in my country to give ocular demonstration in such cases, before so many beautiful women; but if all of them would retire, except the young lady to whom I pointed, (selecting the youngest and handsomest), I would satisfy her curiosity. (154)

Instead of pressing their interest in seeing Park's body at a time when he was fully in their power, the women responded with a politeness that might compare favorably with that of women in European polite society. They went "away laughing," and the woman he had "compliment[ed]" sent him "some meal and milk for [his]...supper" (154). According to his account, the African women showed sexual license, but never licentiousness.

Park's representation of African women and African sexuality occupied the most liberal and sentimental end of the spectrum in British accounts of this time, while Bruce's occupied the illiberal, sensationalist end.[39] Both, though, articulated concerns about British (as well as African) limits to the body and about the ways that extended and intensive encounters with other peoples, lands, and cultures could dislocate and relocate the self. In both cases, the sexuality of Africans and especially female Africans threatened to violate the British male body—to unman the British man—with Bruce's women of Gonder behaving "like the men" and Park's women of Benowm descending upon him en masse and demanding that he display himself to their sexual gaze.[40] Especially in Bruce's case, a British man became weak in the face of African sexual behavior: Africa left him breathless.

And yet, also more clearly in Bruce's passage than Park's, the African behavior was of a lower order than the European. His account implied that since "no European can form any idea" of the African behavior, then perhaps not only African physical life but the African mind differed qualitatively from the European. In this, he followed Voltaire, Hume, and Rousseau, among many others, who already had argued that black minds were different from and inferior to white minds.[41]

The assertion that "no European can form any idea" of African behavior aligned Bruce's passage with polygenetic theories of world populations that were common at this time: theories arguing that Europeans and Africans were different species, with Europeans occupying a more advanced position in the chain of being and Africans—in keeping with the ostensibly extreme nature of Africa—occupying a position just above nonhuman primates.[42] The closeness of Africans to nature gave them a more animal-like experience of life than Europeans, according to European polygenetic accounts reaching back to the sixteenth century.[43] In *A Voyage to the River Sierra-Leone* (1788), John Matthews, a naval lieutenant and slave trader who spent two years in Africa, followed standard polygenetic reasoning, for instance, when he asserted that the labor pains of African women were animal-like: "Nature has exempted [African women]...from the pain and sorrow our fair countrywomen experience in childbirth, as they are seldom confined more than a few hours."[44] More directly, he placed African intellect in a hierarchy reaching down to non-human primates: "Trace the manners of the natives, the whole extent of Africa from Cape Cantin to the Cape of Good Hope, and you find a constant and almost regular gradation in the scale of understanding, till the wretched Cafre sinks nearly below the Ouran Outang."[45]

In general, Matthews narrowed the gap between African humans and other nonhuman primates, as when he at once compared black Africans to chimpanzees and anthropomorphized chimpanzees. The appearance of the chimpanzee

> greatly resembles that of an old Negro, except that the hair on their heads is straight and black like an Indian's....They generally take up their abode near some deserted town...and build huts nearly in the form the natives build their houses....If one of them is shot the rest immediately pursue the destroyer of their friend; and the only means to escape their vengeance is to part with your gun, which they directly seize upon with all the rage imaginable, tear it to pieces, and give over the pursuit.[46]

In looking at Africa's human and non-human nature this way, Matthews followed a way of seeing the continent that had been one of the standards in Europe throughout much of the eighteenth century. James Burnett (Lord Monboddo), a judge on the Scottish High Court of Sessions, believed that "Ourang Outangs" were "rational human beings that happened to live in a primitive state."[47] The multivolume

New Collection of Voyages and Travels (1743), a familiar text to many eighteenth-century Britons interested in world geography and exploration, included a plate with a double image that likewise blurred boundaries between African humans and chimpanzees. On the left sits a "Man Ape from Angola"—sluggish, heavy-faced, squinty-eyed, head cocked to the side in apparent befuddlement—and on the right stands a very human "Chimpanzi" with a walking staff—energetic, bright-eyed, apparently fully aware of his surroundings. The indolent, apparently unintelligent "Man Ape" aptly exemplified many late-eighteenth-century representations of African humans.[48] Matthews commented, for example, that while "Nature appears to have been extremely liberal, and to have poured forth her treasures with an unsparing hand . . . in most cases the indolence of the natives prevents their reaping those advantages, of which an industrious nation would possess themselves"; and, further, "The disposition of the natives is nearly similar every where, extremely indolent."[49]

In such representations, Africans generally showed energy—physical or intellectual—only to cause harm. For Matthews, Africans remained indolent unless "excited by revenge," and then they demonstrated "implacable tempers" and showed themselves to be "full of treachery and dissimulation."[50] Bruce commented likewise that "It is impossible to give one not conversant with these people, any conception what perfect masters the most clownish and beastly among them are of dissimulation" (38–9). Even Park, while generally avoiding such language in descriptions of black Africans, described African "Moors" as "a subtle and treacherous race of people" (141).[51] Period literature commonly distinguished between black Africans and Moors. James Rennell, one of the foremost geographers of the time, asserted,

> The contrast between the Moorish and Negro characters, is as great, as that between the nature of their respective countries; or between their form and complexion. The Moors appear to possess the vices of the Arabs, without their virtues; and to avail themselves of an intolerant religion, to oppress strangers: whilst the Negroes, and especially the Mandingas, unable to comprehend a doctrine, that substitutes opinion or belief, for the social duties, are content to remain in their humble state of ignorance. The hospitality shewn by these good people . . . raises them very high in the scale of humanity.[52]

In eighteenth-century European representations, the "treacherous" Moors and other "Mahometans" extended metonymically into monsters. Even as early as Leo Africanus's account these Africans either became monsters themselves or caused what was potentially benign in nature to become monstrous. Writing about the Nile, he said,

> The course of this riuer is in very deed most admirable, and the creatures therein are exceeding strange, as namely sea-horses, sea-oxen, crocodiles, and other such monstrous and cruel beasts...which were not so hurtfull either in the ancient time of the Egyptians or of the Romaines, as they are at this present: but *they became more dangerous euer since the Mahumetans were lords of Egypt.*[53] [My emphasis]

In other words, if the physical characteristics of the land and climate could shape the physical and moral person, as many eighteenth-century writers argued they did, the moral (and specifically religious) person also could shape the character of the physical environment. Other African monsters stood seemingly independent of human morality and religion, though. In the caves of the Atlas mountains, Leo observed,

> are founde many huge and monstrous dragons, which are heauie, and of a slowe motion, because the midst of their body is grosse, but their necks and tailes are slender. They are most venomous creatures, insomuch that whosoeuer is bitten or touched by them, his flesh presently waxeth soft & weake, neither can he by any meanes escape death....Many of our African writers affirme, that the male eagle oftentimes ingendering with a shee woofe, begetteth a dragon, hauing the beake and wings of a birde, a serpents taile, the feet of a woolfe [*sic*], and a skin speckled and partie couloured like the skin of a serpent. Neither can it open the eie-lids, and it liueth in cause. This monster albeit my selfe haue not seene, yet the common report ouer all Africa affirmeth that there is such an one.[54]

As fantastical as this creature was, Leo claimed to have based his description upon empirical observations, albeit secondhand.

Leo's description contributed so much to the British conception of Africa in the early decades of the nineteenth century that Montgomery built upon it in *The West Indies.*[55] In Africa, Montgomery wrote,

> At sunset, when voracious monsters burst
> From dreams of blood, awakened by maddening thirst . . .
> . . . the lorn caves, in which they shrunk from light,
> Ring with wild echoes through the hideous night;
> . . . darkness seems alive, and all the air
> Is one tremendous uproar of despair,
> Horror and agony. (298)

Drawing from the old proto-empiricism of Leo, Montgomery's lines also revealed anxieties over an extreme African nature even as they exerted control over those anxieties by containing the dragon in conventional gothic language. Montgomery's passage projected into Africa European fears about the self in relation to the rest of the world: it interpreted Europe's own "dreams of blood."

If, according to British travel and geographical accounts, African sexuality could unsex British men with its animalism and its inversion of European behavioral conventions, this more monstrous nature, whether connected to human behavior or independent of it, could devour both Africans and Europeans (whose "blood" the monsters presumably must drink when "awakened by maddening thirst"). The fear of being consumed by Africa took many forms, ranging from depictions of African cannibalism to images of African monsters imported into England,[56] such as that of "A Young ALLIGATOR drawn from the Life in *LONDON*"—the "Young" reptile having been made through a trick of pictorial perspective to look enormous and correspondingly dangerous—or various African human freaks like Saartje Baartmans the Hottentot Venus and George Alexander Gratton the Extraordinary Spotted Boy (whom illustrations compared to a spotted dog).[57]

Such freaks and monsters famously disoriented Wordsworth in the London of *The Prelude*, Book 7. As Wordsworth walked through the "thickening hubbub" of the city, he saw "among less distinguishable Shapes," "conspicuous less or more, / . . . all specimens of man / Through all the colours which the sun bestows, / And every character of form and face" (7.227–8 and 235–8).[58] Among the "specimens"—a term that shares some of its semantic range with "species," though Wordsworth stopped well short of arguing for a polygenetic understanding of humans—were various Africans: "Moors" and "Negro Ladies in white muslin gowns" (7.241–3). Allison Hickey observes rightly that "In the midst of the emporium, the poet tries to proceed as if confident that the colorful array of 'specimens' has been provided for his imaginative consumption, but the somewhat forced insistence on delights and power of choice fails to mask his anxiety about these images."[59] Wordsworth's experience in the crowd led to uncertainties about his own and other selfhoods: "the face of every one / That passes by . . . is a mystery" (7.597–8). The uncertainty then led, unsurprisingly, toward deeper anxiety and fear. When the next African or Afro-Briton—a "silver-collar'd Negro with his timbrel"—appeared in St. Bartholomew's Fair, he was in the company of "All out-o'th'-way, far-fetched, perverted things, / All freaks of Nature";

he participated in "a dream / Monstrous in colour, motion, shape, sight, sound"; and he was a member of a "Parliament of Monsters" (7.677, 688–9, 661–2, 692).

In this scene, Wordsworth feared the loss of the boundaries that decide identity, whether individual, racial, or national. He thus transposed upon London the blankness that signified elsewhere the uncertainty of such boundaries (as well as physical-geographical ones on European maps of Africa and the Americas):

> O blank confusion! And a type not false
> Of what the mighty City is itself
> To all except a Straggler here and there,
> To the whole swarm of its inhabitants;
> An undistinguishable world to men,
> The slaves unrespited of low pursuits,
> Living amid the same perpetual flow
> Of trivial objects, melted and reduced
> To one identity, by differences
> That have no law, no meaning, and no end. (697–705)

As Makdisi observes, in this environment, "Wordsworth's preconceived spatial distinctions break down and dissolve, to be replaced by the flux of a ceaselessly-changing environment, one that never stops its self-transformations long enough to become a safely knowable, chartable, understandable place."[60] Likewise, he could know neither those whom he encountered nor himself, and the unknowability of the self was itself a monster to be feared.[61]

Consuming Africa, Consuming Europe

The fear of this uncertain self was ultimately self-consuming. Romantic writers most often manifested it in descriptions of material consumption, especially the consumption of food. In the literature concerning travels to Africa at this time, you were what you ate; and you could avoid becoming something by refusing to eat it. Consumption—and sometimes non-consumption—of food was transformative: it changed and repositioned the self. Some of the most transformative instances of food occurred in Bruce's *Travels*, where Bruce saw animals butchered and eaten alive. Outside the ruins of Axum, the ancient capital of Abyssinia, he attended a feast in which, he said, Africans ate a live cow: "I saw, with the utmost astonishment, two pieces, thicker, and longer than our ordinary beef steaks, cut out of the higher part of the buttock of the beast. How it was done I cannot possibly say" (40).

According to Bruce, this process of butchering and eating live animals was common, and it demonstrated that he was in a "barbarous country" and that Africans in general were a "barbarous people" (40, 79). At the feast in Gondar where the women ate and drank before engaging in public sex, he saw another cow consumed alive: "All the flesh on the buttocks is cut off them, and in solid, square pieces, without bones, or much effusion of blood; and the prodigious noise the animal makes is a signal for the company to sit down to table" (79–80). The company ate, and

> All this time the unfortunate victim at the door is bleeding indeed, but bleeding little. As long as they can cut off the flesh from his bones, they do not meddle with the thighs, or the parts where the great arteries are. At last they fall upon the thighs likewise; and soon after the animal, bleeding to death, becomes so tough that the cannibals, who have the rest of it to eat, find very hard work to separate the flesh from the bones with their teeth like dogs. (81)

In an important slippage, the eating of a live cow became the eating of human flesh, turning the feast participants into "cannibals."[62] If Africans ate live cattle, the passage implicitly asked, might they not also consume Bruce's body (by all accounts very large and meaty) or any other European's?

Among the various sensational events Bruce described in his *Travels*, many British readers considered the consumption of live animals to be among the most extraordinary. It was so distant from European dietary habits that many readers considered it a lie or a fiction. Bruce noted, "I was told by my friends it was not believed. I asked the reason of this disbelief, and was answered, that people who had never been out of their own country, and others well acquainted with the manners of the world, for they had travelled as far as France, had agreed the thing was impossible, and therefore it was so" (41). For some, like Horace Walpole, the behavior was laughably implausible. "Africa is, indeed, coming into fashion," he wrote to Sir Horace Mann on 10 July 1774. "There is just returned a Mr Bruce, who has lived three years in the court of Abyssinia, and breakfasted every morning with the Maids of Honour on live oxen . . . Oh, yes; we shall have negro butchers, and French cooks will be laid aside."[63]

But Bruce himself, without laughter, figured such eating as highly dangerous to the British and Christian self. In his account, eating live meat was a kind of dark inversion of the Christian Eucharist, a consumption not of the body of a living Christ, but the body of a base, living animal, identifiable with the tenets of a barbarous culture and religion. For related reasons, he avoided even meat from animals butchered after they had been slaughtered. In Gondar, he said, "there was abundance of" meat, but "I could not touch a bit of it, being killed by Mahometans, as that communion would have been looked upon as equal to a renunciation of Christianity" (48). For Bruce, the "cannibal[ism]" inherent in African dietary practices threatened to consume the soul as well as the body.

According to Park's *Travels*, African Moors likewise viewed foods commonly eaten by Europeans as imparting physical, moral, and spiritual identity and as possessing power to harm both body and soul. Taken captive by Ali, Sovereign of Ludamar, Park got word that

> Ali was about to present me with something to eat; and looking round, I observed some boys bringing a wild hog, which they tied to one of the tent strings, and Ali made signs to me to kill and dress it for supper. Though I was very hungry, I did not think it prudent to eat any part of an animal so much detested by the Moors, and therefore told him that I never eat such food. They then untied the hog, in hopes that it would run immediately at me; for they believe that a great enmity subsists between hogs and Christians; but in this they were disappointed; for the animal no sooner regained his liberty, than he began to attack indiscriminately every person that came in his way. (147)

Throughout Park's *Travels*—as throughout Bruce's—food is power. The woman who delivered meal and milk to Park after she and her companions encouraged him to disrobe demonstrated that power. Ali too demonstrated his power over him during the whole of his captivity by feeding him barely enough for him to survive. On the other hand, when Park accompanied a slave coffle toward the African coast, he reported, the slaves looked at him as having power over them because he—or other white Britons—might eat them: "they viewed me at first with looks of horror, and repeatedly asked if my countrymen were cannibals. They were very desirous to know what became of the slaves after they had crossed the salt water" (277). Park best asserted his own power, his own autonomous selfhood, though, by refusing to eat, as when he rejected the pig. Similarly, Bruce asserted his selfhood by rejecting meat, and a female slave in Park's text asserted hers when, having been offered some gruel, "she refused to drink it."[64]

Contemporary British abolitionist writing connected food and power repeatedly and forcefully. The texts presented slavery itself as a form of cannibalism in which Europeans, eating sugar that slaves lived and died cultivating, consumed "blood sugar." Coleridge, Southey, and Ann Yearsley, among others, argued in the 1780s and 1790s that consuming the products of slave labor—sugar in particular—was tantamount to consuming the blood of slaves themselves.[65] Coleridge, for instance, in a March 1796 *Watchman* essay on the slave trade, imagined British Christians asking God to " 'bless the food which thou has given us!' " and then addressed those Christians, observing that

> A part of that food among most of you is sweetened with Brother's Blood.... Did God give food mingled with the blood of the Murdered? Will God bless the food which is polluted with the Blood of his own innocent children?[66]

In America, and from the pen of a slave, the polemic required verbal coding, though it was all the more powerful because its ambiguity called attention to the real threat to the slave's body that such a polemic could entail. In "On being brought from Africa to America," Phillis Wheatley wrote,

> Some view our sable race with scornful eye,
> "Their color is a diabolic dye."
> Remember, *Christians*, *Negroes*, black as *Cain*,
> May be refin'd, and join th'angelic train.[67]

While the end couplet seems to support the dominant pro-slavery argument that Africans were morally fallen and required saving through exposure to European and American Christians, the lines also pun on the sugar "cane" that slaves cultivated and the processes of refining that occurred before the sugar came to the European table. Once "refin'd," the blacks presumably must be consumed at that same table as the cane. (At such a meal, the "Remember[ing]" Christians also would physically re-member, as the bodies of the slaves "join[ed]" with their own). The slippage from ideology-confirming representation to anti-slavery polemic implicit in Wheatley's poem serves as a fine introduction to the broad and complex handling of the issue of cannibalism in period literature.[68]

Like the slave in Africa described by Park, slaves on board ships to the British colonies and in the colonies themselves also sometimes refused to eat; and, in turn, ship captains and slave owners reasserted their power over the slaves' bodies by force-feeding them. William Cowper described one contraption used to compel slaves to eat in "Sweet Meat Has Sour Sauce": "When a Negro his head from his victuals withdraws, / And clenches his teeth and thrusts out his paws, / Here's a notable engine to open his jaws."[69] Cowper's irony critiqued more than forced feeding; it also critiqued the representation and treatment of Africans as animals, "paws" in this context being more than slang for hands or fists.[70]

Southey's ballad "The Sailor who had Served in the Slave Trade" (1798) similarly showed a refusal to eat, followed by a forced feeding on board a slave ship. The titular sailor says,

> some were sulky of the slaves,
> And would not touch their meat,
> So therefore we were forced by threats
> And blows to make them eat.
>
> One woman sulkier than the rest
> Would still refuse her food,—
> O Jesus God! I hear her cries—
> I see her in her blood![71]

More than either Park's or Cowper's description, Southey's showed how power used against the African's body and mind turned against and consumed the British body and mind too. Particularly telling would have been the sailor's assertion that "we were forced by threats / And blows to make them eat." The object of the "threats / And blows" is ambiguous. Did the sailors threaten and flog the slaves? *Who* forced the sailors to force food on them? Did the captain direct the "threats / And blows" against the sailors?—They may have been "forced by threats / And blows" to do something they did not wish to do; at a minimum, the narrating sailor says, "The Captain *made me* tie...up" the sulky woman "And flog [her] while he stood by, / And then *he curs'd me* if I staid / My hand to hear her cry" [my emphasis].[72] The oppressive, enslaving British subject thus finds himself (his self) in the oppressed enslaved African woman.[73]

Despite the clear power differentials between Europeans and Africans, then, Europeans became vulnerable to their own policies and their own representations. If they consumed Africans in the form of slave bodies and blood sugar—or in more displaced forms, such as gold and ivory—they also saw themselves being consumed as a result of their encounter with Africa. If the sailor was consumed by guilt figuratively, others involved in exploring Africa were consumed bodily. Travels into Africa were, after all, extremely dangerous for Europeans. Few of those who ventured into the interior–frequently figured as the "bowels" of the continent—emerged alive.[74] Among the explorers sponsored by the African Association, Park was exceptional in surviving his first trip (though with his body much diminished by hunger and fever). He died on his second trip. Houghton, Hornemann, and others died there as well. As Philip Curtin has shown, Europeans who attempted to set up colonies in Africa also suffered high mortality: "The initial death rate of Europeans sent to the Province of Freedom had been 46 per cent. The Sierra Leone Company lost 49 per cent of its European staff, and the Bulama Island Association lost 61 per cent in the first year."[75] Many European bodies went into Africa and never came back out. Beyond the shores of Africa, the slave trade cost, along with an enormous number of African lives, many Britons. Shipboard disease, while disproportionately devastating to African slaves, killed many European crew members. And many thousands of British soldiers died in the 1790s alone, fighting former slaves who revolted in the West Indies.[76]

Adopting African habits of dress and cultural behaviors could obviate a small amount of danger for Europeans, according to travelers' accounts, though going (or acting) native held its own dangers for the body and selfhood. Hornemann dressed in African clothing to avoid conflicts during his travels, but died nonetheless.[77] Browne, like Hornemann, wore Muslim attire to reduce difficulties, but sheiks threatened him when they discovered the impersonation.[78] Bruce wore "Moorish dress" throughout his travels, and he survived (47).[79] Park, after his own clothes disintegrated from hard wear, also dressed in African clothes given to him by a black merchant who had befriended and protected him. But upon returning from the interior to a European settlement on the African coast, he said, he "lost no time in resuming the English dress" (303). One senses from Park—in this line and in the passage showing him persuade the group of African women not to make him undress—that he saw his European clothing as protecting a vulnerable British body.

The perceived dangers to the body presented by African exploration and trade influenced British representations of the self in Africa. For example, although Park generally claimed to have maintained fine equanimity even in highly threatening circumstances, he occasionally represented himself as powerless. As he worked his way back toward the African coast from the interior, he entered "a vast wilderness, in the depth of the rainy season; naked and alone; surrounded by savage animals, and men still more savage," both of whom might consume him: he was "indeed a stranger in a strange land" (albeit one who was "still under the protecting eyes of that Providence who has condescended to call himself the stranger's friend") (226–7). Bruce, on the other hand, asserted (implausibly) his British *sang froid* when encountering extreme danger. At Masua, he reported, he faced down threats by local Arabs and then heard one of them exclaim, "'A brave man!... *Wallah Englese!* True English, by G—d'" (33). In another famous scene (much doubted by contemporaries, but later authenticated by witnesses), Bruce shot a candle through three Arab shields and heard a king say of himself and his people in relationship to the British, "'We know nothing'" (77). And once again he laughed dangerously at a sheik who tried to compel him to work in his service, explaining to him,

> I was laughing to think that a man set over a province to govern it, like you, should yet know so little of mankind, as to imagine one like me capable of turning renegado....What...could be my inducement to marry here, to change my religion, and live in a country where there is nothing but poverty, misery, famine, fear, and dependence? (203)

Such boasted bravado in his book perhaps betrays more anxiety than confidence. At any rate, on occasion he did represent himself, like Park, as "a stranger, without acquaintance, or protection, having the language but imperfectly, and without power, or controul."[80]

The explorers and writers who sought to consume Africa thus also feared being consumed. Or, in an alternative image also common at the time, those who wished to *penetrate* Africa feared being *penetrated* themselves. These two figures—of consumption and penetration—sometimes came together, as they did in an image of Africa that dates back at least to the ancient Romans and that still was current at the turn to the nineteenth century: an image of Africa as a woman with a cornucopia (to be consumed) and a scorpion (which might penetrate).[81] Some texts emphasized consumption and penetration as unidirectional, as was the case in Southey's first sonnet in the *Poems Concerning the Slave Trade*, which figured Europe drinking from an open African vein and the Niger River functioning as a kind of cafeteria conveyor belt delivering Africa to devouring consumers. The poem opens with a command to stop behavior that has led to the consumption of Africans and Africa:

> Hold your mad hands! for ever on your plain
> Must the gorged vulture clog his beak with blood?
> For ever must your Niger's tainted flood,
> Roll to the ravenous shark his banquet slain?[82]

Most frequently, though, as in Southey's "Sailor who had Served in the Slave Trade," the consumption was reciprocal: the British act of consuming Africa led either to an African act of consuming Britain or a second British act of consuming itself.

Such accounts generally focused on the mouth. And if these accounts commonly considered the eating of food when discussing the relationship between Europe and Africa, they also considered the mouth's other central function: producing language.[83] The accounts of Africa that received the highest contemporary praise and carried the most authority among British readers were the linguistic equivalents of a plain, solid British diet: they were written in plain language and were based closely on what seemed like observable and familiar facts. Park, whose *Travels* achieved more authority than most other contemporary texts, asserted that his narrative was "a plain, unvarnished tale, without pretensions of any kind, except that it claims to enlarge, in some degree, the circle of African geography" (45). The allusion to *Othello* (Othello promises a "round unvarnished tale" of how he won Desdemona's heart) *did* varnish Park's text, of course, making it less plain, but it did so in such familiar, British language—even modernizing Shakespeare's "round" to "plain"—that it only added to the authority of Park's claim.[84] The, July, 1799 *Monthly Review* praised his approach to writing much in the terms that he himself set forth:

> The narrative of Mr. Park is simple: he seems to have described things as he saw them, and to have consulted his senses rather than his imagination; he is unwilling to glut credulity by the narration of wonders; he draws no exaggerated picture of his sufferings and dangers; nor does he ascribe to his own sagacity any event which resulted from chance or accident. The manners, dispositions, and customs of the people are detailed fully and (we believe) faithfully; for if what is described be not real, at least that which is invented is probable.[85]

Browne too asserted that his *Travels* consisted of a "simple narrative of a journey."[86] For him, as for Park, the instability of identity and truth, which accounts of Africa forefronted, made careful empirical description, plain language, and common sense especially necessary. Browne warned that when interviewing Africans in Dar-Fur, if one "Ask[ed] but a leading question,... all the miracles of antiquity, of dog-headed nations, and men with tails,... [would] be described, with their situations, habits, and pastimes."[87] Unless a writer took great care, a text about Africa easily could become outlandish. Dalzel concurred with Browne, noting that many travel accounts and histories of Africa included strange and incredible passages and asserting that he wished to show the "ground of credibility" his own book "stands on, and to give the reader a sufficient confidence in the truth and candour with which the facts are represented."[88] And Jackson asserted that in his own book "the naked truth is stated, without the embellishments of language, or the labour of rhetoric."[89]

On the other hand, Bruce (whom the other writers likely had in mind as a counterexample when making their own claims to truth and simplicity) proclaimed the necessity of representing the extraordinary but true, even if doing so undercut the authority of travel description. He said, "To represent as truth a thing I know to be falsehood, not to avow a truth I ought to declare; the one is fraud, the other cowardice" (42). And, when entering his account of the feast on a live cow, he said, "I cannot avoid giving some account of this . . . banquet, as far as decency will permit me; it is part of the history of a barbarous people; whatever I might wish, I cannot decline it" (79). Although Bruce willingly represented the incredible, his comments upon his willingness show that, like the others, he recognized that credibility was crucial in accounts of Africa and saw that it was difficult to achieve in an unstable world with unstable regional, racial, and individual behaviors and identities.

British Mouths

Africa—as inscribed by British writers who emigrated there, who traveled there on exploratory expeditions, or who wrote about the continent and its people from Britain—is a complex figure of otherness and selfhood, division and continuity, goodness and evil. If African behaviors sometimes seemed to the writers to be beyond the cognitive horizons of Europeans—behaviors of which "no European . . . [could] form any idea"—what these behaviors told Europeans about themselves (their selves) was just as incomprehensible. Europeans at this time attempted to assert control over Africa through various representations of Africans, whether polygenetic ideas that subordinated Africans to Europeans or Edenic ideas that idealized Africans and contained them within the known (primitivist) structures of European culture. They also attempted to assert control over their own selves, selves which, in the face of their ideas of Africa, seemed uncertain, divided, multidimensional.

Like the writers about the French emigration to Britain, writers about Africa indicated that the control of language, including multilingualism, might enable them to negotiate an identity in a world of conflicting spaces. In Africa, British writers depended on the control of language for their survival. Bruce, according to his own account, bowed down antagonists repeatedly with the force of his voice. Park defended his body by charming the women who asked him to undress for them. These and other writers required rhetorical skills in African languages, as well as English, and the most successful of them (which is to say, those who lived to return to England) made learning African languages their first priority. Such was the case with Park, who said, his "first object was to learn the Mandingo tongue, being the language in almost general use throughout this part of Africa" (71). Bruce, too, learned African languages first and only then traveled into the continent.

Language, like food in the world of these travel accounts, was power. In his account, Park translated the numbers one through ten from various African languages, necessary translations for anyone who wished to wield commercial strength on the continent; and he provided Mandingo vocabulary words and a list of questions and answers in Mandingo that could enable Britons to survive ("Blood," "Fever," "Hungry"; "I am sick") and prosper ("Buy," "Gold," "Industrious"; "Are they on board the ship?") (77–8, 106, 109, 307–13).[90] Jackson, too, saw language as power, and his sense entailed more than the physical and commercial. He argued for changing the spelling of various African place names and was particularly pleased that "The learned . . . are now beginning to adopt my orthography of . . . *Timbuctoo* for the old and barbarous *Tombuctoo*."[91] For Jackson, language control would contribute not only to negotiating the complex physical spaces of Africa, but to negotiating the moral universe, enabling one to leave the "old and barbarous behind" and to enter, presumably, the new and civilized.

AFRO-BRITISH MOUTHS

If Britons such as Jackson, who emigrated to Africa, or such as Park, who traveled there, relied deeply on linguistic power, black Africans who emigrated to Britain depended on it still more. Afro-Britons produced representations of themselves, and they played with and reshaped those formed by native Britons, asserting at least limited control over British culture. In other words, in a radical process of dispositioning, they consumed the representations that consumed them; and, having done so, they helped make late-eighteenth-century Britain.

African migration to Britain and British America, of course, had a long history. The British carried about 3,000,000 Africans to the Americas in the 127 years between 1680 and the end of the slave trade in 1807, with the Romantic period seeing Britain's most active period.[92] Between 1791 and 1807, British slave traders carried more African slaves across the Atlantic than traders of all other slave-trading nations combined: 398,719 between 1791 and 1800 and 270,656 between 1801 and 1807; the busiest ten years in the British slave trade occurred between 1797 and 1806.[93]

By 1810, even after the loss of the American colonies, "almost 1 million blacks lived in British territories."[94] Most were in the British West Indies and other colonial lands, but a sizable population lived in England. In 1764, the *Gentlemen's Magazine* estimated that 20,000 men and women of African background lived in London and 30,000 in England.[95] Recently, Carretta has lowered the estimate to "approximately 15,000 Blacks"—or, alternatively, from "fourteen to twenty thousand"—in England in 1772.[96] At any rate, in 1785, the *London Chronicle* noted that the numbers had "greatly increased . . . beyond a doubt."[97]

The Afro-British community, which lived mostly in London, included a highly diverse population. Aside from some important exceptions, Afro-Britons at this time held little social standing or power.[98] Although the British court effectively emancipated slaves in England in 1772, blacks stood in danger of being taken aboard ships bound for the colonies and re-enslaved. Most worked in the servant class, though within this class they occupied a wide range of positions.[99]

The late-eighteenth-century Afro-British writers Ignatius Sancho, Quobna Ottobah Cugoano, and Olaudah Equiano emerged from the middle and upper ranks of this class. Among them, critical tradition has treated Sancho as the most problematic. According to a biographical sketch written by Sancho's friend Joseph Jekyll and published in front of the *Letters of the Late Ignatius Sancho* (1783), Sancho was born in 1729 on a slave ship that had sailed from the coast of Guinea toward the West Indies.[100] After Sancho's mother died from disease and his father committed suicide, his owner took him, at age two, to England, where, in the house of the Duke and Duchess of Montagu, he learned to read. As an adult, he worked as a butler in the Montagu household and, later, as a grocer. In these two positions, he began writing the letters that comprise his volume, corresponding most famously with Laurence Sterne, whose writing style he emulated. He also wrote plays and music.[101] He died in 1780.

Contemporary writers viewed him ambivalently and indicated that he embodied many of the same contradictions they believed inhered within Africa and Africans. Jekyll asserted that Sancho shared with other Africans a tendency toward dissipation and indolence. After the Duchess of Montagu bequeathed Sancho "seventy pounds in money, and an annuity of thirty," Jekyll wrote, "Freedom, riches, and leisure, naturally led a disposition of African texture into indulgence . . . which dissipated the mind of Ignatius."[102] Nonetheless, Jekyll observed that Sancho's letters "exhibit . . . epistolary talent, . . . rapid and just conception, . . . wild patriotism, and . . . universal philanthropy."[103] The letters—along with Sancho's writings of and on music and his drama and poetry—led Jekyll to argue against polygenetic theories or any other ideas of African inferiority: "Such was the man whose species philosophers and anatomists have endeavoured to degrade as a deterioration of the human."[104]

At least two contemporary novels also included extended portraits of Sancho.[105] In the anonymous *Memoirs and Opinions of Mr. Blenfield* (1790), Sancho appeared as Shirna Cambo, "by birth an African" and by temperament and behavior the embodiment of high British values.[106] His "disposition was lively," his "temper generous"; he was an "indulgent father"; and his "philanthropy and integrity were the examples and admiration of his neighbourhood; sensibility was a distinguished feature of his character; his imagination was pure, but unlimited; his conceptions nervous; and his conversation animated and engaging."[107] He also vocally opposed British policy in the slave trade and in Africa generally, even as his opposition arose from English values. He "no sooner felt the ardors of manhood, than he learnt the principles of English freedom—asserted his birth-right of human nature, [and] yielded to no master but virtue and himself."[108] When hearing claims that the British exhibit "charitable dispositions," he "would rise from his chair, with indignation flashing from his eye, and would insist that no charity could deserve praise, which was contradicted by unpardonable barbarity" of the kind shown by the British in Africa.[109] In the novel's account of that "indignation," admittedly, he showed something of the extreme temper that British writers frequently identified as an African characteristic at this time. On the other hand, his temper arose "from, perhaps, a too zealous principle in the cause of virtue."[110] Even his apparent failings resulted from a strength of character.

In the also anonymous *Berkeley Hall: or, The Pupil of Experience* (1796), characters contested the figuration of "Sancho." Some considered him a "black rogue," a "dog" (again with dissipated habits), while others defended him as "*honest* and generous."[111] Here he suffered for the misdeeds of whites and demonstrated—even when he declined to speak—that they were more barbaric than he.

In most contemporary portraits, though, Sancho did speak and did so with great force when opposing the mistreatment of black

Africans. In *An Enquiry Concerning the Intellectual and Moral Faculties and Literature of Negroes* (1810), Bishop Grégoire included him on a list of "men who have had the courage to plead the cause of the unhappy blacks and mulattoes" (i, iii). He, along with Equiano, Cugoano, and Wheatley, had shown "zeal to avenge . . . [his] African compatriots."[112]

More recent criticism of Sancho's life and writings has focused on questions of identity, especially involving how fully he allowed himself or was able to assimilate into British culture. The critical consensus through the 1970s and 1980s is that Sancho assimilated or attempted to assimilate into a British society that exerted a mostly unilateral, hegemonic control over Africa and Africans.[113] Walvin in 1973 calls Sancho "one of the most obsequious of eighteenth-century blacks."[114] André Dommergues observes in 1983 that Sancho, "whose mother tongue was English and who was brought up in an English family[,] had been cut off from his ancestral roots."[115] Mtubani in 1984 argues that "In general, Sancho is at home in white society. However, his attitude was occasionally ambivalent."[116] Edwards in 1985 calls him "a man largely assimilated to English middle-class society," though his letters also "show him both attached to, and detached from the English values of his time."[117] As late as 1996, Myers describes him as "apologetic, complaisant," and "self-debas[ing]," though she suggests that "On the other hand he may have been 'playing a fool to catch wise.'"[118] But in the 1990s and early 2000s, following the direction of postcolonial theory, most critical accounts identify subversion and hybridity in Sancho's writing. As early as 1983, Dommergues, while generally in the assimilative camp, suggests that in moments of anger Sancho "disassociate[s] . . . himself from the English" and reveals a "rebellious attitude."[119] Ellis points out further in 2001 that Sancho clearly does imitate British language use and attitudes in his letters, but that he does so within a neoclassical tradition that values imitation, and the fact that he imitates Sterne's unconventional writing is itself subversive. Thus, "Sancho's imitation of Sterne was not a matter of slavish copying. . . . Rather than a falling away from his own voice, [his] imitation is a kind of inspiration, the mask that allows Sancho's voice to be heard."[120]

While my own analysis of Sancho's writing accords more with the recent criticism than the earlier, it also acknowledges the powerful evidence of assimilation. Sancho's writing, like many contemporary texts by British writers about Africa, shows an African who *at once* continues with and divides from European culture, *at once is assimilated* and distinct, different, resistant to assimilation. If European and

African cultures consumed each other and became each other, there was a clear assimilative process (and within the Anglophone tradition this process tended strongly toward assimilation into British culture rather than African), but there was also a mutual antagonism and violence in such consumption, a rending apart.

Sancho was assimilating and British culture was consuming him, for instance, when he articulated a position nearly identical to that of Montgomery who, for all his opposition to slavery, adopted proto-imperialist objectives when he foresaw "Commerce abroad espous[ing Africans]...with mankind." "Commerce," according to Sancho as well, "was meant by the goodness of the Deity to diffuse the various goods of the earth into every part—to unite mankind in the blessed chains of brotherly love—society—and mutual dependence" (131). But in the same paragraph he resisted commerce in its present and foreseeable forms: British "conduct has been uniformly wicked in the East–West-Indies—and even on the coast of Guinea.—The grand object of English navigators—indeed of all christian navigators—is money—money—money" (130–1). Sancho's contradiction resolved as he prescribed a new kind of African commerce that transformed current British commercial policy, ridding it, it would seem, of the slave trade and of any other exploitative treatment of Africans: he advocated "Commerce attended by honesty" (131).

Sancho's assimilation, then, also entailed a strong reformist critique. If one must be consumed by another culture and if one must consume it, Sancho's letters suggested, one should establish power in the mix. This was the point of another letter in which he celebrated the mix that those contemporaries who wrote against miscegenation most feared: "We will mix, my boy, with all the countries, colours, faiths—see the countless multitudes of the first world...we will mingle with them, and try to untwist the vast chain of Providence—which puzzles and baffles human understanding" (86). What might it have meant to "untwist the vast chain of Providence"? Seemingly it must have been to undo and reconceive the Chain of Being that polygenetic theorists saw as including a racial hierarchy. The "chain," as eighteenth-century Britons conceived it, "puzzles and baffles," and they must work toward a clearer and better understanding of it.

Consumed and consuming, Sancho in many respects already incorporated into his writing and spoken language the mix that he foresaw.[121] His written English was reflective language. It was highly literary and self-conscious, full of rhetorical strategy and play, commenting on language usage itself.[122] For instance, Sancho appropriated the language of the promoters of slavery and applied it (oddly it seems at first) to himself and other Afro-Britons. Combining the two African groups who appeared most frequently in contemporary British literature, he called himself a "Black-a-moor" and, in a version of the stereotype used even by opponents of slavery like Southey, "a coal-black, jolly African" (*Letters* 118, 210). Instead of appropriating such terms ironically to subvert their destructive power as, for instance, the editors of the liberal periodical *Pig's Meat* did when facing down Burke's famous description of the "swinish multitude," he took the role as a given one from which he would operate, within which he would live. But he nonetheless used this apparent subordinate, subaltern position as a point of rhetorical strength. He was more than "a coal-black, jolly African"; he was one "who wishes health and peace to every religion and country throughout the range of God's creation" and thus one who distinguished himself from—and raised himself politically and morally above—less "jolly" British figures: the "raving mad whig" and the "fawning deceitful tory" (*Letters* 210). (The ascribed deceitfulness of the Tory also responded to descriptions of dissimulating Africans.)

Once again he accepted a white British figuration of an African (this time a Shakespearian figuration as mediated by British racist history) when he encountered a bigot on a London street, and he turned this figuration to rhetorical power. As William Stevenson recalls the event in John Nichols's *Literary Anecdotes of the Eighteenth Century* (1815), a man, upon seeing Sancho, declared, "Smoke Othello!" to which Sancho responded, " 'Aye, Sir, such Othellos you meet with but once in a century,' clapping his hand upon his goodly round paunch, 'such Iagos as you, we meet with in every dirty passage. Proceed, Sir!' "[123] Against the racist implications of the bigot who accosted him, Sancho read Shakespeare well and insisted that Othello was a superior individual to the white men who surrounded him. The racist white man, rather than Sancho, was an inferior type, the too common "Iago." The most extraordinary words in his retort, though, may be "Proceed, Sir!" Sancho avoided confronting the man physically; and he used deferential language toward him, calling him "Sir." But, in telling the man to "Proceed," he nonetheless commanded and controlled the man's physical movement, and, since "Proceed" then as now also meant to *continue speaking*, he commanded the man's language use, antagonistic though it may have been. *Continue calling me names*, Sancho demanded, and he embodied those names with power and turned them against the antagonist. The racist epithet, at least in the specific, local instance of this anecdote, contributed to Sancho's strength and diminished that of the man who accosted him.

If Sancho appears to have taken a certain pleasure in consuming the culture that consumed him—"clapping his hand upon his goodly round paunch" as he turned Shakespeare against the racist—in *Thoughts and Sentiments on the Evil and Wicked Traffic of the Slavery and Commerce of the Human Species* (1787) Cugoano demonstrated well-earned anger in doing so. According to his own account, Cugoano was born in "the city of Agimaque, on the coast of Fantyn" in what is now Ghana, around 1757, son to "a companion to the chief."[124] Kidnapped in his early teens, he was enslaved in Grenada and renamed John Stuart before being taken to work as a servant in England, where he learned to read and write.[125] By the mid-1780s he had obtained his freedom, and, as Carretta notes, he became "one of the first identifiable Afro-Britons actively engaged in the fight against slavery."[126] He probably died in 1791 or 1792.

Romantic contemporaries represented him, like Sancho, as an active opponent of slavery. Grégoire included him on his list of black abolitionists, and he recalled the strong language—Carretta and Roxann Wheeler term his book a "jeremiad"—with which he argued that "the stealing, sale and purchase of men, and their detention in a state of slavery, are crimes worthy of death."[127] For all of Cugoano's vituperative language, Grégoire reported, contemporaries regarded him highly for "his piety, his mild character and modesty, his integrity and talents" against standard figurations of Africans who, when angered, showed rash, brutal violence.[128] For sympathetic contemporaries, Cugoano was an integral part of the British body politic, even as he argued for radical transformation of that body. More than Sancho, with his vocal mimicry, though, contemporaries heard from Cugoano a seemingly independent language. "A voice" spoke of the great injustice of slavery, and "this voice was that of Cugoano," Grégoire recalled, singling him out.[129]

More recent criticism emphasizes this oppositional independence in contrast to what many see as Sancho's assimilative tendencies. Folarin Shyllon sees Cugoano as a "leader of the black community."[130] Myers warns that the term "leader" may simply equate "literacy with leadership," but Shyllon, like many other critics, sees Cugoano's language as containing a power, even a violence, that did enable him to lead with words: Cugoano "demolished the tenets of... slavery"; he "flatly denied the... shameless lies" of promoters of slavery; he argued that Africans "were entitled to rebel and fight."[131] According to Shyllon, Cugoano committed himself less peacefully to Christian values than many contemporaries believed he did. Edwards, like Shyllon, sees in Cugoano's *Thoughts and Sentiments* an essential physical strength aimed at resistance: the text contains, he says, "plenty of vigorous rhetoric."[132]

The best recent criticism acknowledges this "vigorous," even aggressive rhetoric, but sees in it a tension with other forces. For Wheeler, Cugoano's writing becomes "Riddled with contradictions raised by the languages of abolition and racial difference."[133] Carretta adds that while "Cugoano's radical stance on slavery" and his "castigat[ion]...of everyone actively or passively involved in the perpetuation" of it seem to indicate that he was an outside resister of British culture, his means of opposing slavery—for example, by adopting "the persona of an Old Testament prophet"—suggests instead that he may have been "more assimilated" into the European cultural body than even Sancho, that he spoke "from the very core" of that body.[134] To the degree that this is so, Cugoano became a man in whom Africa and Britain merged, or as Carretta comments, he "derive[d]...his authority, his right and power to write, from his combined African and British identities."[135]

The authority, right, and power again came from a self that had consumed and had been consumed. If Bruce, Park, and other white British writers focused closely on what they ate and refused to eat in Africa as well as on their fears of being consumed themselves by Africa and Africans, Cugoano maintained a similar focus but represented Europeans more than Africans as having barbarous, potentially cannibalistic eating habits. When kidnappers first captured him, they promised that they were taking him and his companions to a "feast" with some men who turned out to be African slave traders (13). The slave trade involved the consumption of human bodies, rather than the typical fare of feasts, Cugoano indicated: when he and his companions received the promise, they soon discovered that "these villains meant to feast on us as their prey" (13).

When he discovered his kidnappers' treachery, he demonstrated his power in the same way that Park and the enslaved woman in Park's *Travels* did later, by "refus[ing]...to eat or drink for whole days together" (14). The kidnappers again made false promises (that they would return him to his home) to convince him to eat, but the danger of cannibalism remained and seemed to increase when his kidnappers sold him to white European slave traders. His first sight of "several white people" made him "afraid that they would eat me, according to our notion as children in the inland parts of the country" (14).

White cannibalism of Africans was a childish notion, according to this description, but, as Cugoano's comments on feasting showed, adults also understood the connection between the slave trade and the consumption of African bodies. If white slave traffickers did not actually eat him, they consumed his body nonetheless within the slave trade. This consumption, still more than the consumption inherent in the *domestic* African slave trade, was violent. European slave holders controlled Africans with more than the false promises that the African slave holders used; they controlled them with physical brutality. In particular, they frequently brutalized a slave's mouth. In Grenada, for instance,

> For eating a piece of sugarcane, some were cruelly lashed, or struck over the face to knock their teeth out. Some of the stouter ones, I suppose often reproved, and grown hardened and stupid with many cruel beatings and lashings, or perhaps feint and pressed with hunger and hard labour, were often committing trespasses of this kind, and when detected, they met with exemplary punishment. Some told me they had their teeth pulled out to deter others, and to prevent them from eating any cane in future. (16)

African slaves produced sugar, and Europeans ate it and, in the form of "blood sugar," ate them, English sweetened tea being, for Cugoano, the "blood of iniquity" (102). Europeans, especially European slave holders, sought to avoid reciprocal consumption: they would keep the slaves from eating up their investment—and, also by extension, themselves—by knocking out their teeth.

But as Cugoano's book demonstrates still more clearly than Sancho's *Letters* mutual consumption occurred anyway. African mouths repeatedly "committed . . . trespasses" against European-owned food products, and these mouths also spoke back to Europeans. In Cugoano's case, the speech showed that he had consumed British literature on Africa and Africans, and, like white opponents to the slave trade, he turned negative representations of Africa against Europe.[136] He showed that, by consuming Africans, Europeans had assumed the characteristics they had attributed to the Africans. For Cugoano, Europeans, rather than Africans, were "inhuman, barbarous" (37); and Europeans, rather than Africans, were "of the most brutish and depraved nature, led on by the invidious influence of infernal wickedness" (61).[137]

On the other hand, according to Cugoano, Africans embodied the highest values that Britons attributed to themselves in their self-representations.[138] Some of the values were political: "Those people annually brought away from Guinea, are born as free, and are brought up with as great a predilection for their own country, freedom and liberty, as the sons and daughters of fair Britain"; and "it may be said that freedom, and the liberty of enjoying their own privileges, burns with as much zeal and fervour in the breast of an Æthiopian, as in the breast of any inhabitant on the globe" (27–8). And some of the values were moral and religious: "the word of the Lord" speaks to African slaves; and

> it is surely to the great shame and scandal of Christianity among all the Heathen nations, that those robbers, plunderers, destroyers and enslavers of men should call themselves Christians, and exercise their power under any Christian government and authority. I would have my African countrymen to know and understand, that the destroyers and enslavers of men can be no Christians. (60, 66)

On the other hand, Cugoano, by his own account, had committed himself to Christianity, and even unconverted Africans behaved in a more Christian manner than Europeans (17, 23). Cugoano thus ate and spoke with a mouth that was as much British as it was African, and that mouth delivered a critique of Britain formulated out of the language of those who had consumed him and whom he consumed.

OLAUDAH EQUIANO: CONSUMING AFRICA

Of the major late-eighteenth-century Afro-British writers, though, Equiano, who arrived free in Britain after a childhood and early adulthood as a slave, developed the most rhetorically complex account of British, African, and Afro-British selfhood. (Many critics have suggested that he had a hand in writing—and developing the rhetoric and analysis in—Cugoano's *Thoughts and Sentiments.*) Equiano's *Interesting Narrative of the Life of Olaudah Equiano* (1789) engaged with the figurations that dominated white British literature on Africa as well as those that dominated Afro-British accounts. It also developed the most explicit ideas of a selfhood that emerged from mutual British and African consumption and dislocation.

At the end of the *Interesting Narrative*, Equiano commented that Africans occupied "the bowels of Africa" as well as the coasts (234). In Johnson's *Dictionary*, the second definition of the word "bowels" is "The inner part of any thing," and Johnson cites as an example Shakespeare's "bowels of ungrateful Rome" in *Coriolanus.*[139] Johnson's first definition, though, deals directly with the viscera, particularly the lower alimentary canal (the *botulus* or *sausage* of the word's Latin origins): "Intestines; the vessels and organs within the body." In practice, eighteenth-century British writers sometimes combined the two definitions, figuring physical spaces in terms of a human anatomy that included circulatory "vessels and organs": veins, arteries, hearts, and the like. Such was the case in Joseph Addison's *Remarks on Several*

Parts of Italy. When a religious hermit found water emerging from mountain rock, Addison wrote, "by following the veins, he . . . made himself two or three fountains in the bowels of the mountain."[140]

As did Park, Bruce, Sancho, Cugoano, and other writers about Africa, throughout the *Interesting Narrative* Equiano also conflated the human body and physical space, and once again the connection was more than incidental linguistic play. In observing that Africans were in "the bowels of Africa," Equiano indicated that a space defined by the physical and cultural boundaries of such geographical entities as Africa could consume and digest the bodies and subjectivities of a people.[141] More explicitly than the other writers, though, he indicated as well that other physical and cultural spaces—the nations of Europe, for instance—also might consume and digest Africa. These other spaces, Equiano suggested, could benefit by bringing Africa and Africans "into circulation" within their own bodily systems (234). Such a cannibalistic process—a process of ingestion and ultimately of incorporation and circulation—contributed centrally to the production of geographical and cultural identity, according to the *Interesting Narrative*.

Critical accounts of *The Interesting Narrative* often debate whether Equiano had a West African, a British American, or a hybrid identity.[142] Research by Carretta suggesting that Equiano "may have been a native of South Carolina rather than Africa" (as he claimed in the *Narrative*) further complicates the debate; but, while this research requires a full rethinking of previous positions in the identity debates, it presents serious problems mostly for interpretations that essentialize geographical identity in a way that the *Narrative*—as well as this book—actively resists.[143]

If, as Helen Thomas suggests, "the moment *preceding* cultural contact can never be recovered," Equiano as the *Narrative* figured him—that is, as a man writing about African origins long after he had had "cultural contact" with Europe—had already become dislocated and was already part of the circulatory system of European consumerism (inasmuch as he was speaking from within the European culture even when he spoke of a time before he had knowledge of that culture); and yet his irrecoverable origin or heritage in Africa nonetheless actively constituted his identity.[144] In other words, as was also the case with Sancho and Cugoano, Equiano as an African became part of the body that had consumed him.[145]

* * *

In the *Narrative*, Equiano described the constant consumption of food. Equiano and others ate (or carried as food cargo) bullocks, goats, poultry, plantains, eadas, yams, beans, Indian corn, palm wine, pineapples, peppers, honey, poisoned meat and drink, coconuts, sugar, pumpkins, liquor, fish, rice, pork, bread, water, shark, snow, rum, limes, oranges, turkeys, lemons, turtles, salt beef, biscuit, lobsters and other shellfish, grapes, pomegranates, lamb, polar bear, bread, wine, land tortoise, alligator, manatee, and poisoned fish, among other named and unnamed victuals. The book also detailed the eating customs of various cultures (which required people to wash thoroughly before eating, which required men and women to eat separately, etcetera). For Equiano, even more than for Bruce, a culture's dietary features and customs reflected—and produced—moral and social codes. For instance, in the African village of Essaka, a place that Equiano represented as prelapsarian, the unfallen moral and social status of the people related closely to the food they ate: the "manner of living is entirely plain; for as yet the natives are unacquainted with those refinements in cookery which debauch the taste" (49).[146]

The *Narrative* worked with the same figurations of eating as many other accounts of Africa at this time, but worked them to greater rhetorical effect. For instance, when cultures with different diets and eating rituals came into contact, eating became the site of power demonstrations and contests still more explicit and elaborate than in other texts. The slave traders on the ship that took Equiano from Africa showed their power by eating fish that they caught and "toss[ing] . . . the remaining fish into the sea again" instead of feeding the hungry slaves (58). When Equiano and other slaves refused to eat, on the other hand, the traders treated the refusal as a challenge to their ownership of the slaves' bodies (56). The *Narrative*, still more than the other contemporary texts, exhibited both the power of forcing a person to eat and the power of refusing a person food, as was the case too when Equiano encountered a slave whose owner forced her to wear an iron muzzle when she worked as a cook (62–3).

As seen in Cugoano's *Thoughts and Sentiments*, in culinary terms there may be no better way of exerting power over the people of an alternative culture than by eating them. And as seen in the accounts of Park, Bruce, and other British explorers of Africa, as well as throughout the history of imperialist discourse, a nearly equal way of exerting power over such a people is to represent them as potential eaters of you. As Geraldine Murphy, among others, has noted, much "Proslavery discourse offered accounts of cannibalism" by Africans; and Europeans used these accounts to justify the commodification and commercial consumption of humans as slaves.[147] The practice of representing Africans as potential cannibals occurred also in European social and political documents that ostensibly took neither a pro- nor an anti-slavery position. Thus, where Equiano wrote that the people of Essaka "practised circumcision like the Jews, and made offerings and feasts on that occasion in the same manner as they did" (41) (a representation of the ritual that would have familiarized the practice to European readers who knew the Biblical history of the Jewish Patriarchs), a pictorial representation of circumcision titled "The Admission of their Youth to the State of Manhood" on Robert Sayer's *A New and Correct Map of Africa* (1754) parallelled the "youth" being circumcised with a goat being slaughtered for a feast so closely that the "youth" too appeared as if he was being prepared for cooking.[148]

Early in the *Narrative*, Equiano famously challenged dominant English-language representations of African cannibalism by discussing a childhood fear that the white sailors who enslaved him planned to eat him:

> When I was carried on board [the slave ship,]...I was immediately handled, and tossed up, to see if I were sound.... When I looked round the ship...and saw a large furnace of copper boiling, and a multitude of black people of every description chained together, every one of their countenances expressing dejection and sorrow, I no longer doubted of my fate....I asked...if we were not to be eaten by those white men with horrible looks, red faces, and long hair. (55)

Equiano represented these fears as innocent unworldliness, though Equiano's story—like Cugoano's account of his childhood fears of cannibalism—had a polemical function. Such a function was similar to that of accounts of European cannibalism in much transatlantic anti-slavery literature, particularly accounts of blood sugar such as Coleridge's and Wheatley's.

Some readers now take Equiano's representation of his fears on the slave ship at face value, seeing them as a "striking reversal" of white fears, fears that were "much better motivated" than the whites' since Equiano was treated so brutally.[149] But others note in the *Narrative* what William Mottolese calls patterns of "careful appropriation and mimicry" and Murphy calls the "turn[ing of]...tables on the slave traders' accounts"—patterns and acts that suggest that such reversals were rhetorically strategic.[150] Or as Henry Louis Gates, Jr., has put it: "Under the guise of the representation of his naïve self, [Equiano]...is naming or reading Western culture closely, underlining relationships between subjects and objects that are implicit in commodity cultures."[151] Such rhetorical strategies are the alimentary equivalent of what Pratt has described as "reciprocal vision," in which a foreign "other" engages in "anti-conquest" by returning the gaze of a British or European imperialist, thereby reversing "Eurocentered power relations and cultural norms, especially norms about seeing and being seen."[152] This rhetorical strategy, in other words, amounts to reciprocal eating.

But rhetorical tropes such as appropriation/mimicry, turning of tables, and naming namers, even while they valuably highlight how Equiano resisted imperialist discourse, fail to account for the full progression of ways that he represented cannibalism and for the circumstance that the (Anglophone) narrator who spoke about cannibalism already had been "eaten and digested" by imperial culture and had "become . . . an integral part of the eating organism"[153]: in other words, for the circumstance that he had become part of the system from which he appropriated, one of those who positioned the table that he turned, one of the namers whom he named. A survey of instances in which Equiano mentioned cannibalism directly or used figures of speech involving cannibalism shows him representing himself as a man who not only had been consumed by other humans but who also consumed them.

Equiano first raised the familiar spectre of African cannibalism only to dispel it. Although men like Bruce would continue to allude with fear or disgust to African cannibalism, as Equiano described it, it was an empty threat, used to make fun of people who were acting grouchy: "We had a saying among us to any one of a cross temper, 'That if they were to be eaten, they should be eaten with bitter herbs'" (41). Having reconfigured imperialist representations of African cannibalism as a joking matter, Equiano described serious childhood fears of being eaten by the slave traders after they carried him on board the slave ship and passed him around to see if he was "sound." Then, after making the passage from Africa to Barbados, the fear of being eaten returned. While he represented the earlier fear as the product of childhood naivete, in a pattern similar to one in Cugoano's text he now indicated that there was collective fear among all the new slaves on board the ship, including the adults:

> merchants and planters . . . made us jump, and pointed to the land, signifying we were to go there. We thought by this we should be eaten by these ugly men, as they appeared to us. . . . [A]t last the white people got some old slaves from the land to pacify us. They told us we were not to be eaten, but to work. (60)

If Equiano were to have discussed cannibalism no further, accounts of appropriation, mimicry, table turning, and naming of namers would suffice.

When Equiano next mentioned cannibalism, though, he showed that such accounts are insufficient. On board the Industrious Bee sailing from Virginia to England, Equiano—now the slave of Captain Pascal—faced the threat of cannibalism again when provisions ran low: "In our extremities the captain and people told me in jest they would kill and eat me, but I thought them in earnest, and was depressed beyond measure, expecting every moment to be my last" (64–5). Equiano may have passed off the threat as a "jest," but few eighteenth-century British readers would.

As these readers would have known from highly publicized events, British voyagers did resort to cannibalism to avoid starvation when they ran out of provisions. This need-driven act was sufficiently common to become a "socially accepted practice" among sailors, according to A.W. Brian Simpson.[154] And while the readers would have known that the sailors often selected the person to be consumed by lottery, they also would have known that Equiano, as an African, would have had a greater than even chance of losing the draw, had one been required. On board the Peggy in the winter of 1765 famished sailors consumed an African shipmate after apparently conducting such a spurious lottery. According to the ship captain, David Harrison,

> The little time taken to cast the lot, and the private manner of conducting the decision, gave me some strong suspicions that the poor Ethiopian was not altogether treated fairly;—but, on recollection, I almost wondered that [the other sailors]...had given him even the appearance of an equal chance with themselves.[155]

In the extremity of hunger at least, these sailors consumed the body of an African enthusiastically, engaging in what Harrison calls "a luxurious banquet" and remaining "busy the principal part of the night in feasting."[156] Similarly, in the *Shipwreck of M. Pierre Viaud* (English translation 1771), when Viaud, his wife, and his slave faced starvation, Viaud's "eyes fell on [his]...black. They lingered there with a kind of greed"; and then (in an act that recalls the image from Sayer's map but with a white European committing the violence), "I drew my knife and, with all my strength, sank it in his throat and widened the wound," after which he and his wife cooked and ate the man.[157] Then, in *Letters on the Slave Trade* (1791), published two years after *The Interesting Narrative*, Thomas Cooper recounted how a ship captain used cannibalism to control slaves who were refusing to eat:

> he obliged all the negroes to come upon deck, where they persisted in their resolution of not taking food; he caused the sailors to lay hold upon one of the most obstinate, and chopt the poor creature into small pieces, forcing some of the others to eat a part of the mangled body, withal swearing to the survivors, that he would use them all, one after another, in the same manner, if they did not consent to eat.[158]

In light of such instances as these, the threat of cannibalism in Equiano's *Narrative* (or for that matter Cugoano's *Thoughts and Sentiments*) becomes suddenly real, and this shift at once shows that Equiano was not so naïve after all and reveals a contradiction at the heart of European representations of Europe and of Africa.[159]

Even as Equiano's account of his shipmates' jests about cannibalism highlighted the fact that such sailors—and by extension European culture and ideology—consumed men like himself, though, he indicated that the very process of being consumed and incorporated into the European "body" lessened his fear of being consumed. Soon he could announce that the "fear,...which was the effect of my ignorance [of Europeans], wore away as I began to know them" (77). And soon, wishing to consume more of Europe into himself so as to become a more constitutive part of the European "body" (if not to become European himself), he began also to cannibalize his European acquaintances, at least figuratively: he started to "relish" their company and desired "to imbibe their spirit" (77–8, 93). Such a wish involved more than the oppositional, contesting relations implied by tropes such as reversal, appropriation and table turning: it involved material consumption, incorporation and circulation.

Having become incorporated and constitutive, Equiano in his *Narrative* started to wield much of the same rhetorical power against the European body that it wielded against him. He morally condemned European overseers of plantations for their cannibalistic behaviors as "human butchers" (105). He showed that European fears of actual cannibalism by non-Europeans were as naïve as his own initial fears of cannibalism appeared to be. Such was the case when Equiano's ship foundered on the Bahama Banks and the crew saw "some very large birds, called flamingos," which, "from the reflection of the sun, appeared to us...as large as men" and which "our captain swore...were cannibals" (152). The captain's certainty "created a great panic" until Equiano led the crew toward the birds and rousted them to flight (152). The progression of passages on cannibalism—with Equiano figuring himself as eaten, as eater, and as a man who calmed others' fears about being eaten—suggests that Europe had consumed the body of Equiano and that he became so much a part of Europe that he could assume the kind of position of intellectual and moral confidence that once appeared to be Europe's own.

The dispositioned body of Equiano as represented by the *Narrative* was more than the body of a native of Essaka, then; it was also European: a body from Essaka who nonetheless could assert that England was "where my heart had always been" (147). Equiano evidently would have had his readers understand the body, as substantial as it might be, to be a floating signifier—or a circulating signifier.[160] He noted (and was grateful) that the signification of his body had not been fixed and determined by the Igbo Embrenché mark "signifying . . . grandeur," a mark which, he said, some Africans created by "cutting the skin across the top of the forehead, and drawing it down to the eye-brows," or by other African scarification (32, 54).[161] He noted (and was more grateful) that, despite the prevalence of flogging slaves, his own body never had received "the marks of any violence of that kind" (an odd assertion since he earlier described being "flogged . . . severely") (147, 56). Equiano argued that skin color, in particular, was unstable. He quoted John Mitchel's comment that " 'The Spaniards, who have inhabited America, under the torrid zone, for any time, are become as dark coloured as our native Indians of Virginia' " (44). And he passed for white himself on two occasions: when he "whitened [his] . . . face" to deceive watchmen who had been hired to keep him from serving a writ of *habeas corpus* to a West Indian plantation owner who had kidnapped another African in England, and when a Miskito Indian called him "white" (180, 204).

If, as such passages suggest, Equiano's body, consumed and incorporated by Europe, became part of the European body with European tastes and habits, he also started to consume himself. No where is such auto-cannibalism more evident in the *Narrative* than in his *buying of himself*, his purchasing of his own manumission (135).[162] This purchase came at enormous cost inasmuch as it required Equiano to authorize the economic system that enslaved him.[163] According to his own descriptions, he did not so much obtain "freedom" as purchase himself as a slave: he became "my own master" (137) and hired out his own body just as his previous masters had done, "consent[ing] . . . to slave on as before" (141). As Equiano repeatedly showed, "freedom" itself was a misnomer for the condition he achieved by purchasing his manumission. Inasmuch as "freedom" provided no guarantee of fair treatment by whites and no guarantee that he would remain free of slavery, Equiano realized that "the state of a free negro" was equal to or "in some respects even worse" than the state of the slave since free blacks "live in constant alarm for their liberty; which is but nominal" (122).[164]

The culture that incorporated Equiano as a consumable good, then, irrevocably transformed him. As the *Narrative* shows, even if he helped to constitute that culture, he constituted it not as a man from Essaka, Benin, but as an African-Anglo-American. David Howes observes that "The idea that goods 'substantiate' the order of culture . . . [is] thrown into confusion . . . in situations of *cross*-cultural consumption. For when goods cross borders, then the culture they 'substantiate' is no longer the culture in which they circulate."[165] Equiano's case suggests even more clearly than Sancho's or Cugoano's that the new cultures also altered the goods themselves through alternative use and valuation. Because the culture that enslaved Equiano altered him and incorporated him into its systems, even Equiano's resistance to that culture operated within its systems and often looked little different from full participation within and collaboration with it. He gained power (very limited power) against those who enslaved him only by working the same consumer market system that they worked. Having decided to "commence merchant" by purchasing and reselling a glass tumbler, for instance, Equiano quickly developed a trade practice that reproduced the practices of the dominant culture, even as he sought to undercut the power structures of that culture (116). To the end, Equiano worked within the European economy while also resisting it, as when he accepted a position as commissary of a group repatriating Africans to Sierra Leone. The repatriation scheme suffered from many of the same "flagrant abuses" (economic, human rights, broadly social) that affected Equiano throughout the *Narrative*, though he achieved two successes against the dominant social forces that opposed him. He earned fifty pounds sterling, which was "Certainly . . . more than a free negro would have had in the western colonies!!!" (231) And he used the failed scheme as a platform from which to raise a public protest (227–31).

With this second, rhetorical success—and with similar rhetorical successes—Equiano came closest to transforming himself materially from a consumed consumer into an actively resistant (though never autonomous) producer of the culture in which he lived. When faced with injustice, Equiano spoke and wrote, thereby shaping private and public policy. "I could not silently suffer government to be thus cheated [in the Sierra Leone scheme], and my countrymen plundered and oppressed, and even left destitute of the necessaries for almost their existence," he recalled; "I therefore informed the Commissioners of the Navy" about the abuses (228). Then he wrote letters, objecting to "misrepresentations" of himself and requesting "redress" for the wrongs against him; and he received the redress (230). Still later, he wrote to Queen Charlotte petitioning "on behalf of my African brethren" for the end of West Indian slavery (231–2). Finally, in what Gates describes as the result of a "movement from slave-object to author-subject," he wrote a very public book (which made him wealthy).[166]

While such rhetorical acts represented a culmination of Equiano's increasing power as a producer of material culture, earlier instances in which he verbally resisted oppression in less public circumstances also showed him producing or attempting to produce material change. For instance, he quoted British law early in the *Narrative* when Captain Pascal illegally sold him to Captain James Doran in England. He told Doran: "I have been baptized; and by the laws of the land no man has a right to sell me: and I added, that I had heard a lawyer, and others at different times, tell my master so" (93–4). When Pascal and Doran challenged his assertion, Equiano commented that it was "very extraordinary that other people did not know the law as well as they"—to which Doran said, Equiano "talked too much English" (a remark that recalls also the power of multilingualism in accounts of the French emigration) (94). While Equiano's "English" made Pascal and Doran aware that Equiano knew much about his own social condition, it resulted only in physical violence against him. Later, though, when two white men attempted to kidnap him into slavery after he bought his manumission, Equiano again revealed verbally that he was aware of both his social condition and theirs, and they also observed that he spoke "too good English" and then departed, leaving him physically unmolested (159).

As Equiano increasingly produced European-British culture, he also increasingly represented himself as non-British and gained advantage by doing so. Instead of representing himself as "almost an Englishman" as he did earlier (77), he now represented himself as "an obscure African" when discussing the Sierra Leone controversy, and he signed his letter to the Queen "The oppressed Ethiopian" (229, 232).[167] To gain agency, to re-appropriate his Africanness (albeit an Africanness that circulates through Europe), it seems to have been necessary that he distinguish the specific constitutive function that he had within European culture. By the end of the *Narrative*, Equiano's status as a member of the English body politic depended upon his contribution as an African (an African whom Europe had consumed). The full title of the *Narrative* reflected this status: *The Interesting Narrative of The Life of Olaudah Equiano, or Gustavus Vassa, The African. Written by Himself.* The key words were the conjunctions and articles. The *Narrative* recounted the experiences of Equiano "or" Gustavus Vassa, suggesting an opposition between African and European identities, but the qualification following the European name then challenged this opposition. He was Gustavus Vassa, The African. The European name Gustavus Vassa (which, Equiano said, he at first "refused to answer to" [64])[168] became part of who he was as an African just as his origins became part of who he was as a European. Equiano told "The" life story of this complex subjectivity, not "my" life story; and the definite article allowed that what he told was not just a story that he himself had made and experienced but the story that had been made collectively by himself and those who purchased that life before he purchased it back for himself and it again became *mine*. "The" life he described was, further, more than his own; in many respects it was generally that of "The African" in a late-eighteenth-century Western world under the dominant influence of European culture and especially the slave trade.[169] The final phrase, "Written by Himself," while asserting rhetorical agency (an assertion much doubted by the anti-abolitionist press which argued that Equiano did not write the *Narrative*), also once again begged the question: who was "Himself"?

The title, like the rest of the *Narrative*, spoke forcefully of Equiano's emigrant condition in late eighteenth-century Britain. While Equiano's speaking mouth, like the rest of his body, was consumed by European cultural ideology and consumed it, his mouth functioned—and still functions—as what Pasi Falk calls "an intermediary channel [since it both consumed and produced] to be controlled and thus as the site of judgment."[170] Like the presence of the multilingual characters in Smith's poetry and prose, Equiano's presence in the cultural body was felt most when he spoke, when he wrote. He was most powerful, most dangerous to slaveholders, when he demonstrated that, by the logic of consumption itself, in cannibalizing him his enslavers transformed him from material good back into living body and living voice. Equiano's most radical move in the *Narrative* was in highlighting an African-European mouth and its insistence upon eating and speaking.

Afterword

Equiano and the other turn-of-the-century writers on African–British emigration ask much the same question as the writers on the British–American and the French–British emigrations: what constitutes physical, mental, moral, and spiritual selfhood in a time and space of instability and uncertainty?

Writers about the most violent migrations describe the material body as a consuming and consumable subject/object. The literature concerning the forced migrations of Black Africans does so; and so does, for example, the literature about the forced migration of British convicts transported to Australia. In his *Conciones ad Populum* (1795), Coleridge describes the transported convicts as physical consumers (as eaters or non-eaters), and he highlights the relation between food and socioeconomic power as fully as the writers about African–British emigrations do. Governmental policies cause poverty and hunger, he writes, but if men "pick their countrymen's Pockets" so as to feed themselves, "they are . . . transported to Botany Bay. And here we cannot but admire the deep and comprehensive Views of Ministers, who having starved the wretch into Vice send him to the barren shores of new Holland to be starved back into Virtue."[1] The woman, whom the government has transported because in England she has needed to "prostitute for Bread," likewise will be "famine-bitten into Chastity" in Australia.[2]

Writers about the least physically violent migrations generally emphasize the mental, moral, and spiritual self as a transforming and transformable entity. The Pantisocrats do so; and so do many writers who compose explicitly imaginative (fictional) utopian migration texts. Aratus's *A Voyage to the Moon Strongly Recommended to All Lovers of Real Freedom* (1793), James Henry Lawrence's *The Empire of the Nairs; Or the Rights of Women. An Eutopian Romance* (1811), and G.A. Ellis's *New Britain* (1820) draw from the material conditions of British bodies in the Romantic-period world, and yet their imagined voyages and migrations are more to ideational than to physical spaces.[3] Thomas Erskine's *Armata: A Fragment* (1817), for instance, describes a "New Land" that does not appear "on any accredited map": a land that has "*no* latitude . . . or longitude."[4] Still, the text remains topical and materially grounded, with Erskine's narrator discovering his new space "On the evening of the day which was to become memorable by the triumphant termination of the immortal battle of Waterloo, [a day that ushered in] . . . a new æra in the history of the world."[5]

The accounts of Romantic migration—whether from France to England, Africa to England, England to the Americas, England to Australia, or England to an imaginary utopian space—belong to a single body of literature that engages deeply with Romantic-period concerns even as it represents displacements from the sites where the greatest historical events occurred: France of the Terror, England of domestic political oppression, the British slave colonies. As the Romantic writers understood, physical, social, and imaginative displacement relates directly to emplacement. These writers and their characters did more than turn away; they also turned toward.

* * *

In *The Age of Migration*, Stephen Castles and Mark J. Miller describe the late-twentieth- and early-twenty-first-century "emergence of international migration as a force for social transformation," a process in which "Migration . . . bring[s] a new cultural diversity, which often brings into question national identity."[6] Castles and Miller note that the most authoritative studies say that between 150 and 185 million people (more than two percent of the world population) are emigrants, living for over a year away from their nation of birth.[7] I have suggested that the language and conceptual horizons of Romantic migration literature at once have contributed to the language and conceptual horizons of late-twentieth- and early-twenty-first-century discussions of migration and have provided a means to critique this language and these horizons.

For instance, pledging to review British immigration policy in April, 2004, Tony Blair denied, as Charlotte Smith did, that Britain would function as an ideal retreat for those seeking to come from other parts of Europe—saying that the United Kingdom would be neither a "fortress" against nor an "open door" to immigrants—though Smith went further than Blair and imagined an alternative Britain and Europe that could serve the needs of all inhabitants.[8] Blair's assertion that, "in the enlarged European Union," "No-one will be able to come to the UK . . . simply to claim benefits or housing" bounces hard against Smith's transnational and translingual ideals and harder against Wordsworth's 1803 argument that, in England, "all might come and go that would."[9]

In May, 2006, on the other hand, George W. Bush revealed that he either had internalized a historical contradiction or had learned to capitalize politically off it when he declared that the United States could function as *both* a fortress against *and* an open door to immigrants. "America remains what she has always been: the great hope on the horizon, an open door to the future, a blessed and promised land," he said in May, 2006, but, even as it continues as such a land, "the United States must secure its borders."[10]

In a *New York Times* series on Border Crossings, Jason DeParle describes a woman who has moved back and forth between her native Cape Verde and the Netherlands as having "her shoes on one shore, her mind on another and her innocence lost somewhere in between"; and he as easily could be describing Wordsworth's Female Vagrant, back in England after her voyage to America.[11] While each migration is particular to its historical situations and geographical locations, reading migration across historical periods may be as informative as reading them across geographical spaces.

British Romantic experiences and representations of emigration show that it leads to no promised land, but that it does offer a variety of promises: for destructive and productive instability, transformation, and new ways of conceiving selfhood and otherness. The literature of Romantic migration also investigates the value of its own promises, particularly concerning language. It investigates its own affirmation that language—especially literary language—can clarify all that is at stake in intra-cultural and intercultural contacts, conflicts, and encounters.

Notes

Preface

1. Roe, "Pantisocracy," 92. "An earlier usage . . . was the seventeenth-century sense of emigration as the migration of departure of the soul from the body at death or through an ecstatic rapture. . . . The two senses of emigration—physical removal and spiritual elation—coincided for dissenters like William Hazlitt (father of the critic), Richard Price, Joseph Priestley, Thomas Cooper and Coleridge, for whom religious liberty was an inspiring motive to emigrate."
2. Thomas Poole, quoted by Sandiford, *Thomas Poole*, 97–9.
3. White, *Natural History*, 131.
4. Hearne, *Journey*, 4.74.
5. Belknap, *History*, 3.6; Kendall, *Travels*, 2.54.252; cf. Roe, "Pantisocracy," 92.
6. Erickson, *Leaving*, 90; Horn, "British Diaspora," 30.
7. Birkbeck, *Letters from Illinois*, 133.
8. Makdisi, *Romantic Imperialism*, xii.
9. Leask, *British*, 33.
10. Suleri, *Rhetoric*, 4–5.
11. Drayton, "Knowledge," 238.
12. Rzepka, *Self*, 12; and cf. 21.
13. As David Bromwich comments, the concepts that many "share today about the distinctness of personal identity seem so plain a given that we are apt to assume they were always so: that this kind of self-consciousness was known, quite literally, in earlier times and that it was known to carry a peculiar importance"; Bromwich, "Note," 66. Critical literature on the Romantic self is extensive. Of the book-length studies published in the last twenty-five years on the topic, Rzepka's *Self* is among the best. Other important studies include Michael O'Neill's *Romanticism and the Self-Conscious Poem*, Andrew M. Cooper's *Doubt and Identity in Romantic Poetry*, and Paul Michael Privateer's *Romantic Voices: Identity and Ideology in British Poetry, 1789–1850*.
14. See Fortier, *Migrant*, 2.

Introduction: Deposing, Disposing, Dispositioning

1. The information that appears in this account of Louis XVI is generally available, though I especially make use of Andress, *Terror*; Schama, *Citizens*; and Doyle, *Oxford*.
2. Schama, *Citizens*, 552.
3. Ibid.; Andress *Terror*, 26.
4. Andress, *Terror*, 34.
5. Schama, *Citizens*, 554; Andress, *Terror*, 37.
6. Schama, *Citizens* 670; Andress, *Terror*, 148.
7. Ibid.

1 The French Immersion: Cross Currents of Selfhood

1. Carpenter, *Refugees*, 18; Roberts, *Counter-Revolution*, 5–6.
2. Carpenter, *Refugees*, 29–48, 195; Greer, *Incidence*, 115.
3. Greer, *Incidence*, 63–91, 111; Roberts, *Counter-Revolution*, 5.
4. Toby Benis addresses the French emigration in Romantic literature in "'Likely Story,'" 291–306; as does Carpenter, *Refugees*, 133–54.
5. Coleridge, "Priestley," ln. 2; *The Watchman*, 41; *Lectures on Revealed Religion*, "Lecture 2," 124; *Essays on His Times*, 1.76, 180, 341.
6. Carpenter, *Refugees*, 134.
7. Mary Moorman describes Wordsworth's move from Orleans to Blois as a "migration," but not his move from England to France; Moorman, *William*, 1.178.
8. Moorman, *William*, 1.170; also Reed, *Early Years*, 123–38; and Johnston, *Hidden*, 292ff.
9. Wordsworth, *Thirteen-Book*, 9.18, 35–7; further references to the *Prelude* will be to this edition, unless otherwise noted, and citations will appear parenthetically in the text.
10. Moorman, *William*, 1.181–2; Curtis, "Wordsworth," 145.
11. For the "Spy-Nozy" affair, see Coleridge, *Biographia Literaria*, 1.193–4. Further citations of *Biographia Literaria* will appear parenthetically in the text.
12. Nicholas Roe cites "HO 42/41. Domestic Correspondence George III, June–Dec. 1797"; Roe, *Wordsworth*, 249–50.
13. Holmes, *Coleridge*, 61.
14. Coleridge, *Letters of Samuel Taylor Coleridge*, 1. 89. Further citations of Coleridge's *Letters* will appear parenthetically in the text. Other prominent Romantic writers had close connections to the emigration as well. For instance, Jane Austen's "favorite cousin Eliza was married to the comte of Feullide in 1781 and often spent time in England with the Austen family. Early in the Revolution Feullide sent his wife to England and emigrated to Turin. He returned to

France to save family possessions and was guillotined on 22 February 1794"; Carpenter, *Refugees*, 152.

15. Carpenter, *Refugees*, 191.
16. Coleridge, *Lectures*, 124.
17. Coleridge, *Essays*, 1.180.
18. Smith, *Emigrants*, 2.382–4 and 387–95. Further citations of this poem will appear parenthetically in the text.
19. Young made his observation in his 1813 *General View of the Agriculture of the County of Sussex*, 62; but he also published a shorter text on Sussex in 1793, the same year that Smith published *The Emigrants.*
20. Barber, "Necessary," 3; Tunnicliff, *Topographical*, iv–v; Wiley, *Romantic Geography*, 29.
21. Harley, "Brighton Map."
22. Benis, "'Likely Story,'" 298.
23. Matthew Bray argues that Smith's children's book *Minor Morals* (1798) "opposes the idea that physical barriers between nations should carry any ideological significance"; "Anglo-Saxon Yoke," 155. Smith's geographical inscription, strategic and polemical as it is, precedes what Edward Soja has described as the nineteenth-century turn to foundationalist ideas of "the concrete and subjective meaning of human spatiality"; *Postmodern Geographies*, 79. Although no postmoderns themselves, Smith and many of her contemporaries recognized, as Soja and other postmodern geographers would recognize later, that "the organization and meaning of space is a product of social translation, transformation, and experience"; Soja, *Postmodern Geographies*, 80. For other evidence that Smith uses place names for strategic purposes, see Harries, "'Left Field,'" 466. See Wiley, *Romantic Geography*, for discussion of Wordsworth's similar geographical sense, likely influenced by Smith, whom Wordsworth met in November, 1791, and whose poem *The Emigrants* he likely read between May, 1793, and May, 1794; Moorman, *William*, 1.170 and Wu, *Wordsworth's Reading, 1770–1799*, 128.
24. Cf. Benis, "'Likely Story,'" 292 and 295.
25. Smith indirectly refers to this mindset in her dedication to William Cowper, when she suggests that different people have different ideas of what France and French nationhood are. Praising French "Emigrants of all descriptions" throughout England, Smith says that their "conduct…has been such as does honour to *their* nation" (133). The emphasis on "their" is Smith's and it suggests more than an opposition to England, "our nation" (133): it points toward the irony that "*their* nation" currently is not their own. "*Their* nation" is a Catholic monarchy that no longer exists: the monarch is dead, and the domes of the Catholic church are falling. The French revolutionaries have changed the geographical coordinates of what *was* the emigrants' nation to make the nation serve their own ideological

needs and interests. In 1789–90, the French revolutionaries, led by the cartographer the Comte de Cassini, remapped France into departments. For the cultural implications of this remapping, see Corbin, "Paris-Province," 436–8; and Schama, *Citizens*, 475–7.

26. Curran, "I Altered," 201.
27. *Emigrants* 1.110–11; *Desmond*, 314. In *Desmond*, emigrants argue that Revolutionary France erases institutional reference points. D'Hautville, uncle of Desmond's friend Montfleuri, says that it is "'utterly impossible...to continue in this lost and debased country [France], from which every thing valuable is gone....Would they not erase my arms? change my description? tear down the trophies of my house?'" (142).
28. *European Magazine*, 245–6.
29. See Carpenter, "London"; and *Refugees*; also Weiner, *French Exiles*, 1. As early as 1792, newspaper accounts indicated that London was becoming the emigration capital; see Parry, *Historical and Descriptive Account*, 328. For an account of Smith taking refugees into her house, see Fletcher, *Charlotte Smith*, 191.
30. Carpenter, *Refugees*, 14–15; Auckland, qtd. in Carpenter, *Refugees*, 210. Smith may refer to this reputation when describing an emigrant Abbé who "Still smiles and flatters, and still talks of Hope; / Which, sanguine as he is, he does not feel," and again when referring to the "native gaiety" that the French exiles now have "forgot[ten]" (1.150–1 and 2. 240).
31. Carpenter, *Refugees*, 13.
32. Responding to the perceived threat, the British government attempted to control widespread emigrant movement by passing the Aliens Act of January, 1793, requiring emigrants to notify local Justices of the Peace every time they relocated their residence; Carpenter, *Refugees*, 35–8 and passim. Smith's emigrant hero Armand D'Alonville sets himself up as a tutor in her 1794 emigrant novel *The Banished Man*. Smith also addresses the threat of Jacobins on English soil, albeit satirically, in *The Banished Man*.
33. Relhan, *Short History*, 44. Texts promoting Sussex seawater continued to appear well into the nineteenth century; see Parry's 1833 *Historical and Descriptive Account*, for example, or Harwood's 1828 account of the "Curative Influence of the Southern Coast of England," cited by Parry, *Historical and Descriptive Account*, 101–2.
34. Lee, *Ancient and Modern History*, iii. In an August 1789 letter, Smith notes that her mother-in-law "talk'd much of coming down to Brighton under the idea that the sea air would be of great use to her & that she might be able to use the hot baths"; *The Collected Letters of Charlotte Smith*, 22.
35. Quoted in Melville, *Brighton*, 24.
36. Cowper, "Retirement," 109–26, ln. 515–20; also Melville, *Brighton*, 28.
37. In a 1793 review of *The Emigrants*, the *European Magazine* says that Smith is visible "almost at the bottom of every page";

European Magazine 24 (1793): 42. Judith Pascoe argues that by "employ[ing]... the plight" of the French (Marie Antoinette in particular), "Smith is able to theatricalize her own situation, to project small-scale aggravations onto a larger stage"; *Romantic Theatricality*, 109. Sarah Zimmerman argues that Smith, having already established herself as a "popular cultural figure," tries to "lend [the emigrants]... some of the sympathy she has generated for herself" by connecting herself to them; *Romanticism*, 57.

38. Curran, "I Altered," 200.
39. Smith seems to be about twenty miles to the west of Brighton now. She remembers (consistently in the past tense) having "play'd" on "the banks of Arun" as a child; and she now (in the present) can "see [the river] / Make its irriguous course thro' yonder meads" (2.332–4). While Smith does not explain why she changes location, her new position in a place that has sustained past happiness perhaps enables her to sketch a map of a future happiness. For more discussion of Smith's self-positioning in this poem, see Labbe, *Romantic Visualities*, 33.
40. Smith comments in *Beachy Head* that there are "strong winds from the south-west"; *Beachy Head*, 437, 480fn. In representing the sheltering capacities of the topography, she again is engaging with what appears to have been a popular geographical representation of the region; in 1795 William Lee commented that "the *South Downs*... shelter the town [of Brighthelmston] from the bleak winds of the east, north, and north-west"; *Ancient and Modern History*, 434.
41. The Normandy region, with many royalist inhabitants, experienced a large number of executions and a high degree of oppression in 1793–94.
42. Smith, *Desmond*, 73; *Emigrants*, 133, 1.347, and 1.50.
43. The reviewer for *The Critical Review* notes that Smith "wishes for a retired hut, sheltered by the steep chalky hills that lie in prospect before her," but that "This wish is checked by the recollection, that no situation... can shut out care"; *Critical Review*, 300.
44. Cf. Bray, "Anglo-Saxon Yoke," 156, and Lee, *Ancient and Modern History*, 435.
45. Smith, *Beachy Head*, 121–6 and passim. In this poem, Smith explicitly denies a contemporary threat—"let not modern Gallia form from hence / Presumptuous hopes"—but implicitly shows that such a threat exists, as when she comments on the beacon system that still can pass an alarm in the case of an invasion; 143–4, 227–8.
46. Lee, *Ancient and Modern History*, 490.
47. Quoted in Parry, *Historical and Descriptive Account*, 67.
48. Quoted in ibid.
49. *Gentlemen's Magazine*, 784.
50. Quoted in Parry, *Historical and Descriptive Account*, 67.
51. Smith entertains ideas of such a French–British combination as early as *Desmond*, 315.

52. See Anderson, "*Beachy Head*," 574; and Fletcher, *Charlotte Smith*, 331.
53. Smith, *Beachy Head*, 1–4.
54. Ibid., 5–10.
55. Zimmerman, *Romanticism*, 64.
56. Smith, *Beachy Head*, 403–9.
57. Ibid., 481n.
58. Wallace, "Picturesque Fossils," 91.
59. Smith, *Beachy Head*, 507, 520, 574–5.
60. Ibid., 506–10, 541; cf. Anderson, "*Beachy Head*," 547.
61. Zimmerman, *Romanticism*, 58.
62. In November 1792 (the same month cited as the "TIME" of Book One of *The Emigrants*; p. 135), Smith hoped that the National Convention might "bring about a reconciliation" between the emigrants and the French revolutionaries; the "emigrants should suffer the loss of a very great part of their property & all their power. But they should still be considerd as Men & Frenchmen"; *Collected Letters*, 49.
63. Although early reviewers of *The Banished Man* saw in it a shift by Smith toward political conservatism and Loraine Fletcher follows this line of analysis, most recent criticism has argued instead that Smith still supports the early principles of the French Revolution while condemning the violence and tyranny of the early 1790s; see Fletcher, *Charlotte Smith*, 168, and Miller, "Truth and Deception," 348. My analysis is consistent with this second position.
64. Benis, "'Likely Story,'" 292.
65. Cf. Keane, *Women Writers*, 93.
66. Smith, *The Banished Man*, 1.1; cf. Keane, *Women Writers*, 92. Further citations of *The Banished Man* will appear parenthetically in the text.
67. Also see 1.67–8, 76, 108, 177, 189, 205; 3.78.
68. Andress, *Terror*, 26.
69. D'Alonville himself is "of Picardy" (1.174).
70. See Mansel, "Coblenz to Hartwell," 2. Keane observes that "Koblenz was an important gathering place for emigrants," but does not explore the importance of the place for *The Banished Man*; *Women Writers*, 93.
71. Weiner, *French Exiles*, 31; Carpenter, *Refugees*, 24. The reports of spendthrift emigrants were widespread. For instance, *The Morning Chronicle* for 5 January 1791 reported that "The King of Sardinia has certainly intimated to the Count d'Artois that he ought forthwith to return to France, and ought not by his contumacy reduce his family to ruin. . . . The burden of their maintenance has perhaps more than any other motive occasioned this resolution"; quoted in Carpenter, *Refugees*, 212n.
72. The deeds do maintain value in the narrative, though; see 4.329.
73. In the years surrounding the publication of *The Banished Man*, three partitionings of Poland—in 1772, 1793, and (a year after the novel's

publication) 1795—provided stark examples of how political and geographical changes could transform individuals and the spatial (particularly spatio-social, -political, and -economic) identities of societies. Carlowitz embodies these transformations in the novel. For Smith's contemporaries, Carlowitz's exile would have associated him with a class of poor, unlanded nobility who supported a Polish constitution, established in 1791, that increased Polish autonomy and was decidedly progressive (it included limited electoral reform, followed "English principles of ministerial accountability and monarchical irresponsibility," abolished slavery, etcetera; Lukowski and Zawadzki, *Concise History of Poland*, 100–1; also see Prazmowska, *History of Poland*, 127, and Lukowski, *Partitions of Poland*). The poor, landless nobles later would support the revolt led by Thaddeus Kosciusko in 1794 against a Russian occupying/partitioning army. Carlowitz's lack of country—similar to D'Alonville's, though emerging from revolutionary politics opposed to his—causes D'Alonville to question the absolutes of his own political identity and to sympathize with his political opposition. He acknowledges to Carlowitz that "'Had I been Polonese, I might have thought and have acted as you have done. Had you been a native of France, you would have seen her monarchy exchanged for anarchy infinitely more destructive and more tyrannical, with the same abhorrence as I have done'" (2.51–2).

74. On nationalistic figurations, see Jerinic, "Challenging Englishness," 64; also, Colley, *Britons*, 250.
75. Cf. Stanton, *Charlotte Smith's Prose*, 174 ; and Fletcher, *Charlotte Smith*, 219.
76. On the other hand, evidence of England's enlightenment comes from English letters (2.13).
77. Marin, *Utopics*, 195.
78. Weiner, *French Exiles*, 73; Mansel, "Coblenz to Hartwell," 5.
79. They encounter the Rosenheim family, who seem to be following the French court.
80. Weiner, *French Exiles*, 73.
81. Carpenter, *Refugees*, 117–18.
82. Schama, *Citizens* 297–8; Carpenter, *Refugees*, 117–18 and 231n, quoting Sabatier de Cabre on 23 November 1792. The principle villain in *The Banished Man*—Baron Rosenheim's castle almoner Heurothosen, who "'ought to have . . . taken care'" to bring Rosenheim's deeds to Koblenz but forgets to do so—appears to be at least a partial caricature of the forgetful and morally slack Comte.
83. Compare with the botanical and geological precision of *Beachy Head*. On Smith's botanical figurations, see Kelley, "Romantic Exemplarity," 233–4.
84. Mrs. Denzil then quotes Rousseau : "'Ajouter à tout cela les illusions de l'optique les pointes des monts diférmment éclairs, le clair obscur du

soleil et des ombres, et tous les accidens de lumière qui en réfultoient le matin et le soir; vous aurez quelque idée des scenes continuelles qui ne cesserent d'attirer mon admiration, et qui sembloient m'être offerts en un vrai theater: car la perspective des monts êtant verticale. Frappe les yeux tout a la fois, et bien plus puissamment que celle des plaines qui ne fe voit qu'obliquement en fuyant et don't chaque objet vous en chache un autre.'" (4.333–4). Smith appends a note that "The translation [of this passage is already]...in every body's hands who does not speak French" and so she will provide none (4.333). Thus, she is playing with a *well-known* figuration; and she is speaking an other's language.

85. Keane uses a different definition of utopia—one that conflates utopianism with ideological idealism—when she concludes that "The novel's grounding in Europe's immediate history...precludes a more Utopian projection [than the one created by the "little society" at the novel's conclusion,] and the tranquility and autonomy of the small republic seems...fragile"; *Women Writers*, 96. I argue, though, that the novel is not "ground[ed]" in immediate history, but that it has a critically unstable relation to it.
86. Benis, "'Likely Story,'" 292.
87. Also a "'friendly society'"; 4.337.
88. As a reviewer for *The British Critic* implies and as many subsequent critics have noted, despite its publication date, *The Wanderer* is in many senses a novel of the 1790s; Review of *The Wanderer*, 385.
89. Croker, Review of *The Wanderer*, 130; Doody, *Frances Burney*, 333.
90. Cutting, "Defiant Women," 519; Pearson, "Crushing the Convent," 132.
91. Doody, *Frances Burney*, 332.
92. Lynch, "Domesticating Fictions," 62.
93. Kristina Straub comments on divisions within *The Wanderer* of a different, though related, kind: this novel, she writes, "explore[s]...the cultural paradoxes implicit in women's socially sanctioned means to personal power"; *Divided Forms*, 8.
94. Schama, *Citizens*, 682; Doody, *Frances Burney*, 200; Hemlow and Douglas, Introduction, 2.x–xiv.
95. Doody, *Frances Burney*, 288.
96. Burney, *The Wanderer*, 4; also see Jerinic, "Challenging Englishness," 63. Further citations of *The Wanderer* will appear parenthetically in the text.
97. Also Burney, *Journals and Letters*, 6.716–17; cf. Zonitch, *Familiar Violence*, 113.
98. In Burney, *Wanderer*, xv; also 19, 26.
99. Ellis, *Post Office*, 49.
100. Ibid., 74, 71.
101. Ibid., 122; Joyce, *History of the Post Office*, 241, 315, 327.

102. Doody, in Burney, *Wanderer*, xvi. Notably, the name of Juliet's English counterpart Elinor—Elle-in-nor—has some of the same self-negating potential. Nonetheless, Elinor calls attention to Juliet's absence of certain identity, calling her " 'a chimera . . . an existence unintelligible, a character unfathomable, a creature of imagination, though visible,' " a woman of " 'false appearance, and lurking disguise! without a family she dare claim, without a story she dare tell, without a name she dare avow!' " (181) The initials "L.S." themselves signify little or nothing: Juliet has "fixed upon [them] by accident" (391).
103. The narrator conspicuously declares that Ellis is the "appellation [which], now, will be substituted for that of the Incognita" (*Post Office*, 91). Nearly 300 pages later, the narrator announces that "the borrowed name of Ellis will now be dropt," replaced by Juliet (*Post Office*, 389).
104. When Juliet does receive the anticipated letter (addressed to "L.S."), it affords her " 'no consolation! on the contrary, it tells me that I must depend wholly upon myself' "; and yet her sense of self remains uncertain (123). The novel indicates that while a person, and especially an woman, may wish to establish " 'self-dependence' " in England (273), English law and custom make it impossible for figures such as Juliet.
105. Cf. Jerinic, "Challenging Englishness," 68.
106. In what turns out to look occasionally like providential geography in this book, the Admiral turns out to be Juliet's uncle (835).
107. Doody, in Burney, *Wanderer*, xix.
108. Zonitch does see what amounts to a sought-after utopian alternative in this novel: "a community of women . . . to replace or at least offer an alternative to male-dominated versions of authority and protection"; "Burney explores in *The Wanderer* a new species of 'replacement' that evolves out of both the concept of a women's community and the structures of bourgeois authority: female economic independence"; *Familiar Violence*, 114, 115.
109. Burney, *Diary and Letters*, 4.298. I am grateful to Andrea Richards for helping me track down information concerning English sea bathing.
110. Cf. Mary Louise Pratt on "contact zones"; *Imperial Eyes*, 6–7.
111. On Juliet's selfhood, cf. Straub, *Divided Forms*, 176, 178; Zonitch, *Familiar Violence*, 119; and Epstein, "Marginality," 206–7. Though "fixed," Juliet returns to Europe at the end, coming back to England only when "A rising family . . . put[s] an end to foreign excursions" (870–1).
112. Burney, *Brief Reflections*, facsimile reprint in More, *Considerations*, 17. Further citations will appear parenthetically in the text.
113. Burney offers also a third (again negative) alternative: a " 'bleak northern strand, where life is mere existence, where the genial board has never welcomed the wearied traveler, where freezing cold

benumbs even the soft affections of the heart, and where, from the first great law of self-preservation, compassion is monopolized by internal penury and want' " (*Brief Reflections*, 16).

114. Given Burney's penchant for name play, the closeness between Juliet's last name—Granville—and Greville, the maiden name of Frances Anne Crewe, is noteworthy. As Claudia L. Johnson comments, Greville prompted Burney to write her *Reflections*: she "led the 'Ladies of Great Britain' in raising money to aid emigrant French clergy and appointed Dr. Burney as the honorary secretary. At her request, he urged Hannah More and Frances Burney to write appeals on behalf of the banished priests and to donate the proceeds to charity for their relief"; in More, *Considerations*, iii. Juliet Granville may be part of Burney's effort to write Greville into the annuls of British history.
115. Although "race" could mean a distinct species or genus of animals (as in the "human race"), the term dominantly referred to a subcategory within a species. If Burney uses the former meaning here, the latter meaning inflects it strongly, as my subsequent discussion shows (and as her own use of the term elsewhere in the "Reflections" also indicates).
116. In "Burney and Race Relations," Doody and Mack demonstrate Burney's strong opposition to slavery; in Burney, *Wanderer*, 884–7.
117. Ibid., 886.
118. See Jones, *Longman Companion*, 36; Grégoire, *Memoir*, 106; Hunt, Introduction, 24; Sepinwall, *Abbé Gregoire*, 93.
119. See Jones, *Longman Companion*, 14–72; Ott, *Haitian Revolution*, 140; Parry and Girard, *France Since 1800*, 16.
120. Ott, *Haitian Revolution*, 141.
121. Davis, "Impact of the French and Haitian Revolutions," 6.
122. Ott, *Haitian Revolution*, 141.
123. Ibid., 140; and see 143.
124. Cf. Lynch, "Domesticating Fictions," 60–2.
125. Cf. Deborah Lee, who finds in Wordsworth an extended, if displaced, consideration of black Africans and slavery; *Slavery*.
126. Quoted by Moorman, *William*, 1.571.
127. *Poems in Two Volumes*, passim; also Moorman, *William*, 1.571.
128. Wordsworth, "It is not to be thought of that the Flood," ln. 5.
129. To my knowledge, the *Morning Post* version has not been anthologized. It appears in Curtis, "Wordsworth," 144.
130. Cf. Sepinwall, *Abbé Gregoire*, 96; Johnston, *Hidden*, 301.
131. Grégoire, *Memoir*, 106.
132. Roe, *Wordsworth*, 66; Hunt, 24.
133. Sepinwall, *Abbé Gregoire*, 74.
134. Legouis, *William Wordsworth*, 9–10.
135. Johnston argues that Wordsworth "probably talked with Grégoire on more than one occasion," that he was Grégoire's "acquaintance," and, eventually, that he had a "close association and friendship" with

him; *Hidden*, 323, 379, 435, 442. For most others, the acquaintance is more speculative.

136. Roe, *Wordsworth*, 67; Wordsworth, "Letter to the Bishop," 32; also see Johnston, *Hidden*, 307.
137. Cf. Johnston, *Hidden*, 308, 389.
138. Wordsworth, "The Banished Negroes."
139. Many anthologies treat the historical issue silently, simply citing Wordsworth's 1827 note; critics occasionally turn the omission into a positive assertion of "Napoleon's 1802 expulsion of blacks from France following slave rebellions in the Caribbean colonies"; Lynch, "Domesticating Fictions," 61. As Curtis notes, "John Gibson Lockhart..., in his *History of Napoleon Buonaparte*, first published in 1829 and reprinted often in this century, cited Wordsworth's poem as the 'source' for the information that Napoleon banned Negroes from France in 1802"; "Wordsworth," 144. On the other hand, more recent studies of the French emigration by Greer, Carpenter, Weiner, and others make no mention of a banishment of blacks.
140. Curtis, "Wordsworth," 144.
141. Ibid., 145.
142. Ibid.
143. In *Letter to the Bishop of Llandaff* (1793), Wordsworth considers the French elite blameworthy; for example, 53–54. Although Wordsworth's thinking had changed greatly in the ten years that separated his writing of the *Letter* and the publication of "Banished Negroes," his visit to France in 1802 would have brought him face to face with his earlier political self.
144. In Lecture 2 from *Lectures on Revealed Religion*. Coleridge blames the emigrants for their own exile; 123–4.
145. When Wordsworth reprinted "The Banished Negroes" under the new title "September 1st, 1802" in his 1807 *Poems, in Two Volumes*, he reduced the woman's complexity. Under the new title, she no longer stands in for the plural "Negroes"; she no longer is "more than tame," but is "pitiably tame"; and she is no longer one of "us": rather, she speaks to "us" and does not "murmur...at the unfeeling Ordinance."
146. Curtis, "Wordsworth," 145.
147. Reed, *Middle Years,* 153–4; Dorothy Wordsworth, *Journals*, 124–5.
148. Wordsworth was thinking about Annette at this time; Dorothy Wordsworth, *Journals*, 127–8; Legouis, *William Wordsworth*, 66.
149. Wordsworth, "The Emigrant Mother," *Poems in Two Volumes,* ln. 2, 5.
150. Wordsworth's account of Vaudracour and Julia in Book 9 of *The Prelude* (the same book in which he discusses the "Band of Emigrants in Arms") famously parallels the story of his relationship with Annette Vallon and seems to be the source of many critical accounts that blame him for failing his lover. At the end of the account, Wordsworth again denies guilt: "Theirs be the blame who

caused the woe, not mine!" (9.852) Far more men than women emigrated from France, but women did emigrate as well: about 85.5 percent of the emigrants were men and 14.5 percent women; Greer, *Incidence*, 113.

151. Wordsworth, "Emigrant Mother," 9–14.
152. Ibid., 23–4, 28, 46, 59–63.
153. Ibid., 75–6.
154. Ibid., 90.
155. Ibid., 91–5.
156. Wordsworth, "Exiled French Clergy," 402.
157. Wordsworth, "Festivals," 12–14; cf. Hill, "Wordsworth," 64.
158. Cf. Hill, "Wordsworth," 60, 62.
159. Bellenger, *French Exiled Clergy*, 3; cf. Hill, "Wordsworth," 61.
160. Catholic emancipation occurred the following year, in 1829.

2 Imagining America

1. The best recent account is in Chandler, *England in 1819*, 441–80. Also see Mazzeo, "Anglo-American," 59–78.
2. Giles, *Transatlantic Insurrections*, 119.
3. Cohen, Introduction, Cobbett, *A Year's Residence*, 7; Lamb, *Letters*, 1.9.
4. Lloyd, "To ******," 41, 32–4, 37–8.
5. Earlier, in 1785–86, Robert Burns—motivated by his failed love affair with Jean Armour and by debts that threatened to land him in prison—obtained an appointment as a subordinate overseer on a Jamaica sugar plantation and tried to book passage to emigrate, though he never sailed; Kinghorn, "Robert Burns and Jamaica," 70, 73; McIntyre, *Dirt & Deity*, 69. While he saw himself becoming "exiled, abandoned, forlorn," he also idealized the West Indian spaces where he planned to live: the "charms o' the Indies," he wrote, included the "sweet... lime and the orange, / And the apple on the pine"; Burns, *Letters*, 1.35.
6. Todd, *Mary Wollstonecraft*, 37, 295–302; Mazzeo, "Anglo-American," 63.
7. Cole, *William Cobbett*, 55.
8. In a letter written to George and Georgiana between February and May 1819, Keats commented: "I see Cobbet has been attacking the [Birkbeck] Settlement but I cannot tell what to believe—and shall be out at elbous till I hear from you"; Keats *Letters*, 2.60. Cobbett had attacked Birkbeck in his *Weekly Register* 34 (6 and 13 February 1819): 603–66; and had reprinted the attack in his 1819 *A Year's Residence in the United States of America*, 285–320.
9. Representations of America as a space of bounty, often offset only slightly by counter-representations of America as a dangerous wasteland, contributed to the motivation of British emigrants of many

classes and ideological orientations at least since the early 1600s; De Wolfe, Introduction, 13. Blake and Paine, among others, saw America as a regenerative space before the French Revolution.

10. Cf. Mkarshall, "British North America," 372.
11. As Romantic criticism arguing for a Romantic ideology in the 1980s and early 1990s and the criticism that has countered the formulations of this ideology in subsequent years has shown, idealization and the resistance to idealization are central to—and often simultaneous within—Romantic literature.
12. See Flanders, *Atlas*, 77, 87.
13. Lewis and Clarke completed their transcontinental journey in 1805.
14. Seale, *Map*, 204–5.
15. Dalrymple, *Map*; cf. Swift, *Historical Maps*, 99.
16. Pinkerton, *Modern Geography*, 2.215; also Wiley, *Romantic Geography*, 11.
17. Williams notes that "The story of the search for a passage in the eighteenth century is one of credulity and some duplicity, of hopes raised and dashed, of the misdirection of practical seamen by those 'closet navigators' or armchair geographers much reviled in the explorers' journals"; *Voyages of Delusion*, xviii.
18. Ibid., 275, 277.
19. Quoted in Williams, *Voyages of Delusion*, 280.
20. Equiano, *Interesting Narrative*, 172. Explorers who were seeking to find a passage through or around North America from America's western coast commonly used the term "northeast passage" at the time. The captain of Equiano's ship may have been seeking to go east toward Asia, rather than west.
21. Williams, *Voyages of Delusion*, 283.
22. Ibid., 362.
23. Wordsworth, *Excursion*, 136. Further citations of *The Excursion* will appear parenthetically in the text.
24. Shelley, *Frankenstein*, 5–6. The geography of *Frankenstein* opposes the "country of eternal light" to England, which is presumably dark; 186.
25. Park reproduces the "List of Land Purchases," *Joseph Priestley*, 52–7.
26. See Brownstone and Franck, *Facts*, 95, 97; Horn, "British Diaspora," 31; cf. Johnston, *British Emigration Policy*, 6; Cobbett, *The Emigrant's Guide*, para. 33.
27. Many of the emigrants, it is true, headed for the best-established metropolitan areas, where they could find goods, services, and physical and social safety familiar from life in Britain. Thomas Cooper wrote in 1794 that "In Boston, New York, Philadelphia, and Baltimore, the state of society is much the same as in the large towns of Great Britain" (*Information*, 48). Paine and Cobbett sought such spaces, spaces that were not London, but were still recognizably British in their orientations. Most of the authors, though, looked to remove

themselves further. Priestley and the Pantisocrats, while choosing to be near the Susquehanna River and thus to maintain access to Philadelphia, also chose to go far upriver to Northumberland, a place difficult to reach (and often inaccessible during winter; see Cooper, *Information*, 108). Those who looked to settle in Illinois, Indiana, or Kentucky on the western frontier, as the Pantisocrats initially did and as George Keats did, were willing to leave the familiar further behind.

28. Johnston, *Hidden*, 2; Horn, "British Diaspora," 32.
29. Brownstone and Franck, *Facts*, 90; Flanders, *Atlas*, 76; and Shepperson, *Emigration*, 4. Johnston notes that "the Passenger Act of 1803 . . . was inspired by a fear that emigration from the Highlands was on the increase. At the dawn of an era of mass emigration strong objections were still heard to the departure of even a small number"; *Hidden*, 2. Brownstone and Franck suggest more generally that the Act "was primarily used to limit immigration to the United States, by driving up the price of passage"; *Facts*, 90. Significantly (especially to analysis of social and property-based movements such as Pantisocracy), as awareness grew of the hardships of indentured servitude (which remained legal until 1819) and as increasingly insurmountable financial blocks appeared to emigration by the poor, American emigration became largely a middle-class venture. Horn notes that the "majority of those" who emigrated after 1780 were "farmers and artisans of middling status"; "British Diaspora," 49.
30. Brownstone and Franck, *Facts*, 90; also Berthoff, *British Immigrants*, 5. The actual number of emigrants to America from Britain in the 1790s is notoriously hard to ascertain; Brownstone and Franck, *Facts*, 95; Flanders, *Atlas*, 76; Horn, "British Diaspora," 32. The British government, for all its concern with limiting the departure of its population, did not keep emigration records, and the U.S. government started maintaining immigration statistics only in 1820. Most estimates show a severe decline in the numbers during this time. For instance, whereas more than 125,000 people emigrated from Britain to America between 1761 and 1776, a total of fewer than 43,000—British *and* non-British—appear to have come between 1790 and 1799; De Wolfe, Introduction, 3; Flanders, *Atlas*, 76; cf. Horn "British Diaspora," 50. Much changed at the end of the Napoleonic Wars. "Between 1820 and 1870, American officials counted some three and a half million immigrants arriving from the United Kingdom"; Berthoff, *British Immigrants*, 5.
31. Coleridge, *Collected Letters*, 1.112–13, 115; also see Courtney, *Young Charles Lamb*, 90. Further citations of Coleridge's *Letters* will appear parenthetically in the text. Two years latter, Cobbett tapped into the same conception when he edited a volume of letters titled Look Before You Leap. The Newberry Library catalogue lists this text as "probably edited by William Cobbett." The language of the

Preface and of one of the letters in the volume is consistent with Cobbett's other work at this time.

32. Cobbett, *Emigrant's Guide*, 1.
33. Cobbett, *Look Before You Leap*, iv.
34. Wordsworth, "Tintern Abbey," 63. Unless otherwise noted, all citations of *Lyrical Ballads* poems will be from this edition and will appear parenthetically in the text. As Benis observes, many of the 1798 *Lyrical Ballads* poems "consider people on the move whose motives and desires are incomprehensible or mysterious," so much so that their psychological stability is in question; *Romanticism on the Road*, 239. A reading of this movement in relation to the Pantisocratic emigration scheme makes the "motives and desires" more comprehensible, though, and shows that psychological instability is consistent with a general process of destabilization that occurs during times of migration.
35. Conversely, the imagination of the American emigrant was sometimes that of the *Lyrical Ballads*: see *Sketches in Verse* by Robert Hutchinson Rose, who lived in a British settlement on the banks of the Susquehanna near where the Pantisocrats had planned to settle. The volume includes a poem titled "A Lyrical Ballad" which is a pastiche of "We Are Seven" and other Wordsworth poems.
36. Coleridge, *Biographia Literaria*, 2. 5. Further citations of *Biographia Literaria* will appear parenthetically in the text.
37. Coleridge, *The Friend*, 2.224.
38. Ibid., 2.225–6.
39. See also Nigel Leask's excellent article "Pantisocracy," 39–58.
40. Coleridge, *The Friend*, 2.224.
41. Cottle, *Reminiscences*, 5.
42. Eugenia observes too that "Pantisocracy, although usually dismissed with a casual paragraph in any discussion of Coleridge, presents a chapter in the poet's development which deserves to be more fully investigated"; "Coleridge's Scheme," 1069.
43. Quoted in Sandiford, *Thomas Poole*, 98.
44. Ibid., 98–9.
45. Cottle, *Reminiscences*, 3.
46. Poole, quoted in Sandiford, *Thomas Poole*, 97.
47. Cf. Roe, "Pantisocracy," 94; Marrs, Jr., "Introduction," 1 xxxi; Southey, *New Letters*, 1.84 fn5; Coleridge, *Letters*, 1.114, 122; Sandiford, *Thomas Poole*, 97. Further citations of Southey's *Letters* will appear parenthetically in the text.
48. Cf. Roe, "Pantisocracy," 90.
49. Poole, quoted in Sandiford, *Thomas Poole*, 97.
50. Cottle, *Reminiscences*, 7.
51. Poole, quoted in Sandiford, *Thomas Poole*, 98.
52. Brissot de Warville, *New Travels*, 361.
53. Quoted in Sandiford, *Thomas Poole*, 97.

54. Cottle, *Reminiscences*, 2. Additionally, as Nigel Leask notes, Pantisocracy would have been "a *colonial*, as well as radical-democratic enterprise"; "Pantisocracy," 44. Cf. McKusick, "'Wisely Forgetful,'" 108.
55. And see Courtney, *Young Charles Lamb*, 88.
56. Quoted in Sandiford, *Thomas Poole*, 98.
57. Cf. McKusick, "'Wisely Forgetful,'" 108. Cobbett comments on "the *sickening toothless dames*" of America in *Look Before You Leap*, 132.
58. Quoted in Sandiford, *Thomas Poole*, 98.
59. Ibid.
60. Lewis Patton observes, "Though [Pantisocracy is] often dismissed as a callow whim, the plan, as the long-unpublished Lectures on Revealed Religion help to show, was based on a profound awareness of the defects of established, so-called Christian society"; in Coleridge, *Watchman*, xxvii.
61. Cf. Erdman, *Blake*, 50.
62. Cottle, *Reminiscences*, 2–3. In more restrained language, Cottle notes that the Pantisocrats hoped to establish "a state of society free from the evils and turmoils that then agitated the world, and to present an example of the eminence to which men might arrive under the unrestrained influence of sound principles"; *Reminiscences*, 2.
63. Quoted in Pratt, "Pantisocratic Origins," 36.
64. Coleridge less happily reported that Mary Evans considered the possibility that he had lost his mind; 1.112. The idea that the Pantisocrats had been "called into life and action" would echo through Wordsworth's *Prelude* passage describing poets and thinkers who "Were call'd upon" to participate in governing the French Revolutionary world. Coleridge in extremity (as the plans for the community were falling apart) said, a member must "disregard 'his father and mother and wife and children and brethren and sisters, yea, and his own Life also'" in support of Pantisocracy; *Letters* 1.164. Nonetheless, "every individual [was]...at liberty, whenever he please[d]..., to withdraw from the society"; Poole, quoted in Sandiford, *Thomas Poole*, 98.
65. When facing Southey's arguments for the Wales alternative, Coleridge responded, "As to the Welch scheme—pardon me—it is nonsense—We must go to America, if we can get Money enough"; Coleridge, *Letters*, 1.132, also 150 and 155. He eventually did agree to consider Wales, but, for him, America was clearly the best place for Pantisocracy.
66. Paine, *The Rights of Man*, 394.
67. Ibid., 395; also cf. Brissot de Warville, *New Travels*, 31–2.
68. Imlay, *Topographical Description*, 3; Eugenia, "Coleridge's Scheme," 1075–6. Also see Courtney, *Young Charles Lamb*, 88; Whalley, "Coleridge and Southey," 324–40; and Roe, "Pantisocracy," 93, for discussion of Coleridge's and Southey's reading during the early- and mid-1790s.

69. Brissot de Warville, *New Travels*, 215; cf. Eugenia, "Coleridge's Scheme," 1072.
70. Cf. Courtney, *Young Charles Lamb*, 88. Cottle commented fifty years later, "It will excite merely an innocent smile in the reader at the extravagance of a youthful and ardent mind, when he learns that Robert Lovell stated with great seriousness, that, after the minutest calculation and inquiry among practical men, the demand on their labour would not exceed two hours a day; that is, for the production of absolute necessaries"; 7. Adam Smith observed that much of "the whole annual produce" of every country goes to the "idle" rather than toward "maintaining the industrious"; *Inquiry*, 54.
71. Courtney, *Young Charles Lamb*, 88.
72. Tim Fulford has done considerably the best work on the British Romantic engagement with American Indians. See "Romantic Indians," 139–50; and *Romantic Indians.*
73. Brissot de Warville, *New Travels*, 32.
74. Ibid., 419, 213–14.
75. Ibid., 418.
76. Imlay, *Topographical Description*, 549, 352–3.
77. Bartram, *Travels*, 113, 490, 213.
78. In planning to settle in Northumberland, Pennsylvania, the Pantisocrats may well have worried about the activities of the Indian tribes of the Six Nations, whose current boundaries were upriver on the Susquehanna; see Aldam and Wallis, *Map.* The Pantisocrats probably would have interacted with Indians, if only rarely. Indians had occupied Northumberland during the War for American Independence; and as recently as 1791 the U.S. government sent Thomas Proctor, who owned land in Northumberland, to give a "last solemn warning" to Indians of the Six Nations whom they accused of "carrying on . . . wanton depredations"; Holt, *Joseph Priestley*, 187; Proctor, *Narrative*, 569.
79. Roe, "Pantisocrac," 93; Holt, *Joseph Priestley*, 185; Graham, *Revolutionary in Exile*, 33. Cf. Maurice M. Kelley, who argues that Priestley and Cooper "sought to sell land rather than to reform society and establish Utopia"; "Thomas Cooper and Pantisocracy," 219–20. Some recent publications suggest that Priestley himself was not deeply involved in the plans to develop the settlement—the impetus for the settlement coming rather from Cooper and from Priestley's sons Joseph, Jr., Henry, and William—but for the British Romantics the senior Priestley's name and reputation were the ones that most mattered. Moreover, in his recent biography, Robert Schofield sees Priestley in a central role and sees the failure of the settlement emerging from outside rather than inside: Priestly

> hoped to establish a community of English "rational Christians," . . . with himself as minister and head of a college. These plans failed, as the abortive treason trials of Thomas

> Hardy, John Horne Tooke, and John Thelwall reduced the threat of persecution in England and stemmed the expected flood of liberal, Dissenting emigrants. (*Enlightenment* 275)

A letter from Priestley to Cooper also indicates that he had a "firm intention of establishing a settlement for his fellow refugees from England—'an asylum for my christian and Unitarian friends'...a rallying point for the Englishmen...emigrating to America in great numbers" (qtd. in Graham, *Revolutionary in Exile*, 35).

80. Park, *Joseph Priestley*, 14–15; and Maurice Kelley, "Romantic Exemplarity," 218–20. As Park points out, Brissot's travels in America were themselves part of a land-acquisition and settlement project for "founding an ideal community in the New World"; *Joseph Priestley*, 14. Priestley's correspondence indicates that, before emigrating to America, Priestley considered creating a settlement in "an abandoned French monastery in Toulouse"; Park *Joseph Priestley*, 13. Like the Pantisocrats, Priestley failed to commit his settlement plans to paper, noting in a letter only belatedly that the "scheme of a large settlement for English emigrants, projected by Mr. Cooper,...is given up"; Joseph Priestley, *Scientific Autobiography*, 286. But, in contrast to the Pantisocratic scheme, Priestley's does have an extensive paper trail in the form of the land records including the aforementioned tract names.
81. Priestley, *Autobiography*, 129.
82. As Jenny Graham notes, "The news [of Priestley's decision to abandon the settlement plans] was communicated in a letter to Lindsey of 14 September [1794], and undoubtedly created consternation in England"; *Revolutionary in Exile*, 63.
83. Cooper, *Information*, 208.
84. Ibid., 105. "Delight" is the most frequently mentioned feature of Northumberland at this time. Poole, as seen, reported that the Pantisocrats were headed for a "delightful part of the new back settlements." Shortly after arriving in Northumberland, Priestley commented that "nothing can be more delightful, or more healthy than this place"; 52.
85. Ibid., 105–6.
86. Ibid., 106.
87. Brissot de Warville, *New Travels*, 359–60.
88. Ibid., 338.
89. See Graham, *Revolutionary in Exile*, 8.
90. Barbauld, "To Dr. Priestley," 125, ln. 16121.
91. Coleridge, "Priestley," 1–2, 5–10, 13–14. Further citations of Coleridge's poems will be from the first volume of the *Complete Poetical Works* unless otherwise noted and will appear parenthetically in the text.
92. Coleridge, *The Complete Poems*, 473n.
93. Coleridge also had ties to Priestley through the Wedgewood family, particularly Thomas, who, following the example of his father, patronized Priestley's scientific work and also patronized Coleridge, Wordsworth, and many others. See Schofield, "Commentary," 375–6.

94. Graham, *Revolutionary in Exile*, 38.
95. Morse, *The American Gazetteer*, 383. Richard Holmes writes, albeit with insufficient discrimination between various planned American communities, that "the Susquehanna scheme did become a reality in other hands, and had a considerable influence on radical thinking in England at this time"; *Coleridge*, 89.
96. Coleridge repeatedly met with "a most intelligent young Man who has spent the last 5 years of his Life in America—and is lately come from thence as An Agent to sell Land," and although he was less skeptical of the land agent's sales job than he might have been, he did ascertain specific information about emigration and settlement costs, climate, and health care; *Letters*, 1.99.
97. I do not mean to suggest that Pantisocracy was ever in any way a realistic plan; rather, it was consistent with a reasonable perception of reality at the time. Clavière asked, "Suppose that wise and enlightened men planned the organization of a society before it actually had a single member, foresaw as far as possible all aspects of its future developments, set up institutions which would promote public and private virtue, and mapped out the economic growth of the state on the basis of the nature of the area. Must we say that such men would be mere utopians?"; Brissot de Warville, *New Travels*, 38.
98. Leask, "Pantisocracy," 53.
99. Dorothy Wordsworth, *Letters*, 221.
100. Reed, *Early Years*, 249, 267.
101. Leask, "Pantisocracy," 54; also see Roe, "Pantisocracy," 96.
102. In a letter to Poole dated the following day, Coleridge backed away from his position, saying that he had declared it in " 'a wildly-wailing strain' " and stating that "my Country is my Country; and I will never leave it, till I am starved out of it"; *Letters*, 2.710–11.
103. The language of Pantisocracy remained in Coleridge's mind when writing about this house in the West Indies. His comment that "we should not leave three such men behind us" echoes Southey's comment (in a letter promoting Pantisocracy) that upon emigrating to America "we shall not leave our superiors behind"; Southey, *Letters*, 1.72. Also see Tim Fulford on Coleridge's need for community; *Coleridge's Figurative Language*.
104. Coleridge, *Friend*, 1.224.
105. On the other hand, Eugenia suggests that "The topic of Pantisocracy died out after the year 1801, and with it passed from Coleridge's writing the chance references to this possible aspect of American life"; "Coleridge's Scheme," 1084.
106. Cf. "On the Prospect of Establishing a Pantisocracy in America," which has been doubtfully attributed to Coleridge; Coleridge, *Complete Poems*, 448n. The language echoes that of Cooper in his *Some Information Concerning America*, which Coleridge knew well, but it lacks Coleridge's tone and style.

107. Leask, "Pantisocracy," 40.
108. Eugenia, "Coleridge's Scheme," 1084.
109. Mazzeo, "Anglo-American," 67.
110. Imlay, *The Emigrants*, 246; Mazzeo, "Anglo-American," 66.
111. Cooper, *Some Information*, 135.
112. If the chasm of "Kubla Khan" resonates with the sounds of nightmare, entering into the Pantisocratic settlement would be like waking "From the Precipices of distemper'd Sleep, / On which the fierce-eyed Fiends their Revels k[eep]"; Coleridge, "Pantisocracy," 11–12.
113. Myers, "Sentiment," 76.
114. Fulford, *Coleridge's Figurative*, 4; McKusick, "'Wisely,'" 122. The Pantisocrats' widespread and notorious talk about Pantisocracy indicates that they were attempting to bring about a new space at least partly through the power of language. In Llanvillin, Coleridge reported, "I preached Pantisocracy and Aspheterism with so much success that two great huge fellows, of Butcher like appearance, danced about the room in enthusiastic agitation"; *Letters*, 1.88. Toward the end of "Kubla Khan," Coleridge declares his wish to construct his own spatio-linguistic structure: "with music loud and long, / I would build that dome in air"; 45–6. This "dome in air," I suggest, is yet another articulation of the Pantisocratic settlement—perhaps an early version of the "air-castles" of *The Friend*—that he was alternately displacing into Nether Stowey, the West Indies, Italy, the South of France, and the Lake District during this period; *Friend*, 2.224. All who see Coleridge's dome in "Kubla Khan" must cry out to

    Weave a circle round him thrice,
    And close your eyes with holy dread,
    For he on honey-dew hath fed,
    And drunk the milk of Paradise. (51–4)

    Had he been able to inhabit the Pantisocratic millenarian paradise on the banks of the Susquehanna, on the other hand, the situation would have been still more extreme and more ideal. In a Pennsylvania "cottag'd Dell / . . . / . . . / . . . Wizard Passions [would] weave a holy Spell" apparently with him and his companions mutually inside the circle, sharing in the holiness; "Pantisocracy," 5–8. In this sense, the displacement of Pantisocracy in "Kubla Khan" also diminishes its values.
115. Roe, "Pantisocracy," 96.
116. Earlier, in "Effusion XXXV, Coleridge struggles with religious principles that are heterodox in Britain, but that might have had freedom to grow in Pantisocratic America, where everyone was "to enjoy his own religious . . . opinions." Written shortly after Coleridge argued that a Pantisocratic settlement would not succeed

in England or Wales and the settlement scheme fell apart, the poem not only gestures toward Coleridge's failure to migrate to a place where he could regenerate body and mind, but explores the possibility of his reconciling himself to English institutional religion, to an English place (a cottage that for all its attractions is not a log-dwelling), and to a political environment where one might achieve personal tranquility, albeit (as so much of his other writing of this period shows) a tranquility always surrounded by institutional violence. Thus he represents regenerative Pantisocratic values as the "shapings of an unregenerate mind" and praises both the orthodox God who has given him "PEACE, and this COT" and Sara Fricker, the woman he had agreed to love in a Pantisocratic society but whom he struggled to love in Britain; 47, 56. Fulford argues that Coleridge's theological position in this poem depends upon that of his prospective Susquehanna neighbor, Priestley; *Coleridge's Figuration*, 56.

117. Cf. Richardson and Hofkosh, "Introduction," 1.
118. Brissot de Warville, *New Travels*, 295.
119. Ibid., 295–6.
120. Southey asked, "what is the origin of moral evil?" and answered, "individual property"; *Letters*, 1.70.
121. Brissot de Warville, *New Travels*, 295.
122. Ibid., 296–7.
123. The poetry of other Pantisocrats also deals directly or indirectly with the values and goals of Pantisocracy. For instance, as Lynda Pratt notes, in *Madoc* "Southey's descriptions of the society founded by Capac, with its emphasis upon the annihilation of 'individual property,' transmute Incan civilization into the ideal Pantisocratic state"; "Pantisocratic Origins," 35.
124. See Wiley, *Romantic Geography*.
125. Reed, *Early Years*, 344, 176. Reed also argues that the poem "was almost certainly sent in" to the *Morning Post* by Coleridge; 212.
126. Godwin, *Enquiry*, 244–5.
127. Oddly, he says that he has not "often" seen such a man, allowing that he at least possibly has occasionally seen one in his travels away from England.
128. While the account of the Female Vagrant contains a strong critique of Pantisocracy, Coleridge nonetheless valued *Salisbury Plain* very highly; Wordsworth, Cornell *Lyrical Ballads*, 343; Coleridge, *Biographia Literaria*, 1.80. Since Wordsworth drafted the lines on the Female Vagrant at least by 1793 and possibly earlier, Coleridge in his poems largely responded to a critique of Pantisocracy already implicit in Wordsworth's poem.
129. Or, rather, since Wordsworth wrote his lines first, his ship forges the path, and Coleridge's follows.
130. Cf. Magnuson, *Coleridge*, 77.

131. As Roe points out, this phrase "would have gained a topical resonance from the practice of transporting convicts and reformists to Botany Bay"; *Wordsworth and Coleridge*, 128. Since the poem is set during or shortly after the American War for Independence, the phrase also resonates with earlier (prewar) transportations to the American colonies.
132. Wiley, *Romantic Geography*, 37–47, 81–106. Roe also sees Pantisocracy in "Wordsworth's 'Home at Grasmere,'" as does Leask; Roe, "Pantisocracy," 96; Leask, "Pantisocracy."
133. See, for instance, Wright, *Widow*. Also see Fulford, "Romantic Indians," 145.
134. Cf. Johnston, *Hidden*, 726.
135. Cf. Benis, *Romanticism on the Road*, 101.
136. Cf. Fulford, "Romantic Indians," 147.
137. Ibid.
138. Ibid., 174.
139. Bewell, *Wordsworth*, 199.
140. For other discussion of Wordsworth and Hearne, see Wiley, *Romantic Geography*, 110, 147.
141. Such lines have contributed to the frequent critical perception of the Indian Woman as "a stock exotic figure, overlaid with sentimentalist and primitivist associations," though Bewell also shows that she critiques such stock representations; 197.
142. Wordsworth, "Ruth," 191–208. Further citations of "Ruth" will appear parenthetically in the text.
143. Bartram, *Travels*, 356–7.
144. Wiley, *Romantic Geography*, 145.
145. Wordsworth, *Excursion*, 62. Further citations of this poem will appear parenthetically in the text.
146. My analysis is a geographical analogue to Geoffrey Hartman's comment that "The Solitary has lost his 'excursive power,' and with it his chances to be renewed"; *Wordsworth's Poetry*, 306.
147. For an excellent discussion of the British engagement with America during this time, see Chandler, *England in 1819*, 441–80.
148. Johnson, *Letters*, v.
149. Ibid., ix.
150. Ibid., viii, 84.
151. Ibid., vi. For an account of pastoral idyll—albeit one disrupted eventually by violent bloodshed—on the banks of the Susquehanna, also see Campbell, *Gertrude*.
152. Birkbeck, *Notes*, 8.
153. Birkbeck, *Letters*, 19.
154. Ibid., 25.
155. Ibid., 133.
156. Shelley, *Lodore*, 54.
157. Owen, "Address."

3 CONSUMING AFRICA: EMBODYING ANTITHESIS

1. For instance, Mungo Park wrote, "whatever difference there is between the Negro and European in the conformation of the nose and the colour of the skin, there is none in the genuine sympathies and characteristic feelings of our common nature"; *Travels*, 120.
2. Browne, *Travels*, viii.
3. Torgovnick, *Gone Primitive*, 11; also Nichols, "Mumbo Jumbo," 97.
4. Fulford et al., *Literature*, 100; also see Fulford and Lee, "Mental Travellers," 132.
5. Dalzel, *History of Dahomy*, v.
6. Ibid. Such language also anticipated Wordsworth's arguments in the Preface to the *Lyrical Ballads.*
7. Browne, *Travels*, 425.
8. Lee, *Slavery*, 31.
9. The various impulses toward self and not-self relate closely to Coleridge's sense that Africa is at once divided from and continuous with Europe. Contemporary writers figured the migration between these two spaces as being at once between two radically different worlds and as being, essentially, no migration at all but a deeper reaching into the values already inherent in each native space.
10. Campbell, *Romantic Ethic*, 9. Also see McKendrick et al., *Consumer Society*, 13.
11. Morton, *Poetics of Spice*, 105.
12. Porter argues that, from the seventeenth century, "Wealth was the life-blood, the vital spirits, of the incorporated nation"; "Consumption: Disease of the Consumer Society?" *Consumption*, 58. Porter's use of the anatomical metaphor is more than incidental: William Harvey's early-seventeenth-century "discovery of the circulation of the blood," he observes, "perhaps underwrote the mercantilist credo that opulence grew out of the velocity of commercial transactions, providing employment and 'exercise' for the social organism"; 58.
13. Hallet, "Introduction," 6.
14. Beaufoy, *Plan of the Association*, 42–4.
15. Park, *Travels*, 67. Further citations of Park's *Travels* will appear parenthetically in the text.
16. *Records of the African Association, 1788–1831*, 177.
17. Ibid., 216. See Fulford and Lee's "Mental Travellers" for a fine short account of Banks and his importance to the Romantics. They argue persuasively that Banks "opened . . . spaces within the minds of Britons, mental geographies that seemed to place the real geographies of foreign realms within their knowledge and power"; 119–20.
18. Cf. Fulford et al., *Literature,* 98–9.
19. Wordsworth, *Peter Bell*, 6, 96, 86. Further citations of *Peter Bell* will appear parenthetically in the text.

20. Wu, *Wordsworth's Reading, 1800–1815*, 162.
21. Jackson, *Timbuctoo and Housa Territories*, ix.
22. *Records of the African Association, 1788–1831*, 47.
23. Ibid., 132.
24. Equiano and Cugoano, among others, volunteered to embark on African explorations; Sandiford, *Measuring the Moment*, 95.
25. *Records of the African Association, 1788–1831*, 103.
26. Marsters, "Introduction," Park, *Travels*, 10; Hallet, "Introduction," 7; also see Lupton, *Mungo Park*, 24–5; and cf. Matthews, *Voyage*, 51.
27. Cf. Marsters, "Introduction," 10.
28. Jackson, *Timbuctoo and Housa Territories*, 269.
29. Ibid., 270.
30. *Records of the African Association, 1788–1831*, 117–18.
31. Cf. Nichols, "Mumbo," 100; and Marsters, "Introduction," 3.
32. Coleman, *Romantic Colonization*, 65.
33. *Records of the African Association, 1788–1831*, 132.
34. Coleridge, *Lecture on the Slave-Trade*, 240.
35. Southey, *Poems*, 9–11.
36. Nussbaum, "Being a Man," 68. Nussbaum writes specifically about "black masculinity," though these "monstrous racial fictions" also extend across genders and beyond the human.
37. Cf. Fryer, *Staying Power*, 139.
38. Bruce, *Travels*, 75. Further citations of Bruce's *Travels* will appear parenthetically in the text.
39. Pratt, "Pantisocratic Origins," 74.
40. These British men, in the midst of their self-described penetrations into the African interior, could themselves be penetrated; and in many senses they were: to penetrate Africa was to be penetrated by Africa.
41. Curtin, *Image of Africa*, 42.
42. See Kitson, "Romanticism and Colonialism," 18–19; and Curtin, *Image of Africa*, 41–3.
43. Fryer, *Staying Power*, 137–8.
44. Matthews, *Voyage*, 99. On the other hand, he added, "In their domestic amusements [African women]...in some respect imitate the good country housewife in England"; 99.
45. Ibid., 159. For Coleridge's belief in physical and intellectual hierarchies, cf. Fulford et al., *Literature*, 144–6. Montgomery, though, wrote against polygenetic arguments in *The West Indies* when he asked about the black African, "Is he not *man*...?" (298)—a line that alluded to Josiah Wedgewood's 1787 plaque (the design of which was used as a seal Society for Effecting the Abolition of the Slave Trade) of a kneeling black man who asked, "Am I not a man and a brother?"; see Myers, *Reconstructing*, 41. For another set of representations that advocated a polygenetic conception of race, see Long, *History of Jamaica*, 353–4.
46. Matthews, *Voyage*, 41–2.

47. Fryer, *Staying Power*, 139.
48. For the eighteenth century, a "man ape" was "a primate with both human and ape-like characteristics" (*OED*).
49. Matthews, *Voyage*, 63, 96; also see Curtin, *Image of Africa*, 224 and 253.
50. Matthews, *Voyage*, 63.
51. Cf. Nichols, "Mumbo," 101. Elsewhere, for Park, "Moors [are] . . . very indolent"; 150.
52. Rennell, *Geographical Illustrations*, 396.
53. Leo Africanus, *History*, 935–6.
54. Ibid., 953–6.
55. Further citations of *The West Indies* will appear parenthetically in the text.
56. Bruce, *Travels*, 81.
57. Cf. Edwards, "Black Personalities," 42.
58. In suggesting that the "sun bestows" skin color, Wordsworth contributed to the idea, current at this time, that climate caused changes in pigmentation. His implication that "character" was discernible in "form and face" contributed to the equally common idea that body and skull types reflected intellect; see Fulford et al., *Literature*, 127–48.
59. Hickey, "Dark Characters," 287; cf. Makdisi, *Romantic Imperialism*, 31.
60. Makdisi, *Romantic Imperialism*, 23.
61. Wordsworth's concerns with the interblending of identities also bring his lines close to—though, as is the case with polygenesis, not fully into alignment with—discussions of miscegenation. During this time, European fears often did appear in arguments against miscegenation; see Mtubani, "Black Voice," 85. Park and Bruce carefully finessed themselves out of situations in which sex with Africans might have occurred. Those—like Joseph Banks—who were rumored to have had sex with non-Europeans on their travels suffered damage to their reputations; see Fulford and Lee, "Mental Travellers."
62. And it lowered them beyond primates on the Chain of Being, making them comparable (like the Extraordinary Spotted Boy) to dogs, a particular insult for Muslims.
63. Quoted in Bruce, *Travels*, 11.
64. Park, *Travels*, 284.
65. Morton, *Poetics of Spice*, 171–206; Coleman, "Conspicuous Consumption," 348–9.
66. Coleridge, *The Watchman*, 138–9; also see Morton, *Poetics of Spice*, 174; and Coleman, "Conspicuous Consumption," 348.
67. Wheatley, "On Being Brought," ln. 5–8.
68. Betsy Erkilla notes as well that Wheatley "knew the art and necessity of speaking with a double tongue"; "Revolutionary Women," 205. The process of refining sugar also is ideological; for instance, the refining would start in the colonies where the sugar cane was turned

into "crude brown muscavado" and would continue in factories in British ports; Walvin, *Fruits of Empire*, 126. Refinement thus can be mapped as a process of increasing Europeanization.

69. Cowper, "Sweet Meat," 81–2, ln. 22–4.
70. At this time, monkeys and other nonhuman primates were said to have paws.
71. Southey, "The Sailor," 288–92, ln. 65–72.
72. Ibid., 73–6.
73. Montgomery, *The West Indies*, 311.
74. Equiano, *Interesting Narrative*, 234; Golberry, *Travels in Africa*, 2.209; Curtin, *Image of Africa*, 178. Further citations from Equiano's *Interesting Narrative* will appear parenthetically in the text.
75. Curtin, *Image of Africa*, 177.
76. Makdisi, *Romantic Imperialism*, 32.
77. *Records of the African Association, 1788–1831*, 185.
78. Browne, *Travels*, 18–19.
79. Also see Jackson, *Timbuctoo and Housa Territories*, 296.
80. Bruce, *Travels*, 55.
81. See Curtin, *Image of Africa*, 178; and Golberry, *Travels*, 2.209.
82. Southey, "Hold Your Mad Hands," 1–4.
83. Wordsworth's scene at St. Batholomew's Fair also involved mouths, which, though expressive, contradicted speech and, though involving food, opposed eating: tents and booths at the Fair "vomit[ed]" people; 7.694.
84. Cf. Pratt, "Pantisocratic Origins," 74–5. Intriguingly, Park assumed the voice of a black African (Othello), or, more precisely, the voice of a white Briton's figuration of a black African (*Shakespeare's* Othello) in this allusion.
85. Quoted in Marsters, "Introduction," 17.
86. Browne, *Travels*, v.
87. Ibid., vi–vii.
88. Dalzel, *History of Dahomy*, vi.
89. Jackson, *Timbuctoo and Housa Territories*, 276.
90. Park also depended upon—and at moments seems to have been subordinate to—his multilingual black servant, an ex-slave from Jamaica who spoke both Mandingo and English; *Travels*, 86.
91. Jackson, *Timbuctoo and Housa Territories*, xiii.
92. Rawley with Behrendt, *Transatlantic Slave Trade*, 143; Adams and Sanders, *Three Black Writers*, 1.
93. Rawley with Behrendt, *Transatlantic Slave Trade*, 143; also Richardson, "The British Empire," 440.
94. Morgan, "Black Experience," 465.
95. *Gentlemen's Magazine*, 493; also Walvin, *England, Slaves and Freedom*, 46; Adams and Sanders, *Three Black Writers*, 1.
96. In Sancho, *Letters*, xxx. Citations of Sancho's *Letters* will appear parenthetically in the text.

97. *London Chronicle*, 117; also Adams and Sanders, *Three Black Writers*, 1, and Myers, *Reconstructing*, 18–37.
98. Exceptions included the violinist George Polgreen Bridgetower, for whom Beethoven wrote the *Kreutzer* sonata and who played in the Prince of Wales's private orchestra in Brighton; see Edwards, "Black Personalities," 41; Mtubani, "Black Voice," 86.
99. Walvin, *Black Atlantic*, 107. Despite the treatment the Incognita receives when wearing blackface in *The Wanderer*, black servants were fashionable; Walvin, *Making*, 105. For the complex status that black Britons held in London during the Romantic period, see Walvin's *Black and White*, 132–43; also Myers, *Reconstructing*, 9.
100. In Sancho, *Letters*, 5–9.
101. His published music included *A Collection of New Songs*.
102. In Sancho, *Letters*, 6. John Duncombe in a review of Sancho's *Letters* in the *Gentlemen's Magazine* also called attention to Sancho's "dissipation" even as he professed to "throw a veil" over it; Nichols, *Literary Anecdotes*, 109.
103. In Sancho, *Letters*, 8.
104. Ibid.; and see 9.
105. Ibid., xviii.
106. *Memoirs*, 45.
107. Ibid., 46, 48.
108. Ibid., 47.
109. Ibid., 49–50.
110. Ibid., 51.
111. *Berkeley Hall*, 102–3, 107.
112. Grégoire, *Enquiry*, 168.
113. Cf. Ellis, "Ignatius Sancho's *Letters*," 199–200.
114. Walvin, *Black and White*, 61.
115. Dommergues, "Ignatius Sancho," 190.
116. Mtubani, "Black Voice," 87.
117. Edwards, "Black Writers," 52–3. Edwards later questions the degree to which Cugoano assimilated; 53.
118. Myers, *Reconstructing* 133; and see Shyllon, *Black People in Britain*, 193.
119. Dommergues, "Ignatius Sancho," 192.
120. Ellis, "Ignatius Sancho's *Letters*," 202.
121. His biographical circumstances indicate how fully he had become British, but they also indicate how much power he had achieved in the process. Known as the "black Englishman," he was the first known Afro-Briton to receive an obituary in major British newspapers; Sancho, *Letters*, xiv. He also was the first (and, in the eighteenth century, only) Afro-Briton to vote; Ellis, 207.
122. Cf. Nussbaum, "Being a Man," 68; and Dommergues, "Ignatius Sancho," 196.
123. Cited by Nussbaum, "Being a Man," 64–5.

124. Cuguouno, *Thoughts and Sentiments*, 12.
125. Ibid., 13–17.
126. Ibid., xviii.
127. Ibid., xxii.
128. Wheeler, "'Betrayed,'" 17; Grégoire, *Enquiry*, 19.
129. Grégoire, *Enquiry*, 189.
130. Shyllon, *Black People*, 173.
131. Myers, *Reconstructing*, 134; Shyllon, *Black People*, 174.
132. Edwards, "Black Writers," 57.
133. Wheeler, "'Betrayed,'" 17.
134. In Cugoano, *Thoughts and Sentiments*, xxiv.
135. Ibid., xxvi.
136. Cf. Sandiford, *Measuring the Moment*, 94–5. While Cugoano wrote much of *Thoughts and Sentiments*, he seemingly had assistance from other writers. The collaborative authorship adds more dimensions to the multi-faceted self-representation(s) in the text. Sandiford further analyzes the relation between Cugoano's representations of the British and Britons' self-representations, though he occasionally views Cugoano's equally figurative representations of Africa as emerging from an "ineradicable [and essentially accurate] fund of memories"; 93.
137. Cf. Sandiford, *Measuring the Moment*, 94.
138. Compare Cugoano, *Thoughts and Sentiments*, xxv.
139. Although Johnson does not highlight this meaning, Shakespeare's usage here—addressing the Roman leadership as well as the place—also is consistent with the then common definition of "bowels" as "the seat of the deepest emotions." See Erickson, *Language of the Heart*, 1.
140. Addison, *Remarks*, 517. Veins of water and veins in rock are common figures of speech in their own right, but Addison used the bowels-vein combination repeatedly when describing physical spaces, suggesting a self-conscious body-space conceit. Cf. his comment on Italy as "a country that has...many veins [of marble] in its bowels"; 367.
141. Whereas most critical accounts of the *Interesting Narrative* argue that the textuality of Equiano's self-representation removes him from the exigencies of the material world—"liberating the author from the constraints of corporeality," as Susan Marren has put it; revealing him in a "rhetorical performance" that transcends "fact," according to Adam Potkay—I argue that there can be no such liberation and that rhetorical performances occur within specific historical and geographical relations: that Equiano's performance is inseparable from the circumstances of its production; Marren, "Between Slavery and Freedom," 94; Potkay, "History, Oratory, and God," 604.
142. Sabino and Hall argue that Equiano neither "permanently [n]or temporarily acculturated to Anglo-Christian values"; "The Path Not Taken," 8. Caldwell argues that "it is necessary to grant Equiano the full British voice and identity he considered his own";

"'Talking Too Much English,'" 280. William Mottolese sees in Equiano a "hybrid, diaspora identity"; "'Almost an Englishman,'" 160. Marren, though, argues that Equiano develops "a mode of articulation of newly imagined, radically nonbinary subjectivities"; "Between Slavery and Freedom," 95. Srinivas Aravamudan notes that the "credibility" of Equiano's *Narrative* "is anchored within an identitarian literary history" and argues that "Equiano's readers...witness his difference prior to acculturation"; *Tropicopolitans*, 235. Potkay, on the other hand, sees Equiano as rooted deeply in a "Christian...and colonial world" (one without cultural or linguistic "creolization"); "History, Oratory, and God," 602. Vincent Carretta has argued that Equiano was "conscious" that he was "both African and British in identity"; Carretta, "'Property of Author,'" 139.

143. Carretta, "Olaudah Equiano," 96, 103; also see Aravamudan, "Equiano Lite," 617–18. Carretta has continued to find evidence that Equiano was born in South Carolina.
144. Thomas, *Romanticism*, 231.
145. Sandiford observes rightly that "just as food, eaten and digested, in time becomes an integral part of the eating organism, so...we may perceive an unconscious succumbing to that assimilation which was the fate of the New World slave"; *Measuring the Moment*, 123. I argue, though, for a greater degree of conscious and strategic awareness on Equiano's part. Elspeth Probyn asks, "Do we eat what we are, or are we what we eat?" and "in eating, do we confirm our identities, or are our identities reforged, and refracted by what and how we eat?"; *Carnal Appetites*, 11. Maggie Kilgour also talks about the eater being constituted by the eaten; *From Consumption to Cannibalism*, 7.
146. Cf. Overton, "Countering Crusoe," 308.
147. Murphy, "Olaudah Equiano," 559; cf. Overton, "Countering Crusoe," 306; and see Kilgour, *From Consumption to Cannibalism*, 5.
148. Cf. Potkay, "History, Oratory, and God," 607–8. Sayer, *New and Correct Map of Africa*.
149. Overton, "Countering Crusoe," 306; and cf. Aravamudan, *Tropicopolitans*, 253, Sandiford, *Measuring the Moment*, 123, and Coleman, *Romantic Colonization*, 348; also Arens, *The Man-Eating Myth*, 10–13; and Howes, "Introduction," 1.
150. Mottolese, "'Almost an Englishman,'" 160; Murphy, "Olaudah Equiano," 562.
151. Gates, Jr., *Signifying Monkey*, 156.
152. Pratt, "Pantisocratic Origins," 81–5.
153. Sandiford, *Measuring the Moment*, 123.
154. Simpson, *Cannibalism and the Common Law*, 145; also see Sanborn, *Sign of the Cannibal*, 40; and Kitson, "'The Eucharist of Hell,'" 13.
155. Harrison, "The Melancholy Narrative," 269.
156. Ibid.

157. Viaud, *Shipwreck*, 92–4. Viaud's account was published repeatedly and its authenticity was debated widely through the end of the eighteenth century; 1–8.
158. Cooper, *Considerations on the Slave Trade*, 8–9.
159. For a discussion of how British cannibalism was "convention-bound" and, under certain circumstances, became a "legitimate, normal, and even normative procedure," see Obeysekere, "'British Cannibals,'" 639–40.
160. Cf. Rust, "Subaltern as Imperialist," 32–3.
161. For a discussion of Equiano's misrepresentation of Embrenché, see Afigbo, *Ropes of Sand*, 152. For a discussion of Afigbo, see Aravamudan, *Tropicopolitans*, 252.
162. Cf. Rust, "Subaltern as Imperialist," 25.
163. Also, consider Equiano's decision to buy slaves "all of my own countrymen" when starting a plantation with Dr. Irving (221).
164. Equiano quickly showed (though did not explicitly acknowledge) that his assertion upon his purchase of his manumission that he was "as in my original free African state" was ill founded (159).
165. Howes, "Introduction," 2.
166. Gates, Jr., *Signifying Monkey*, 157; also see Carretta, "Property." As Campbell observes, the increase in novel reading and the expansion of the book market contributed to the "eighteenth-century consumer revolution"; Romantic Ethic, 26. Mottolese—following "Gates, Bhabha, Hall, and other Africanist and postcolonial critics"—comments that "the encounter with the English book is a significant moment in the formation of a new identity in hybridity, a new subjectivity within the experience of diaspora"; "'Almost an Englishman,'"169.
167. See Carretta's research into Equiano's various namings; "Olaudah," 103, and "Property," 139; also Aravamudan, *Tropicopolitans*, 244–5.
168. Equiano's assertion about refusing to answer to the name Gustavus Vassa presents one of the many important complexities in relationship to Carretta's research into his nativity. Carretta has shown that Equiano's birth name in fact may have been Vassa and that he may have adopted Equiano only around the time of publishing the *Interesting Narrative*.
169. Cf. Carretta, "Olaudah," 104.
170. Falk, *Consuming Body*, 15.

AFTERWORD

1. Coleridge, *Conciones ad Populum*, 68–9. "After the [American] Revolution, Botany Bay replaced America as the principal destination of Britain's convicts. Nearly 12,000 men and women were transported between 1787 and 1810, at the rate of 500 to 1,500 a year, and another 17,400 were banished between 1811 and 1820"; Horn, "British Diaspora," 34.

2. Coleridge, *Conciones*, 69.
3. Even these texts relate to physical geography (or cosmography). For the best recent collection of Romantic-period utopian texts, see Claeys, *Modern British Utopias*. Also valuable is Hayden, *Seven American Utopias*.
4. Erskine, *Armata*, 2.
5. Ibid., 7. Erskine describes a New World, a twin of the earth, attached as by an umbilical cord to the South Pole.
6. Castles and Miller, *Age of Migration*, 2–3.
7. Ibid., 4.
8. "Blair Pledges Immigration Review."
9. Ibid.
10. Bush, "Immigration Reform." In January, 2004, he said, "[O]ur country is a welcoming society.... Every generation of immigrants has reaffirmed the wisdom of remaining open to the talents and dreams of the world"; "Bush Calls on Changes for Illegal Workers."
11. DeParle, "In a World on the Move."

Works Cited

Adams, Francis D. and Barry Sanders. *Three Black Writers in Eighteenth Century England*. Belmont, CA: Wadsworth, 1971.

Addison, Joseph. *Remarks on Several Parts of Italy, &c. in the Years 1701, 1702, 1703. The Works of Joseph Addison*. 2 vols. Ed. Henry G. Bohn. London: G. Bell, 1906.

Afigbo, Adiele. *Ropes of Sand: Studies in Igbo Hostory and Culture*. Ibadan: Oxford UP, 1981.

Aldam, John and John Wallis. *Map of the State of New York, With Parts of the Adjacent States, Made in 1793–4. Proceedings* 5.1. Albany: New York Commissioners of Indian Affairs, 1794.

Anderson, John. "*Beachy Head*: The Romantic Fragment Poem as Mosaic." *Huntington Library Quarterly* 63.4 (2000): 547–74.

Andress, David. *The Terror: The Merciless War for Freedom in Revolutionary France*. New York: Farrar, Straus and Giroux, 2005.

Anonymous. *Berkeley Hall: or, The Pupil of Experience*. London: T. Tindal, 1796.

Anonymous. *Memoirs and Opinions of Mr. Blenfield*. London: W. Lane, 1790.

Aratus. *A Voyage to the Moon Strongly Recommended to All Lovers of Real Freedom*. London, 1793.

Aravamudan, Srinivas. "Equiano Lite." *Eighteenth-Century Studies* 34.4 (2001): 615–19.

———. *Tropicopolitans: Colonialism and Agency, 1688–1804*. Durham: Duke UP, 1999.

Arens, W.W. *The Man-Eating Myth: Anthropology & Anthropophagy*. New York: Oxford UP, 1979.

Barbauld, Anna Letitia. "To Dr. Priestley. Dec. 29, 1792." *The Poems of Anna Letitia Barbauld*. Ed. William McCarthy and Elizabeth Kraft. Athens: U of Georgia P, 1994. 125.

Barrell, John. *The Idea of Landscape and the Sense of Place, 1730–1840: An Approach to the Poetry of John Clare*. Cambridge: Cambridge UP, 1972.

Barber, Peter. "Necessary and Ornamental: Map Use in England Under the Later Stuarts, 1660–1714." *Eighteenth-Century Life* 14 (November 1990): 1–28.

Bartram, William. *Travels Through North & South Carolina, Georgia, East & West Florida, the Cherokee Country, the Extensive Territory of the Muscogulges, or Creek Confederacy, and the Country of the Chactaws: Containing an*

Account of the Soil and Natural Productions of Those Regions, Together with Observations On the Manners of the Indians. Philadelphia: James & Johnson, 1791.

Beaufoy, Henry. *Plan of the Association.* 1788. In *Records of the African Association, 1788–1831.* Ed. Robin Hallet. London: Thomas Nelson and Sons, 1964. 42–5.

Belknap, Jeremy. *The History of New Hampshire, 1784–92.* 3 vols. Boston: Belknap and Young, 1792.

Bellenger, Domini Aidan. *The French Exiled Clergy in the British Isles after 1789: An Historical Introduction and Working List.* Bath: Downside Abbey, 1986.

Benis, Toby R. " 'A Likely Story': Charlotte Smith's Revolutionary Narratives." *European Romantic Review* 14.3 (September 2003): 291–306.

———. *Romanticism on the Road: The Marginal Gains of Wordsworth's Homeless.* New York: St. Martin's P, 2000.

Berthoff, Rowland Tappan. *British Immigrants in Industrial America, 1790–1950.* New York: Russell & Russell, 1953.

Bewell, Alan. *Wordsworth and the Enlightenment: Nature, Man, and Society in the Experimental Poetry.* New Haven: Yale UP, 1989.

Birkbeck, Morris. *Letters from Illinois.* London: James Ridgeway, 1818.

———. *Notes on a Journey in America, from the Coast of Virginia to the Territory of Illinois.* 1818. New York: Da Capo P, 1970.

"Blair Pledges Immigration Review." 27 April 2004. BBC News. http://news.bbc.uk/2/hi/uk_news/politics/3661261.stm. Accessed 18 January 2007.

Bray, Matthew. "Removing the Anglo-Saxon Yoke: The Francocentric Vision of Charlotte Smiths Later Works." *Wordsworth Circle* 24.3 (Summer 1993): 155–8.

Brissot de Warville, J.P. *New Travels in the United States of America, 1788.* 1791 French ed., 1794 1st English trans. Ed. Durand Echeverria. Trans. Mara Soceanu Vamos and Durand Echeverria. Cambridge: Harvard UP, 1974.

Bromwich, David. "A Note of the Romantic Self." *Raritan.* 14.4 (Spring 1995): 66–74.

Browne, William George. *Travels in Africa, Egypt, and Syria, from the year 1792 to 1798.* London: T. Cadell junior and W. Davies; and T. N. Longman and O. Rees, 1799.

Brownstone, David M. and Irene M. Franck. *Facts about American Immigration.* New York: H.W. Wilson, 2001.

Bruce, James. *Travels to Discover the Source of the Nile.* 1790. Ed. C.F. Beckingham. New York: Horizon P, 1964.

Burney, Frances. *Brief Reflections Relative to the Emigrant French Clergy.* London: Thomas Cadell, 1793. Facsimile reprint in More, Hannah. *Considerations on Religion and Public Education.* Los Angeles: William Andrews Clark Memorial Library, 1990.

———. *The Diary and Letters of Madame D'Arblay.* Vol. 4 of 6. Ed. Charlotte Barrett. London: Macmillan, 1905.

———. *The Journals and Letters of Fanny Burney (Madame D'Arblay).* 12 vols. Ed. Joyce Hemlow and Althea Douglas. Oxford: Clarendon P, 1972–84.

———. *The Wanderer; or Female Difficulties.* 1814. Ed. Margaret Anne Doody and Robert L. Mack. Oxford: Oxford UP, 1991.

Burns, Robert. *The Letters of Robert Burns.* 2 vols. Ed. J. de Lancey. Oxford: Clarendon P, 1931.

"Bush Calls on Changes for Illegal Workers." 8 January 2004. http://www.cnn.com. Accessed 18 January 2007.

Bush, George W. "Immigration Reform." 15 May 2006. http://www.whitehouse.gov/news/releases/2006/05/20060515–8.html. Accessed 18 January 2007.

Caldwell, Tanya. "'Talking Too Much English': Languages of Economy and Politics in Equiano's *The Interesting Narrative.*" *Early American Literature* 34:3 (1994): 263–82.

Campbell, Colin. *The Romantic Ethic and the Spirit of Modern Consumerism.* Oxford: Basil Blackwell, 1987.

Campbell, Thomas. *Gertrude of Wyoming.* London: Longman, Hurst, Rees, and Orme, 1809.

Carpenter, Kirsty. "London: Capital of Emigration." In *The French Émigrés in Europe and the Struggle Against Revolution, 1789–1814.* Ed. Kirsty Carpenter and Philip Mansel. New York: St. Martin's P, 1999.

———. *The Refugees of the French Revolution: Émigrés in London, 1789–1802.* New York: St. Martin's P, 1999.

Carretta, Vincent. "Introduction." Ignatius Sancho's *Letters of the Late Ignatius Sancho, and African.* Ed. Vincent Carretta. New York: Penguin, 1998. ix–xxxii.

———. "Olaudah Equiano or Gustavus Vassa? New Light on an Eighteenth-Century Question of Identity," *Slavery and Abolition* 20.3 (December 1999): 96–105.

———. "'Property of Author': Olaudah Equiano's Place in the History of the Book." *Genius in Bondage: Literature of the Early Black Atlantic.* Ed. Vincent Carretta and Philip Gould. Lexington: UP of Kentucky, 2001.

Castles, Stephen and Mark J. Miller. *The Age of Migration, Third Edition: International Population Movements in the Modern World.* New York: Guilford P, 2003.

Chandler, James. *England in 1819: The Politics of Literary Culture and the Case of Romantic Historicism.* Chicago: U of Chicago P, 1998.

Claeys, Gregory. *Modern British Utopias, 1700–1850.* 8 vols. London: Pickering & Chatto, 1997.

Cobbett, William, ed. *Look Before You Leap; Or, a Few Hints to Such Artizans, Mechanics, Labourers, Farmers and Husbandmen, As Are Desirous of Emigrating to America, Being A Genuine Collection of Letters, from Persons Who Have Emigrated.* London: W. Row, Walker, and J. Barker, 1796.

Cobbett, William. *The Emigrant's Guide; In Ten Letters, Addressed to the Tax-Payers of England, Containing Information of Every Kind, Necessary to Persons Who Are About to Emigrate; Including Several Authentic and Most Interesting Letters From English Emigrants, Now in America, To Their Relations in England.* London, 1829.

Cobbett, William. *Observations on the Emigration of Dr. Joseph Priestley: to which is Addred, a Comprehensive Story of a Farmer's Bull.* In *Peter Porcupine in America: Pamphlets on Republicanism and Revolution.* Ed. David A. Wilson. Ithaca: Cornell UP, 1994. 52–86.

———. *Weekly Register* 34 (6 and 13 February 1819): 603–66.

———. *A Year's Residence in the United States of America, Treating of the Face of the Country, the Climate, the Soil, the products, the Mode of Cultivating the Land, the Prices of Land, of Labour, of Raiment; of the Expenses of Housekeeping, and of the usual Manner of Living; of the Manners and Customs of the People; and of the Institutions of the Country, Civil, Political and Religious.* 1819. Carbondale, IL: Southern Illinois UP, 1964.

Cohen, J.M. Introduction to William Cobbett's *A Year's Residence in the United States of America, Treating of the Face of the Country, the Climate, the Soil, the products, the Mode of Cultivating the Land, the Prices of Land, of Labour, of Raiment; of the Expenses of Housekeeping, and of the usual Manner of Living; of the Manners and Customs of the People; and of the Institutions of the Country, Civil, Political and Religious.* 1819. Carbondale, IL: Southern Illinois UP, 1964.

Cole, G.D.H. *The Life of William Cobbett.* Westport, CT: Grenwood P, 1947.

Coleman, Deirdre. "Conspicuous Consumption: White Abolition and English Women's Protest Writing of the 1790s." *ELH* 61:2 (Summer 1994): 341–62.

———. *Romantic Colonization and British Anti-Slavery.* Cambridge: Cambridge UP, 2005.

Coleridge, Samuel Taylor. *Biographia Literaria.* 2 vols. Ed. James Engell and W. Jackson Bate. Princeton: Princeton UP, 1983.

———. *Collected Letters.* Vols. 1 and 2. Ed. Earl Leslie Griggs. Oxford: Clarendon P, 1956.

———. *The Complete Poetical Works.* 2 vols. Ed. Ernest Hartley Coleridge. Oxford: Clarendon P, 1968.

———. *The Complete Poems.* Ed. William Keach. New York: Penguin, 1997.

———. *Conciones ad Populum, or Addresses to the People* (1795). *Lectures 1795 on Politics and Religion.* Vol. 1. Ed. Lewis Patton and Peter Mann. *The Collected Works of Samuel Taylor Coleridge.* Princeton: Princeton UP, 1971.

———. *Essays on His Times in The Morning Post and The Courier.* 3 vols. Ed. David V. Erdman. *The Collected Works of Samuel Taylor Coleridge.* Princeton: Princeton UP, 1978.

. *The Friend* 2 pts. Ed. Barbara E. Rooke. *The Collected Works of Samuel Taylor Coleridge.* Vol. 4. General Ed. Kathleen Coburn. Princeton, NJ: Princeton UP, 1978.

———. *Lay Sermons.* Ed. R.J. White. Vol. 6. General Ed. Kathleen Coburn. Princeton, NJ: Princeton UP, 1972.

———. *Lectures on Revealed Religion.* "Lecture 2." *Lectures 1795 on Politics and Religion.* Vol. 1. Ed. Lewis Patton and Peter Mann. *The Collected Works of Samuel Taylor Coleridge.* Princeton: Princeton UP, 1971.

———. "Lecture on the Slave-Trade." *Lectures 1795: On Politics and Religion.* Ed. Lewis Patton and Peter Mann. Princeton: Princeton UP, 1971. 231–51.

———. *Letters of Samuel Taylor Coleridge.* Vol. 1. Ed. Earl Leslie Griggs. Oxford: Clarendon P, 1956.

———. *The Notebooks of Samuel Taylor Coleridge.* Vol. 2 (Text). Ed. Kathleen Coburn. New York: Pantheon, 1961.

———. *The Watchman.* Ed. Lewis Patton. *The Collected Works of Samuel Taylor Coleridge.* Princeton: Princeton UP, 1970.

Colley, Linda. *Britons: Forging the Nation, 1707–1837.* New Haven: Yale UP, 1992.

Cooper, Andrew M. *Doubt and Identity in Romantic Poetry.* New Haven: Yale UP, 1988.

Cooper, Thomas. *Considerations on the Slave Trade; and the Consumption of West Indian Produce.* London, 1791.

———. *Some Information Respecting America.* London: J. Johnson, 1794.

Corbin, Alain. "Paris-Province." In *Realms of Memory: Rethinking the French Past.* Vol. 1. Trans Arthur Goldhammer. Ed. Pierre Nora. New York: Columbia UP, 1996.

Cottle, Joseph. *Reminiscences of Samuel Taylor Coleridge and Robert Southey.* 1847. Highgate: Lime Tree Bower P, 1970.

Courtney, Winifred F. *Young Charles Lamb, 1775–1802.* New York: New York UP, 1983.

Cowper, William. "Retirement." *Poetical Works.* Ed. H.S. Milford. London: Oxford UP, 1971. 109–26.

———. "Sweet Meat Has Sour Sauce: or, The Slave-Trade in the Dumps." In *Slavery, Abolition and Emancipation: Writings in the British Romantic Period.* Vol. 4 (Verse). Ed. Alan Richardson. London: Pickering & Chatto, 1999. 81–2.

Croker, John Wilson. Review of *The Wanderer. Quarterly Review* 11 (April 1814): 125–30.

Cugoano, Quobna Ottabah. *Thoughts and Sentiments on the Evil of Slavery, and Other Writings.* Ed. Vincent Carretta. New York: Penguin, 1999.

Curran, Stuart. "The I Altered." In *Romanticism and Feminism.* Ed. Anne K. Mellor. Bloomington: Indiana UP, 1988. 185–207.

Curtin, Philip D. *The Image of Africa: British Ideas and Action, 1780–1850.* Madison: U of Wisconsin P, 1964.

Curtis, Jared. "Wordsworth and 'The Banished Negroes.'" *The Wordsworth Circle* 18:3 (Summer 1987): 144–5.

Cutting, Rose Marie. "Defiant Women: the Growth of Women in Fanny Burney's Novels." *Studies in English Literature, 1500–1900* 17:3 (Summer 1977): 519–30.

Dalrymple, Alexander. *Map of the Lands around the North Pole.* N.p.: 1789.

Dalzel, Archibald. *The History of Dahomy.* London, 1793.

Davis, David Brion. "Impact of the French and Haitian Revolutions." *The Impact of the Haitian Revolution in the Atlantic World.* Ed. David P. Geggus. Columbia, SC: U of South Carolina P, 2001. 3–9.

DeParle, Jason. "In a World on the Move, a Tiny Land Strains to Cope." *New York Times* (24 June 2007).

De Staël, Madame. *Corinne, or Italy*. 1807. Trans. and ed. Sylvia Raphael. Oxford UP, 1998.

De Wolfe, Barbara. Introduction. *Discoveries of America: Personal Accounts of British Emigrants to North America during the Revolutionary Era*. Ed. Barbara de Wolfe. Cambridge: Cambridge UP, 1997. 1–37.

Dommergues, André. "Ignatius Sancho (1729–1780), the White-Masked African." *History and Historiography of Commonwealth Literature*. Ed. Dieter Riemenschneider. Germany: Gunter Narr Verlag Tubingen, 1983. 189–97.

Doody, Margaret Anne and Robert L. Mack. "Burney and Race Relations." In Frances Burney. *The Wanderer*. Ed. Margaret Anne Doody and Robert L. Mack. Oxford: Oxford UP, 1991.

Doody, Margaret Anne. *Frances Burney: The Life in the Works*. New Brunswick, NJ: Rutgers UP, 1988.

Doyle, William. *The Oxford History of the French Revolution*. Oxford: Oxford UP, 1990.

Drayton, Richard. "Knowledge and Empire." *The Eighteenth Century. The Oxford History of the British Empire*. Vol. 2. Ed. P.J. Marshall. Oxford: Oxford UP, 1998. 231–52.

Edwards, Paul. "Black Personalities in Georgian Britain." *History Today* 31 (September 1981): 39–43.

———. "Black Writers of the Eighteenth and Nineteenth Centuries." In *The Black Presence in English Literature*. Ed. David Dabydeen. Manchester: Manchester UP, 1985.

Ellis, G.A. *New Britain. A Narrative of a Journey, by Mr. Ellis, To a Country So Called By Its Inhabitants, Discovered in the Vast Plain of the Missouri, in North America, and Inhabited by a People of British Origin, Who Live Under an Equitable System of Society, Productive of Peculiar Independence and Happiness. Also, Some Account of Their Constitution, Laws, Institutions, Customs and Philosophical Opinions: Together With a Brief Sketch of Their History from the Time of Their Departure from Great Britain*. London: W. Simpkin and R. Marshall, 1820.

Ellis, Kenneth. *The Post Office in the Eighteenth Century: A Study in Administrative History*. London: Oxford UP, 1958.

Ellis, Markman. "Ignatius Sancho's *Letters*: Sentimental Libertinism and the Politics of Form." *Genius in Bondage: Literature of the Early Black Atlantic*. Ed. Vincent Carretta and Philip Gould. Lexington: UP of Kentucky, 2001. 199–217.

Epstein, Julia. "Marginality in Frances Burney's Novels." *The Cambridge Companion to the Eighteenth-Century Novel*. Ed. John Richetti. Cambridge: Cambridge UP, 1996.

Equiano, Olaudah. *The Interesting Narrative of the Life of Olaudah Equiano*. Ed. Vincent Carretta. New York: Penguin, 1995.

Erdman, David V. *Blake: Prophet against Empire*. New York: Dover P, 1954.

Erickson, Charlotte. *Leaving England: Essays on British Emigration in the Nineteenth Century*. Ithaca: Cornell UP, 1994.

Erickson, Robert A. *The Language of the Heart, 1600–1750*. Philadelphia: U of Pennsylvania P, 1997.

Erkilla, Betsy. "Revolutionary Women." *Tulsa Studies in Women's Literature* 6 (1987): 189–221.

Erskine, Thomas. *Armata: A Fragmant*. 4th ed. London: John Murray, 1817.

Eugenia, Sister. "Coleridge's Scheme of Pantisocracy and American Travel Accounts." *PMLA* 45:4 (December 1930): 1069–84.

European Magazine 22 (September 1792): 245–6.

Falk, Pasi. *The Consuming Body*. London: Sage Publications, 1994.

Flanders, Stephen A. *Atlas of American Migration*. New York: Facts on File, 1998.

Fletcher, Loraine. *Charlotte Smith: A Critical Biography*. New York: St. Martin's Press, 1998.

Fortier, Anne-Marie. *Migrant Belongings: Memory, Space, Identity*. Oxford: Berg, 2000.

Foucault, Michel. "What Is an Author?" *Language, Counter-Memory, Practice: Selected Essays and Interviews*. Trans. Donald F. Bouchard and Sherry Simon. Ed. Donald F. Bouchard. Ithaca: Cornell UP, 1977. 113–38.

Frank, Catherine. "Wandering Narratives and Wavering Conclusions: Irreconciliation in Frances Burney's *The Wanderer* and Walter Scott's *Waverley*. *European Romantic Review* 12:4 (Fall 2001): 429–56.

Fryer, Peter. *Staying Power: The History of Black People in Britain*. London: Pluto P, 1984.

Fulford, Tim. *Coleridge's Figurative Language*. New York: St. Martin's P, 1991.

———. "Romantic Indians and Their Inventors." *European Romantic Review* 17:2 (April 2006): 139–50.

———. *Romantic Indians: Native Americans, British Literature, and Transatlantic Culture, 1756–1830*. Oxford: Oxford UP, 2006.

Fulford, Tim and Debbie Lee. "Mental Travellers: Joseph Banks, Mungo Park, and the Romantic Imagination." *Nineteenth-Century Contexts* 24:2 (June 2002): 117–37.

Fulford, Tim, Debbie Lee, and Peter J. Kitson. *Literature, Science and Exploration in the Romantic Era: Bodies of Knowledge*. Cambridge: Cambridge UP, 2004.

Fulford, Tim and Peter J. Kitson, eds. *Romanticism and Colonialism: Writing and Empire, 1780–1830*. Cambridge: Cambridge UP, 1998.

Fulford, Tim et al. eds. *Travels, Explorations, and Empires: Writings from the Era of Imperial Expansion, 1770–1835*. 8 vols. London: Pickering and Chatto, 2001–.

Gates, Jr., Henry Louis. *The Signifying Monkey: A Theory of Afro-American Literary Criticism*. Oxford: Oxford UP, 1988.

Gentlemen's Magazine 34 (1764): 493.

Giles, Paul. *Transatlantic Insurrections: British Culture and the Formation of American Literature, 1730–1860*. Philadelphia: U of Pennsylvania P, 2001.

Gilroy, Amanda, ed. *Romantic Geographies: Discourses of Travel, 1775–1844*. Manchester: Manchester UP, 2000.

Godwin, William. *Enquiry Concerning Political Justice, With Selections from Godwin's Other Political Writings*. Ed. K. Codell Carter. Oxford: Clarendon P, 1971.

Golberry, S.M.X. *Travels in Africa Performed during the Years 1785, 1786, and 1787.* 2 vols. London: 1803.

Graham, Jenny. *Revolutionary in Exile: The Emigration of Joseph Priestley to America, 1794–1804. Transactions of the American Philosophical Society.* Philadelphia: American Philosophical Society, 1995.

Greer, Donald. *The Incidence of the Emigration during the French Revolution*. Gloucester, MA: Peter Smith, 1966.

Grégoire, Henri. *An Enquiry Concerning the Intellectual and Moral Faculties and Literature of Negroes, Followed With an Account Of the Life and Works Of Fifteen Negroes and Mulattoes Distinguished In Science, Literature and the Arts.* Trans. D.B. Warden. 1810. College Park, Maryland: McGrath, 1967.

———. *Memoir in Favor of the People of Color or Mixed-Race of Saint Domingue*. 1789.

Excerpted in *The French Revolution and Human Rights: A Brief Documentary History*. Ed. and trans. Lynn Hunt. New York: St. Martins P, 1996. 105–6.

Hallet, Robin. "Introduction." *Records of the African Association, 1788–1831*. Ed. Robin Hallet. London: Thomas Nelson and Sons, 1964. 1–41.

Harries, Elizabeth. "'Out in Left Field': Charlotte Smith's Prefaces, Bourdieu's Categories, and the Public Sphere." *Modern Language Quarterly* 58.4 (December 1997): 457–73.

Harley, J.B. Annotation. "Brighton Map. Sheet 87." *Reprint of the First Edition of the One-Inch Ordnance Survey of England and Wales*. Newton Abbot, Devon: David & Charles, 1968.

Harrison, David. "The Melancholy Narrative of the Distressful Voyage and Miraculous Deliverance of Captain David Harrison, of the Sloop, Peggy, of New York, on his Voyage from Fyal, One of the Western Islands, to New York." In *In the Trough of the Sea: Selected American Sea-Deliverance Narratives, 1610–1766*. Ed. Donald P. Wharton. Westport, CT: Greenwood P, 1979.

Harrison, Gary. *Wordsworth's Vagrant Muse. Poetry, Poverty and Power.* Detroit: Wayne State UP, 1994.

Hartman, Geoffrey. *Wordsworth's Poetry, 1787–1814*. Cambridge, MA: Harvard UP, 1987.

Harvey, David. *The Condition of Postmodernity*. Cambridge: Blackwell, 1989.

Hayden, Dolores. *Seven American Utopias: The Architecture of Communitarian Socialism, 1790–1975*. Cambridge, MA: MIT P, 1976.

Hearne, Samuel. *Journey from Prince of Wales' Fort in Hudson's Bay, to the Northern Ocean...in the Years 1769, 1770, 1771 and 1772.* London: Strahan and Cadell, 1795.

Hemlow, Joyce and Althea Douglas. Introduction. Burney, Fanny. *The Journals and Letters of Fanny Burney (Madame D'Arblay).* Vol. 2 (Courtship and Marriage 1793: Letters 1793) Ed. Joyce Hemlow and Althea Douglas. Oxford: Clarendon P, 1972.

Hickey, Alison. "Dark Characters, Native Grounds: Wordsworth's Imagination of Imperialism." *Romanticism, Race, and Imperial Culture, 1780–1834.* Ed. Alan Richardson and Sonia Hofkosh. Bloomington: Indiana UP, 1996. 283–310.

Hill, Alan G. "Wordsworth and the "Emigré French Clergy, 1790–1827." *The Review of English Studies* n.s. 55:218 (2004): 60–74.

Holmes, Richard. *Coleridge: Early Visions, 1772–1804.* New York: Pantheon, 1989.

Holt, Anne. *A Life of Joseph Priestley.* 1931. Westport, CT: Greenwood P, 1971.

Horn, James. "British Diaspora: Emigration from Britain, 1680–1815." *The Eighteenth Century. The Oxford History of the British Empire.* Vol. 2. Ed. P.J. Marshall. Oxford: Oxford UP, 1998. 28–52.

Howes, David. "Introduction," *Cross-Cultural Consumption: Global Markets, Local Realities.* Ed. David Howes. New York: Routledge, 1996.

Hunt, Lynn. "Introduction." *The French Revolution and Human Rights: A Brief Documentary History.* Ed. and trans. Lynn Hunt. New York: St. Martins. 1996. 1–32.

Imlay, Gilbert. *The Emigrants.* 1793. New York: Penguin, 1998.

———. *A Topographical Description of the Western Territory of North America.* 3rd ed. 1797. Rpt. New York: Augustus M. Kelley, 1969.

Jackson, James Grey. *An Account of Timbuctoo and Housa Territories in the Interior of Africa, By El Hage Abd Salam Shabeeny, With Notes, Critical and Explanatory, by James Grey Jackson.* [London] 1820. London: Frank Cass, 1967.

Jameson, Fredric. *Postmodernism, or The Cultural Logic of Late Capitalism.* Durham: Duke UP, 1991.

Jerinic, Maria. "Challenging Englishness: Frances Burney's *The Wanderer. Rebellious Hearts: British Women Writers and the French Revolution.* Ed. Adriana Craciun and Kari E. Lokke. Albany: State U of New York P, 2000. 63–84.

Johnson, Charles Britten. *Letters from the British Settlement in Pennsylvania.* London, 1819.

Johnston, H.J.M. *British Emigration Policy, 1815–1830: "Shoveling Out Paupers."* Oxford: Clarendon P, 1972.

Johnson, Claudia L. "Introduction." More, Hannah. *Considerations on Religion and Public Education* and Frances Burney's *Brief Reflections Relative to the Emigrant French Clergy.* Facsimile reprints. Los Angeles: William Andrews Clark Memorial Library, 1990.

Johnston, Kenneth. *The Hidden Wordsworth: Poet, Lover, Rebel, Spy.* New York: Norton, 1998.

Jones, Colin. *The Longman Companion to the French Revolution.* New York: Longman, 1988.

Joyce, Herbert. *The History of the Post Office, From Its Establishment Down to 1836.* London: Richard Bentley, 1893.

Keane, Angela. *Women Writers and the English Nation in the 1790s: Romantic Belongings.* Cambridge: Cambridge UP, 2000.

Keats, John. *The Letters of John Keats, 1814–1821.* 2 vols. Ed. Hyder Edward Rollins. Cambridge: Harvard UP, 1958.

Kelley, Maurice W. "Thomas Cooper and Pantisocracy." *Modern Language Notes* 45:4 (April 1930): 218–20.

Kelley, Theresa M. "Romantic Exemplarity: Botany and 'Material' Culture." *Romantic Science: The Literary Forms of Natural History.* Ed. Noah Heringman. Albany: State U of New York P, 2003. 223–54.

Kendall, Edward A. *Travels through the Northern Parts of the United States, in the Years 1807 and 1808.* 3 vols. New York: I. Riley, 1809.

Kilgour, Maggie. *From Consumption to Cannibalism: An Anatomy of Metaphors of Incorporation.* Princeton: Princeton UP, 1990.

Kinghorn, A.M. "Robert Burns and Jamaica." *Review of English Literature* 8:3 (1967): 70–80.

Kitson, Peter J. " 'The Eucharist of Hell'; or, Eating People Is Right: Romantic Representations of Cannibalism." *Romanticism on the Net* 17 (February 2000). http://users.ox.ac.uk/~scat0385/17cannibalism.html. Accessed 4 June 2002.

———. "Romanticism and Colonialism: Races, Places, Peoples, 1785–1800." In *Romanticism and Colonialism: Writing and Empire, 1780–1830.* Ed. Tim Fulford and Peter J. Kitson. Cambridge: Cambridge UP, 1998. 13–34.

Labbe, Jacqueline M. *Romantic Visualities: Landscape, Gender and Romanticism.* New York: St. Martin's P, 1998.

Lamb, Charles. *The Letters of Charles and Mary Anne Lamb.* 3 vols. Ed. Edwin W. Marrs, Jr. Ithaca: Cornell UP, 1975.

Langan, Celeste. *Romantic Vagrancy: Wordsworth and the Simulation of Freedom.* Cambridge: Cambridge UP, 1995.

Lawrence, James Henry. *The Empire of the Nairs; Or the Rights of Women. An Eutopian Romance.* 4 vols. London: T. Hookham and E.T. Hookham, 1811.

Leask, Nigel. *British Romantic Writers and the East: Anxieties of Empire.* Cambridge: Cambridge UP, 1992.

———. *Curiosity and the Aesthetics of Travel Writing, 1770–1840: "from an antique land."* Oxford: Oxford UP, 2000.

———. "Pantisocracy and the Politics of the 'Preface' to the *Lyrical Ballads.*" In *Reflections of Revolution: Images of Romanticism.* Ed. Allison Yarrington and Kelvin Everest. New York: Routledge, 1993. 39–58.

Lee, Deborah. *Slavery & the Romantic Imagination.* Philadelphia: U of Pennsylvania P, 2002.

Lee, William. *Ancient and Modern History of Lewes and Brighthelmston in which Are Compressed the Most Interesting Events of the County at Large, Under the Regnian, Roman, Saxon and Norman Settlements.* Lewes, 1795.

Lefebvre, Henri. *The Production of Space.* Trans. D. Nicholson-Smith. Oxford: Blackwell P, 1991.

Legouis, Emile. *William Wordsworth and Annette Vallon.* USA: Archon Books, 1967.

Leo Africanus. *The History and Description of Africa and of the Notable Things Therein Contained, Written by Al-Hassan Ibn-Mohammed Al-Wezaz Al-Fasi, A Moor, Baptized as Giovanni Leone, But Better Known as Leo Africanus, Done into English In the Year 1600.* [1526] 3 vols. Trans. John Pory. Ed. Robert Brown. London: Hakluyt Society, 1896.

Lloyd, Charles. "To ******." *Blank Verse* [By Charles Lloyd and Charles Lamb]. London: T. Bensley, 1798.

London Chronicle 18 (1785): 117.

Long, Edward. *A History of Jamaica.* 2 vols. London, 1774.

Lowes, Jonathan Livinston. *Road to Xanadu: A Study in the Ways of the Imagination.* Boston: Houghton Mifflin, 1927.

Lukowski, Jerzy and Hubert Zawadzki. *A Concise History of Poland.* Cambridge: Cambridge UP, 2001.

Lukowski, Jerzy. *The Partitions of Poland: 1773, 1793, 1795.* New York: Longman, 1999.

Lupton, Kenneth. *Mungo Park, the African Traveler.* Oxford: Oxford UP, 1979.

Lynch, Deidre. "Domesticating Fictions and Nationalizing Women: Edmund Burke, Property, and the Reproduction of Englishness." *Romanticism, Race, and Imperial Culture, 1780–1834.* Ed. Alan Richardson and Sonia Hofkosh. Bloomington: Indiana UP, 1996. 40–71.

Magnuson, Paul. *Coleridge & Wordsworth: A Lyrical Dialogue.* Princeton: Princeton UP, 1988.

Makdisi, Saree. *Romantic Imperialism: Universal Empire and the Culture of Modernity.* Cambridge: Cambridge UP, 1998.

Mansel, Philip. "From Coblenz to Hartwell: The Émigré Government and the European Powers." *The French Emigrés in Europe and the Struggle against Revolution, 1789–1814.* Ed. Kirsty Carpenter and Philip Mansel. New York: St. Martin's P, 1999. 1–27.

Marin, Louis. *Utopics: Spatial Play.* Trans. Robert A. Vollrath. Atlantic Highlands, NJ: Humanities P, 1984.

Marren , Susan. "Between Slavery and Freedom: The Transgressive Self in Olaudah Equiano's Autobiography." *PMLA* 108:1 (January 1993): 94–105.

Marrs, Jr., Edwin W. "Introduction." *The Letters of Charles and Mary Anne Lamb.* 3 vols. Ed. Edwin W. Marrs, Jr. Ithaca: Cornell UP, 1975. 1: xxv–xcv.

Marshall, Peter. "British North America, 1760–1815." *The Eighteenth Century. The Oxford History of the British Empire.* Vol. 2. Ed. P.J. Marshall. Oxford: Oxford UP, 1998. 372–93.

Marsters, Kat Ferguson. "Introduction." Mungo Park. *Travels in the Interior Districts of Africa*. Ed. Kate Ferguson Marsters. Durham, NC: Duke UP, 2000. 1–28.

Matthews, John. *A Voyage to the River Sierra-Leone, Containing an Account of the Trade and Productions of the Country and of the Civil and Religious Customs and Manners of the People.* London: B. White and Son, 1788. Rpt. London: Frank Cass, 1966.

Mazzeo, Tilar J. "The Impossibility of Being Anglo-American: The Rhetoric of Emigration and Transatlanticism in British Romantic Culture, 1791–1833." *European Romantic Review* 16:1 (January 2005): 59–78.

McIntyre, Ian. *Dirt & Deity: A Life of Robert Burns.* London: HarperCollins, 1995.

McKendrick, Neil, John Brewer, and J.H. Plumb. *The Birth of a Consumer Society: The Commercialization of Eighteenth-Century England.* London: Europa Publications, 1982.

McKusick, James C. "'Wisely Forgetful': Coleridge and the Politics of Pantisocracy." In *Romanticism and Colonialism: Writing and Empire, 1780–1830.* Ed. Tim Fulford and Peter J. Kitson. Cambridge: Cambridge UP, 1998. 107–28.

Melville, Lewis. *Brighton: Its History, Its Follies, and Its Fashions.* London: Chapman & Hall, 1909.

Miller, Judith Davis. "The Politics of Truth and Deception: Charlotte Smith and the French Revolution." *Rebellious Hearts: British Women Writers and the French Revolution.* Ed. Adriana Craciun and Kari E. Lokke. Albany: State U of New York P, 2001. 337–63.

Montgomery, James. *The West Indies.* London, 1809. In *Slavery, Abolition and Emancipation: Writings in the British Romantic Period.* Vol. 4 (Verse). Ed. Alan Richardson. London: Pickering & Chatto, 1999. 279–332.

Morgan, Philip D. "The Black Experience in the British Empire, 1680–1810." *The Eighteenth Century. The Oxford History of the British Empire.* Vol. 2. Ed. P.J. Marshall. Oxford: Oxford UP, 1998. 465–86.

Moorman, Mary. *William Wordsworth: A Biography.* 2 vols. Oxford: Clarendon P, 1969.

More, Hannah. *Considerations on Religion and Public Education. Considerations on Religion and Public Education* and Frances Burney's *Brief Reflections Relative to the Emigrant French Clergy.* Facsimile reprints. Los Angeles: William Andrews Clark Memorial Library, 1990.

Moretti, Franco. *Atlas of the European Novel, 1800–1900.* New York: Verso, 1998.

The Morning Chronicle (5 January 1791).

Morse, Jedidiah. *The American Gazetteer.* 2nd ed., corrected. London: Longman, 1798.

Morton, Timothy. *The Poetics of Spice: Romantic Consumerism and the Exotic.* Cambridge: Cambridge UP, 2000.

Mottolese, William. "'Almost an Englishman': Olaudah Equiano and the Colonial Gift of Language," *Bucknell Review* 41:2 (1998): 160–71.

Mtubani, Victor C.D. "The Black Voice in Eighteenth-Century Britain: African Writers against Slavery and the Slave Trade." *Phylon: A Review of Race and Culture* 45:2 (June 1984): 85–97.

Murphy, Geraldine. "Olaudah Equiano, Accidental Tourist." *Eighteenth-Century Studies* 27:4 (Summer 1994): 551–68.

Myers, Norma. *Reconstructing the Black Past: Blacks in Britain, 1780–1830.* London: Frank Cass, 1996.

Myers, Victoria. "Sentiment and the Pantisocratic Community: Coleridge's Letters to Southey." *The Wordsworth Circle* 29:1 (Winter 1998): 75–9.

New Collection of Voyages and Travels, Into Several Parts of the World, None of Them Ever Before Printed in English. 1711. London: 1743.

Nichols, Ashton. "Mumbo Jumbo: Mungo Park and the Rhetoric of Romantic Africa." *Romanticism, Race, and Imperial Culture, 1780–1834.* Ed. Alan Richardson and Sonia Hofkosh. Bloomington: Indiana UP, 1996. 93–113.

Nichols, John. *Literary Anecdotes of the Eighteenth Century.* Vol. 8. London, 1815.

Nussbaum, Felicity A. "Being a Man: Olaudah Equiano and Ignatius Sancho." *Genius in Bondage: Literature of the Early Black Atlantic.* Ed. Vincent Carretta and Philip Gould. Lexington: UP of Kentucky, 2001. 54–71.

Obeyesekere, Gananath. "'British Cannibals': Contemplation of an Event in the Death and Resurrection of James Cook, Explorer." *Critical Inquiry* 18 (Summer 1992): 630–54.

O'Neill, Michael. *Romanticism and the Self-Conscious Poem.* Oxford: Clarendon P, 1997.

Ott, Thomas O. *The Haitian Revolution, 1789–1804.* Knoxville: U of Tennessee P, 1973.

Overton, Bill. "Countering Crusoe: Two Colonial Narratives." *Critical Survey* 4 (1992): 302–10.

Owen, Robert. "Address to the Inhabitants of New Lanark." London, 1816. Informal Education Archives. http://www.infed.org/archives/e-texts/owen_new_ lanark.htm#address. Accessed 11 November 2005.

Owen, Sidney James. *A Selection from the Despatches, Treaties, and Other Papers of the Marquess Wellesley, K.G., During his Government of India.* Oxford: Clarendon P, 1877.

Paine, Thomas. *The Rights of Man.* In *Two Classics of the French Revolution: Reflections on the Revolution in France and the Rights of Man.* New York: Anchor, 1973. 267–515.

Park, Mary Cathryne. *Joseph Priestley and the Problem of Pantisocracy.* Ph.D. Dissertation. Philadelphia: U of Pennsylvania, 1947.

Park, Mungo. *Travels in the Interior Districts of Africa.* Ed. Kate Ferguson Marsters. Durham, NC: Duke UP, 2000.

Parry, D.L.L. and Pierre Girard. *France Since 1800.* Oxford: Oxford UP, 2002.

Parry, J.D. *An Historical and Descriptive Account of the Coast of Sussex.* 1833.

Pascoe, Judith. *Romantic Theatricality: Gender, Poetry, and Spectatorship.* Ithaca: Cornell UP, 1997.

Pearson, Jacqueline. "Crushing the Convent and the Dread Bastille: The Anglo-Saxons, Revolution and Gender in Women's Plays of the 1790s." *Literary Appropriations of the Anglo-Saxons from the Thirteenth to the Twentieth Century.* Ed. Donald Scragg and Carole Weinberg. Cambridge: Cambridge UP, 2000. 122–37.

Pinkerton, John. *Modern Geography.* 2 vols. London, 1811.

Porter, Roy. "Consumption: Disease of the Consumer Society?" *Consumption and the World of Goods.* Ed. John Brewer and Roy Porter. New York: Routledge, 1993. 58–81.

Potkay, Adam. "History, Oratory, and God in Equiano's *Interesting Narrative.*" *Eighteenth-Century Studies* 34.4 (2001): 601–14.

Pratt, Lynda. "The Pantisocratic Origins of Robert Southey's *Madoc*: An Unpublished Letter." *Notes and Queries* 46 (244): 1 (March 1999): 34–9.

Pratt, Mary Louise. *Imperial Eyes: Travel Writing and Transculturation.* London: Routledge, 1992.

Prazmowska, Anita J. *A History of Poland.* New York and Houndmills, Basingstoke: Palgrave Macmillan, 2004.

Priestley, Joseph. *Autobiography of Joseph Priestley: Memoirs Written by Himself; An Account of Further Discoveries in Air.* Teaneck, NJ: Fairleigh Dickinson UP, 1970.

———. *Scientific Autobiography of Joseph Priestley (1733–1804): Selected Scientific Correspondence.* Ed. Robert E. Schofield. Cambridge, MA: M.I.T. P, 1966.

Privateer, Paul Michael. *Romantic Voices: Identity and Ideology in British Poetry, 1789–1850.* Athens: U of Georgia P, 1991.

Probyn, Elspeth. *Carnal Appetites: FoodSexIdentities.* New York: Routledge, 2000.

Proctor, Thomas. *Narrative of the Journey of Col. Thomas Proctor, to the Indians of the Northwest.* 1791. In *Pennsylvania Archives.* 2nd ser., vol. 4, part 2. Harrisburg, PA: B.F. Meyers, 1876. 551–622.

Radhakrishnan, Rajagopalan. *Diasporic Mediations: Between Home and Location.* Minneapolis: U of Minnesota P, 1996.

Rawley, James A. with Stephen D. Behrendt. *The Transatlantic Slave Trade: A History, Revised Edition.* Lincoln, NE: U of Nebraska P, 2005.

Records of the African Association, 1788–1831. Ed. Robin Hallet. London: Thomas Nelson and Sons, 1964.

Reed, Mark L. *Wordsworth: The Chronology of the Early Years, 1770–1799.* Cambridge: Harvard UP, 1967.

———. *Wordsworth: The Chronology of the Middle Years, 1800–1815.* Cambridge: Harvard UP, 1975.

Relhan, Anthony. *A Short History of Brighthelmston, With Remarks on its Air, & an Analysis of its Waters, Particularly of an Uncommon Mineral One Long Discovered, Though But Lately Used.* 1761. Re-edited Lewes, 1829.

Rennell, James. *Geographical Illustrations.* In Mungo Park. *Travels in the Interior Districts of Africa.* Ed. Kate Ferguson Marsters. Durham, NC: Duke UP, 2000. 319–96.

Review of Charlotte Smith's *The Emigrants. Critical Review* 9 (1794): 209–302.

Review of Charlotte Smith's *The Emigrants. European Magazine* 24 (1793).

Review of Mungo Park's *Travels. Monthly Magazine.* (July 1799).

Review of *The Wanderer. The British Critic* n.s. 1 (April 1814): 385.

Richardson, Alan and Sonia Hofkosh, eds. *Romanticism, Race, and Imperial Culture, 1780–1834.* Bloomington: Indiana UP, 1996.

Richardson, David. "The British Empire and the Atlantic Slave Trade, 1660–1807." *The Eighteenth Century. The Oxford History of the British Empire.* Vol. 2. Ed. P.J. Marshall. Oxford: Oxford UP, 1998. 440–64.

Roberts, James. *The Counter-Revolution in France, 1787–1830.* New York: St. Martin's P, 1990.

Robinson, Mary. "The Alien Boy." 1800. *Selected Poems.* Ed. Judith Pascoe. Peterborough, Ontario: Broadview, 2000.

———. *Hubert de Sevrac, a Romance of the Eighteenth Century.* London: Hookham and Carpenter, 1796.

Roe, Nicholas. "Pantisocracy and the Myth of the Poet." In *Romanticism and Millenarianism.* Ed. Tim Fulford. New York: Palgrave, 2002. 87–102.

———. *Wordsworth and Coleridge: The Radical Years.* Oxford: The Clarendon P, 1988.

Rose, Robert Hutchinson. *Sketches in Verse.* Philadelphia: C.&A. Conrad, 1810.

Russell, Richard. *De Tabe Glandulari, sive De Usu Aquae Marinae in Mornis Glandularum Dissertation.* London: Fletcher and J. Rivington, 1750.

Rust, Marion. "The Subaltern as Imperialist: Speaking of Olaudah Equiano." *Passing and the Fictions of Identity.* Ed. Elain K. Ginsberg. Durham, NC: Duke UP, 1996. 21–36.

Rzepka, Charles J. *The Self as Mind: Vision and Identity in Wordsworth, Coleridge, and Keats.* Cambridge: Harvard UP, 1986.

Sabino, Robin and Jennifer Hall. "The Path Not Taken: Cultural Identity in the Interesting Life of Olaudah Equiano." *MELUS* 24:1 (Spring 1999): 5–19.

Sanborn, Geoffrey. *The Sign of the Cannibal: Melville and the Making of a Postcolonial Reader.* Durham, NC: Duke UP, 1998.

Sancho, Ignatius. *Letters of the Late Ignatius Sancho, and African.* Ed. Vincent Carretta. New York: Penguin, 1998.

———. *Ignatius Sancho (1729–1780), An Early African Composer in England: The Collected Editions of His Music in Facsimle.* Ed. Josephine R.B. Wright. New York: Garland, 1981.

Sandiford, Keith A. *Measuring the Moment: Strategies of Protest in Eighteenth-Century Afro-English Writing.* London: Associated UP, 1988.

Sandiford, Margaret. *Thomas Poole and His Friends.* New York: Macmillan, 1888.

Sayer, Robert. *A New and Correct Map of Africa, done from the latest and best Observations. Humbly Inscribed to his Royal Hughness George Price of Wales.* London, 1754.

Schama, Simon. *Citizens: A Chronicle of the French Revolution.* New York: Vintage, 1989.

Schofield, Robert E. "Commentary." In Priestley, Joseph. *Scientific Autobiography of Joseph Priestley (1733–1804): Selected Scientific Correspondence.* Ed. Robert E. Schofield. Cambridge, MA: M.I.T. P, 1966.

———. *The Enlightenment of Joseph Priestley: A Study of His Life and Work from 1733–1773.* University Park, PA: Pennsylvania State UP, 1997.

Seale, R. *A Map of North America with Hudson's Bay and Straights.* 1748. Rpt. in Glyn Williams. *Voyages of Delusion: The Northwest Passage in the Age of Reason.* London: HarperCollins, 2002. 204–5.

Sepinwall, Alyssa Goldstein. *The Abbé Gregoire and the French Revolution: The Making of Modern Universalism.* Berkeley: U of California P, 2005.

Shelley, Mary. *Frankenstein; or, The Modern Prometheus.* 1818. Oxford: Oxford UP, 1993.

———. *Lodore.* Ed. Lisa Vargo. Toronto: Broadview P, 1997.

Shepperson, Wilbur S. *Emigration & Disenchantment: Portraits of Englishmen Repatriated from the United States.* Norman, Oklahoma: U of Oklahoma P, 1965.

Shyllon, Folarin. *Black People in Britain, 1555–1833.* London: Oxford UP, 1977.

Simpson, A.W. Brian. *Cannibalism and the Common Law: The Story of the Tragic Last Voyage of the Mignonette and the Strange Legal Proceedings to Which It Gave Rise.* Chicago: U of Chicago P, 1984.

Smith, Adam. *An Inquiry into the Nature and Causes of the Wealth of Nations.* Ed. Edwin Cannan. New York: Modern Library, 1937.

Smith, Charlotte. *The Banished Man. A Novel.* 4 vols. London: Cadell and Davies, 1794.

———. *Beachy Head. The Poems of Charlotte Smith.* Ed. Stuart Curran. Oxford: Oxford UP, 1993.

———. *The Collected Letters of Charlotte Smith.* Ed. Judith Phillips Stanton. Bloomington: Indiana UP, 2003.

———. *Desmond.* 1792. Ed. Antje Blank and Janet Todd. Pertersborough, Ontario: Broadview P, 2001.

———. *The Emigrants. The Poems of Charlotte Smith.* Ed. Stuart Curran. Oxford: Oxford UP, 1993.

Soja, Edward. *Postmodern Geographies: The Resurrection of Space in Critical Social Theory.* London: Verso, 1989.

Southey, Robert. *New Letters of Robert Southey.* 2 vols. Ed. Kenneth Curry. New York: Columbia UP, 1965.

———. *Poems Concerning the Slave Trade*. In *Slavery, Abolition and Emancipation: Writings in the British Romantic Period*. Vol. 4 (Verse). Ed. Alan Richardson. London: Pickering & Chatto, 1999. 243–6.

———. "The Sailor Who Had Served in the Slave Trade." *Robert Southey: Poetical Works, 1793–1810*. Vol. 5. Ed. Lynda Pratt. London: Pickering & Chatto, 2004. 288–92.

Stanton, Judith. *Charlotte Smith's Prose*. Ph.D. Dissertation.

Straub, Kristina. *Divided Forms: Fanny Burney and Feminine Strategy*. Lexington: U of Kentucky P, 1987.

Sudan, Rajani. *Fair Exotics: Xenophobic Subjects in English Literature, 1720–1850*. Philadelphia: U of Pennsylvania P, 2002.

Suleri, Sara. *The Rhetoric of English India*. Chicago: U of Chicago P, 1992.

Swift, Michael. *Historical Maps of North America*. London: Public Records Office, 2001.

Thomas, Helen. *Romanticism and Slave Narratives: Transatlantic Testimonies*. Cambridge: Cambridge UP, 2000.

Tobin, Beth Fowkes. *Picturing Imperial Power: Colonial Subjects in Eighteenth-Century Painting*. Durham, NC: Duke UP, 1999.

Todd, Janet. *Mary Wollstonecraft: A Revolutionary Life*. New York: Columbia UP, 2000.

Torgovnick, Marianna. *Gone Primitive: Savage Intellects, Modern Lives*. Chicago: U of Chicago P, 1990.

Tunnicliff, W.A. *A Topographical Survey of the Counties of Hants, Wilts*. Salisbury, 1791.

Viaud, Pierre. *Shipwreck and Adventures of Monsieur Pierre Viaud*. Trans. and ed. Robin F.A. Fabel. Pensacola: U of West Florida P, 1990.

Wallace, Anne D. "Picturesque Fossils, Sublime Geology? The Crisis of Authority in Charlotte Smith's *Beachy Head*." *The European Romantic Review* 13 (2002): 77–93.

Walvin, James. *Black and White: The Negro and English Society, 1555–1945*. London: Allen Lane, 1973.

———. *England, Slaves and Freedom, 1776–1838*. Jackson, Mississippi: UP of Mississippi, 1986.

———. *Fruits of Empire: Exotic Produce and British Trade*. New York: New York UP, 1997.

———. *Making the Black Atlantic: Britain and the African Diaspora*. London: Cassell, 2000.

Weiner, Margery. *The French Exiles, 1789–1815*. London: John Murray, 1960.

Whalley, George. "Coleridge and Southey in Bristol, 1795." *Review of English Studies* 1:4 (October 1950): 324–40.

Wheatley, Phillis. "On Being Brought from Africa to America." *Poems on Various Subjects, Religious and Moral [By Phillis Wheatley, Negro Servant to Mr. John Wheatley of Boston, in New England*]. London: A. Bell, 1778.

Wheeler, Roxanne. "'Betrayed by Some of My Own Complexion': Cugoano, Abolition, and the Contemporary Language of Racialism." In *Genius in Bondage: Literature of the Early Black Atlantic*. Ed. Vincent Carretta and Philip Gould. Lexington: UP of Kentucky, 2001. 17–38.

White, Gilbert. *The Natural History of Selbourne*. Ed. Richard Mabey. New York: Penguin, 1977.

Williams, Glyn. *Voyages of Delusion: The Northwest Passage in the Age of Reason*. London: HarperCollins, 2002.

Wiley, Michael. *Romantic Geography: Wordsworth and Anglo-European Spaces*. New York: St. Martin's Press, 1998.

Wordsworth, Dorothy. *Journals of Dorothy Wordsworth*. 2 vols. Ed. Ernest de Selincourt. London: Macmillan, 1952.

Wordsworth, Dorothy. *The Letters of William and Dorothy Wordsworth: The Early Years, 1787–1805*. Oxford: Clarendon P, 1967.

Wordsworth, William. *Descriptive Sketches*. Ed. Eric Birdsall with Paul M. Zall. Ithaca: Cornell UP, 1984.

———. *The Excursion, 1814*. Oxford: Woodstock Books, 1991.

———. "A Letter to the Bishop of Llandaff." *The Prose Works of William Wordsworth*. Vol. 1. Ed. W.J.B. Owen and Jane Worthington Smyser. Oxford: Clarendon P, 1974.

———. *Lyrical Ballads and Other Poems, 1797–1800*. Ed. James Butler and Karen Green. Ithaca: Cornell University Press, 1992.

———. *Peter Bell*. Ed. John E. Jordan. Ithaca: Cornell UP, 1985.

———. *Poems in Two Volumes, and Other Poems, 1800–1807*. Ed. Jared Curtis. Ithaca: Cornell UP, 1983.

———. *The Poetical Works of William Wordsworth*. Vol. 3. 2nd ed. Ed. Ernest de Selincourt and Helen Darbishire. Oxford: Clarendon P, 1954.

———. *The Thirteen-Book Prelude*. 2 vols. Ed. Mark L. Reed. Ithaca: Cornell UP, 1991.

———. "SONNET. No. I" ("I grieved for Buonaparté"). *Morning Post* (29 January 1803).

———. "SONNET. No. II" ("Is it a Reed"). *Morning Post* (29 January 1803).

———. "SONNET. No. III. TO TOUSSAINT L'OUVERTURE." *Morning Post* (2 February 1803).

———. "SONNET. No. IV. THE BANISHED NEGROES." *Morning Post* (11 February 1803).

———. "SONNET. No. V. AUGUST 15, 1802" ("Festivals have I seen"). *Morning Post* (26 February 1803).

. "SONNET. No. VI" ("IT is not to be thought of that the Flood"). *Morning Post* (16 April 1803).

———. "SONNET. No. VII" ("WHEN I have borne in memory"). *Morning Post* (17 September 1803).

Wright, Joseph. Painting: Joseph Wright of Derby 1734–1797, *The Widow of an Indian Chief Watching the Arms of Her Deceased Husband* (1785). Oil on Canvas. Derby Museum & Art Gallery.

Wu, Duncan. *Wordsworth's Reading, 1770–1799.* Cambridge: Cambridge UP, 1993.

———. *Wordsworth's Reading, 1800–1815.* Cambridge: Cambridge UP, 1995.

Young, Arthur. *General View of the Agriculture of the County of Sussex.* London: Sherwood, Neely, and Jones, 1813.

Zimmerman, Sarah. *Romanticism, Lyricism, and History.* Albany: State U of New York P, 1999.

Zonitch, Barbara. *Familiar Violence: Gender and Social Upheaval in the Novels of Frances Burney.* Newark: U of Delaware P, 1997.

Index